MANAGING FACULTY DISPUTES

A Guide to Issues,
Procedures, and Practices

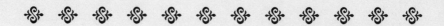

Jane McCarthy
Irving Ladimer
Josef P. Sirefman

MANAGING
FACULTY
DISPUTES

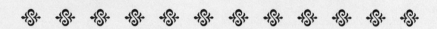

Jossey-Bass Publishers

San Francisco • Washington • London • 1984

MANAGING FACULTY DISPUTES
A Guide to Issues, Procedures, and Practices
by Jane McCarthy, Irving Ladimer, and Josef P. Sirefman

Copyright © 1984 by: Jossey-Bass Inc., Publishers
433 California Street
San Francisco, California 94104
&
Jossey-Bass Limited
28 Banner Street
London EC1Y 8QE

Library of Congress Cataloging in Publication Data

McCarthy, Jane.
    Managing faculty disputes.

    (Jossey-Bass higher education series)
    Bibliography: p. 253
    Includes index.
    1. Collective bargaining—College teachers—United
States. 2. Grievance procedures—United States.
3. Universities and colleges—United States—Administra-
tion. 4. Teacher-Administrator relationships—United
States. I. Ladimer, Irving. II. Sirefman, Josef P.
III. Title. IV. Series.
LB2335.885.U6M32   1984   331.89'04137812'0973   84-47991
ISBN 0-87589-623-5

Manufactured in the United States of America

The paper in this book meets the guidelines for
permanence and durability of the Committee on
Production Guidelines for Book Longevity of the
Council on Library Resources.

JACKET DESIGN BY WILLI BAUM

FIRST EDITION

Code 8433

The Jossey-Bass
Higher Education Series

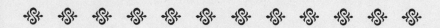

PREFACE

Our book is directed primarily to those who have managerial responsibilities in universities and colleges—trustees, presidents, deans, division and department heads, and other administrators and faculty leaders who participate in governance and academic affairs—and also to professionals in the field of dispute resolution.

The book is a handbook or reference guide that describes the range of faculty disputes that arise on campus and suggests responses for their management. It highlights two general categories of disputes: grievances, which occur with some regularity and involve tenure, promotion, discipline, and compensation; and policy disputes, which arise without pattern as to timing or subject matter and involve retrenchment and reorganization, use of endowment funds, and other disputes over institutional policy. Grievances are amenable to resolution through standard grievance or appeals procedures. Policy disputes, however, by their nature require flexible formats for their resolution.

The emphasis throughout this book is on the *process* of dispute management rather than on substantive solutions to specific problems. For example, the ultimate solution to a problem with the faculty parking lot may require the services of a traffic expert who will lay out new spaces and change existing traffic flows. It is not our intent to furnish such guidance. It is rather to propose a process for conflict resolution that may have as one of its outcomes an agreement to engage such a specialist. Thus, we stress the mechanics of achieving resolutions to numerous and varied problems. We can give fairly definitive advice on designing procedures for regularly occurring grievances; organizations of many kinds have had vast experience in creating and modifying progressive steps toward the resolution of these conflicts. The analysis of management techniques for policy disputes is a new field, however. Although those managing these disputes can draw occasionally on formal experience, the resolution of these conflicts usually requires resilience and the ability to adapt to new and unusual circumstances.

This book is a product of our experiences at the Center for Mediation in Higher Education at the American Arbitration Association in assisting the academic community to prepare procedures to handle either a specific set or a broad range of issues. Since 1979, the center has actively promoted alternatives to litigation. The information we present comes from our contacts with administrators and faculty and from the center workshops on procedural design. From this experience, we have grown to appreciate the extent of the problems that are unfolding, especially on financially beleaguered campuses. Our sense is that too much emphasis is prematurely placed on the substantive aspects of problems; the initial focus should be on the process used to achieve solutions. A previous publication, *Resolving Faculty Disputes* (1981), presented a model procedure and a discussion of procedural elements. The book was limited to one procedural approach for recurring grievances. It was intended as an instructional manual for those engaged in designing grievance mechanisms. *Managing Faculty Disputes* presents a wider spectrum of issues that arise and a broader view of the management options for handling them. Most of the problems we describe will be familiar to those involved in the day-to-day life of educational institutions. This familiarity, however, can foster the sense that these problems are intractable and will always be with us. Thus, we find a need for those involved in dispute management to take a fresh look at their own processes for handling the specific mix of problems characteristic of their institutions.

Part One of the book describes the types of issues that can be handled within a grievance format. Chapter One provides a review of the typical issues involved in professional advancement, such as tenure, promotion, and reappointment. Decisions of this nature rest on numerous factors, including peer review, academic judgments regarding a faculty member's qualifications and performance, and the institution's financial health and its specialized educational focus. The need for balance between confidentiality to protect the evaluation process and candor to demonstrate fairness to the individual is also discussed. Chapter Two deals with discipline and dismissal from two perspectives: (1) the basis for the disciplinary action and (2) the challenge a faculty member may mount to protest the action taken and to seek reversal of an adverse decision. Chapter Three considers the problems that arise out of faculty desires to participate in governance and disputes over compensation and working conditions. In addition, the potential for disputes with respect to part-time faculty, a rapidly growing academic sector, is examined in detail. Chapter Four presents problems that may arise in the management of increasing numbers of university-based, corporate-financed research centers. It highlights the issues that are considered to be the most serious from the viewpoint of participating faculty and their research directors and suggests possible approaches for dealing with these situations.

Part Two provides guidance for those designing procedures to manage the problems described in the previous chapters. Chapter Five discusses the elements that can be incorporated in a faculty complaint process, including the procedural steps of informal negotiations, mediation, the hearing, and possible formats for definitive resolution. An extensive illustration of the way in which procedural revisions should be accomplished, from the question of who should participate in such revisions to the ultimate formulation of policies and procedures, is presented. The primary emphasis throughout is on anticipating problems and offering processes to handle them. Chapter Six, as well as the Resources at the end of the book, draws on

the experiences of college administrators in designing procedures for their distinctly different types of institutions—Northeastern University, Pace University, and Unity College—that
have taken very different approaches for responding to faculty
disputes. The comparison of the tactics of these schools provides the reader with a cross-section of experience in crafting
procedures.

Part Three examines disputes that arise infrequently yet
hold the potential for disrupting the entire campus. Chapter
Seven provides insight into some of the most difficult and vex-
ing problems facing administrators, including those that involve
the academic institution with the politics of the outside world
and internal questions that have the potential to threaten the
existence of the institution, such as retrenchment, reorganization, and leadership changes. Chapter Eight discusses creative responses that administrators can utilize to solve unpredictable conflicts. The basis for these responses is the adaptation of
techniques and steps used in disputes involving individual faculty members—informal negotiation, information sharing, and
mediation. The chapter stresses the importance of providing
channels through which the faculty can express their opinions.
Chapter Nine presents a case study of the participation of faculty at a mid-sized university that needed to solve a serious financial crisis. It outlines the genesis of the crisis, the response of
the faculty, the value of their input, and realistic guidelines for
determining the success of such endeavors.

The final chapter is an overview of management responses
to disputes that can be expected to arise with some degree of
regularity and to those that are unpredictable in their occurrence.

The Resources give specific aid to those designing grievance procedures. They help both in assessing current procedures
and in planning new ones, and they provide models to follow.
The Further Readings list other publications that supply background information for managing faculty disputes.

Although we categorize disputes, we recognize that
many, such as those over alleged discrimination, can arise within
several of the categories. An allegation of discrimination can be
made in connection with individual promotion or tenure deci-

sions (Chapter One), as grounds for claiming unfair discipline or dismissal (Chapter Two), as the basis for challenging the denial of other employment rights (Chapter Three), or as a class action suit (Chapter Seven). Thus, illustrations of disputes involving claims of discrimination are found throughout the book. Similarly, we discuss retrenchment in Part One when it concerns an individual faculty member and in Part Three in connection with broad policy issues that affect the entire institution. In addition, all categories of disputes can involve procedural as well as substantive issues, and therefore we discuss due process in several places.

Throughout the book, descriptions of disputes come from accounts published in the media, such as the *Chronicle of Higher Education* and journals of the leading higher education associations. Specific citations can be obtained by writing to us. This information was collected over a two-year period from the summer of 1981 through the fall of 1983. We chose these examples to illustrate the types of issues that arise with some frequency. An awareness of the common areas of dispute can help designers of resolution processes ascertain the extent and the kinds of issues for which they need to provide plans. Because our purpose is to highlight issues rather than to focus on specific faculty members or administrators, we do not include the names of individuals except where prolonged litigation has brought the issues and individuals into the limelight. Several of the cases cited have not been definitively resolved at this time; the fact that the issues did arise is the primary concern here.

We lay no claim to a magic formula to a sure-fire solution to faculty disputes. Our emphasis is on encouraging decision makers to look for a range of options that may be wider than initial analysis would indicate. We present guidelines and approaches that have been successful in other contexts to enlarge the number of options that can be considered. These considerations are not new. Special publications directed to educators have extensively described the way various battles have been fought. The new element here is our attempt to encourage all those involved in higher education to view these issues and confrontations in the context of a dispute settlement perspective; to consider an extended, planned process rather than an ad hoc one for settling them. To some extent, the skill and wisdom of the faculty and the administration will be demonstrated by the manner in which they work together to fashion appropriate resolutions when these disputes arise.

We are indebted to dozens of educational leaders with whom we discussed the current state of the art of academic dispute management. Comments from more than 200 administrators who responded to our questionnaire on present grievance-handling methods immeasurably enriched the chapters on grievance-procedure design. Members of the advisory board of the Center for Mediation in Higher Education offered encouragement throughout the preparation of the manuscript. The president of the American Arbitration Association, Robert Coulson, was unflagging in his enthusiastic support for this project. Jerome Pescow of the Hofstra University School of Business provided invaluable insights into approaches for dealing with fiscal problems. We could not have prepared the discussion of specific grievance procedures without the cooperation of Jerome Medalie, partner in the law firm Widett, Slater & Goldman, and legal counsel at Northeastern University; Gerald Herman, assistant to the provost at Northeastern University; Robert I. Ruback, in the office of legal counsel at Pace University; and Donald Lord, who commented on the Unity College procedures. We are particularly grateful to the Exxon Education Foundation, whose financial support enabled us to prepare the manuscript. The foundation president, Robert L. Payton, and Arnold Shore, our program officer, provided important assistance in the early stages in shaping the book's approach. A special word of thanks is due to Helen Connolly, whose consistently cheerful and patient work with the manuscript made our efforts less tedious.

New York, New York   Jane McCarthy
August 1984   Irving Ladimer
                                             Josef P. Sirefman

CONTENTS

THE AUTHORS

Jane McCarthy, previously director of the Center for Mediation in Higher Education at the American Arbitration Association, is now with the Municipal Arts Society in New York City. She is the author, with Irving Ladimer, of *Resolving Faculty Disputes,* a 1981 publication that presents a model grievance procedure for handling faculty disputes. She holds a degree in labor economics from the University of Michigan. As a consultant to the Ford Foundation, she pioneered the use of mediation in environmental disputes and has served as a mediator in Washington, D.C., Rhode Island, and Maine. She has also been an investment counselor and the director of public affairs for an independent oil company.

Irving Ladimer is an attorney and former program director of the Research Institute of the American Arbitration Association. He specializes in the design of dispute-resolution methods in the fields of health, medicine, higher education, law, and community relations. He holds J.D. and S.J.D. degrees from George Washington University. As an adjunct associate professor at Mount Sinai School of Medicine, City University of New York, he serves in the faculty senate. He is a consultant to the Center for Mediation in Higher Education.

Josef P. Sirefman is a professor of business law at the Hofstra University School of Business and an active labor arbitrator and mediator in the private and public sectors. He is a member of the National Academy of Arbitrators, has experience as an impartial chair, and serves on a number of contract arbitration panels. He holds a B.A. from the City College of New York, a J.D. from New York University, and an M.B.A. and a Ph.D. in economics from the New York University Graduate School of Business. He serves as the neutral member of the university appeals board under the faculty contract at Hofstra University and is a consultant to the Center for Mediation in Higher Education.

MANAGING FACULTY DISPUTES

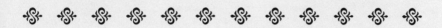

A Guide to Issues,
Procedures, and Practices

PART I

Recurring Disputes

When an institution has an established grievance process for faculty members, disputes typically focus on the application of criteria for evaluating a faculty member's competence and suitability, based on qualifications, performance, and institutional considerations. Faculty covered by a collective bargaining agreement may question the application or interpretation of its terms to specific issues. When an institution does not have a union agreement, disputes typically arise over the meaning and effect of institutional policies, statutes, and practices. In either case it is through the grievance mechanism that stated or implied standards are applied to specific situations. In some instances, faculty members may challenge the procedures themselves. The ultimate objective is to reach a fair decision based on the facts and principles applicable to a particular case.

Disputes managed through a grievance process fall within three major categories: academic advancement (promotion, tenure, and reappointment), discipline (causes and conditions for

1

suspension, dismissal, and other penalties), governance and the employment relationship (professional rights, privileges and benefits of employment, and academic protections). In many instances, these disputes involve both substantive and procedural issues. For example, in a dispute over failure to receive a promotion or in a discharge action, the faculty member may claim inadequate notice, a flaw in the review process, or the use of inappropriate criteria. On a substantive basis, a faculty member may challenge a promotion or dismissal action on the basis of alleged discrimination.

Grievances concerning academic advancement challenge the basis for the unfavorable academic evaluation or administrative denial; in such cases, the grievant seeks a review of the peer judgment or the administrator's decision. In cases involving governance and other aspects of the employment relationship, faculty members claim they were denied conditions to which they feel entitled by institutional policy, contract, or precedent. These cases are akin to promotion and tenure grievances but focus on administrative issues more than professional considerations and usually do not involve peer review. In discipline cases, the grievant denies the charges, offers explanation or justification, or requests a lesser penalty. In tenure and promotion cases, the faculty member's credentials are at issue; in discipline cases, the institution charges a violation of accepted conduct and imposes a sanction.

The first three chapters in Part One discuss the specific grievances that arise within each of these categories. The fourth chapter presents these issues within the context of the new and increasingly important ventures in collaborative research by industry and universities. Collaborative research arrangements involving the creation of institutes present both traditional issues of faculty status and new problems such as conflicts of interest and limitations on academic communications. Those fashioning grievance processes in this new environment need to make them responsive to these special situations.

CHAPTER 1

Professional Advancement:
Tenure, Promotion,
and Reappointment

Career movement in colleges and universities is typically up or out. Until recently, faculty members expected to advance systematically in rank and, in due course, to achieve tenure, which provides protection against dismissal or transfer except for just cause. In effect, tenure spells security within the college and university. In the absence of a tenure system, institutional guidelines or individual contracts that provide an explicit expectation of continued employment may protect faculty members.

Disputes over tenure, promotion, and reappointment arise when a faculty member's expectations for career advancement are thwarted by a negative peer review or a negative decision at the administrative level. Increasingly, economic factors, such as enrollment trends and the extent of tenure in the department, are becoming relevant in tenure decisions. Different opinions exist concerning which sector of the institution should be concerned with such factors, the department at the outset or the president and trustees at the end of the process.

In some institutions, colleagues may take into account factors other than professional qualifications. In any event, peer review is but the first step in the evaluation and is subject to further academic, administrative, and, in public institutions, governmental determinations.

Grievances based on denials of advancement may contend that the reviewers failed to apply the standard criteria and improperly considered other matters. Some departments may seek to retain faculty in their image, while others may actively seek diversity. Some cases allege discrimination, the intrusion of inappropriate political or personal issues, or the consideration of other matters deemed irrelevant to individual academic review, such as financial distress, institutional reorganization, or drastic curriculum revision.

Peer Review and Academic Judgment

To assess suitability for advancement and tenure, departmental colleagues apply specifically stated or implied criteria to the candidate's qualifications and accomplishments. Academic judgments made at the college-wide or university-wide level may differ from those reached at the departmental stage, often for academic or institutional reasons quite apart from those relating to individual performance. In fact, many grievances point to denial in the administrative review, after approval at the peer level. Although the president or other principal officer has the authority to make an independent decision, it is expected that the officer will do so reasonably and consistently.

Qualifications and Performance. Institutional policies or contract provisions usually list the criteria for peer review; these criteria specify qualifications and expected performance. Qualifications include degree attainment or the equivalent, minimum years of service, recognized specialization, and, in some instances, suitability for the institution. Performance generally covers the quality and effectiveness of instruction; recognition for research; and contributions to the institution, community, or professional field. Listed criteria may illustrate or define these factors. For example, research requirements may be met by the number or quality of publications, research grants or contracts awarded, appointment to research committees, and citations in professional sources. Academic judgments also consider the resources required to support the professor as well as the extent to which the professor's field harmonizes with the mission or objectives of the school. General institutional concerns about finances also color these judgments.

Because academic evaluation necessarily involves subjective judgments, most institutions provide criteria to assist peer-review committees. For example, Rutgers University lists the following factors: teaching effectiveness, scholarly or creative activity, and general usefulness to the university. These are, obviously, pointers or guides; they are not specific, unequivocal definitions. They invite evaluation and discussion based on an examination of the individual and comparison with others and are, therefore, subject to honest differences of opinion. Where good faith and honest opinion can be shown and documented, academic judgment within the evaluation process is difficult to attack and is rarely reversed.

Issues involving the application of criteria, however, do arise when there is some alleged failure to interpret properly or consistently or where some factors deemed inappropriate or immaterial are considered in addition to or to the exclusion of others. Examples of issues in disputes over qualifications are the need for terminal degrees, the interpretation of degree equivalence, and the length of service required. Performance disputes concern the fairness of basing judgments about teaching effectiveness on attendance, student ratings, course popularity, and enrollment. Disputes about research requirements arise over the number and type of professional publications and other creative work. Questions about the value of the professor's contribution to the institution, community, or professional field are based on the extent of committee work and public service. Decisions about how much weight to give to each of these criteria in an individual case are an additional source of dispute.

In the matter of degree equivalence, for example, denial of promotion to an associate professor was held to be justified even though the candidate, with neither a doctorate nor a sufficient number of publications, created maps for publication in his field of cartography. In this Rhode Island College case, the arbitrator conceded that the maps were impressive but found "no evidence that the maps attained the stature of outstanding publications" or constituted significant or exceptional contributions to cartography. The grievant claimed that traditional publication could not be expected when the professor's competence called for another form of expression. The arbitrator held that when the candidate does not possess a doctorate, "one must look to other objective, external sources, . . . and [traditional] publication is the natural way" to demonstrate academic achievement.

On occasion a dispute that appears to involve the issue of equivalence may be decided on another basis. A federal judge ordered the University of the District of Columbia to promote a Puerto Rican faculty member to full professor, despite the fact that the faculty member did not hold a doctoral degree. Because the university had previously promoted non-Hispanic faculty members to full professor without the terminal degree, the judge considered the failure to promote in this instance discriminatory.

In a controversy over what constitutes continuing professional achievement, a requirement for full professorship at an independent college in Connecticut, an arbitrator ruled that the college could deny promotion to a faculty member who, for three and a half years after receipt of his doctorate, did not participate in such professional activities as research, publication, or attendance at professional meetings. The provost's interpretation of *continuing* was held to be reasonable and correct despite the fact that the college provided no specific definition of or limitation on this term.

In the area of performance, student evaluations are controversial elements. Many educators believe that student evaluations are among the most objective measures of teaching ability. Those opposed to student ratings stress lack of student competence and the fact that restrictions on academic freedom and the erosion of traditional peer judgment can result from using student ratings. In addition, some faculty believe that student evaluations undermine academic standards and necessitate pleasing students by providing entertainment, giving high grades, retreating from controversial or unpopular issues, and relaxing discipline.

Grievances lodged by faculty increasingly refer to student assessment as an improper basis for withholding promotion, reappointment, or tenure. However, sometimes a faculty member asks that student appraisals be considered. At the University of Colorado at Denver, a professor of art history who was awarded honors for outstanding teaching by students and alumni was nevertheless denied tenure on the basis that his scholarly research on civilization was held unrelated to his specialty.

Although student ratings are clearly relevant, it may be argued that they have been given undue weight. When specified criteria are silent about student evaluations, some institutions do not allow consideration of them, while others permit consideration as long as student ratings are not the sole basis for a decision. However, concern for maintaining enrollment may give students an increasingly important role in assessing teaching ability.

Confidentiality. Disputes involving the fairness of the peer-review process are particularly sensitive because of the tradition of confidentiality and the great reluctance of peer-review committees to permit scrutiny of the way the determinations are made and votes are cast. The confidential aspect of peer review makes it extremely difficult for a faculty member to document allegations of improper evaluation, such as arbitrariness, incomplete review, and discrimination.

Over the years, the federal courts presented with this issue have reached seemingly contradictory conclusions. In a Smith College case, a federal court of appeals ruled that the college, in denying tenure to a faculty member in the English department, need not disclose the individual votes of members of the tenure committee. The court deemed the evidence introduced by the college sufficient to justify denial of tenure, regardless of the voting and committee recommendations. In this case, a native of India claimed the denial of tenure was based on his race and national origin. A similar conclusion was reached in a case involving denial of tenure at the University of Alaska. An assistant professor of fisheries biology charged that his constitutional rights were violated when the committee refused to divulge reasons for the denial of tenure. But, in another case, which aroused public as well as academic controversy, a federal district court ordered tenure-committee members at the University of Georgia to give depositions explaining their votes. The principles of academic privilege and the right to know were thereby cast in opposition. This case became highly publicized when one of the committee members, James A. Dinnan, was fined and served a thirty-day jail sentence rather than comply with the court order.

Some institutions traditionally provide the candidate with only the statement that the evaluation has been unfavorable. This practice is based on the view that complete confidentiality is required in order to fully protect the evaluation process. With the growing concern for individual rights, however, some courts have qualified this principle by insisting that the statement specify the substantive reasons for the decision. If it does not, courts may pierce the veil of confidentiality and insist on additional detail and personal disclosure from the evaluators. For example, in the case of S. Simpson Gray, a black professor who was turned down when he applied for advancement at LaGuardia Community College in New York City, the circuit court of appeals ruled that certain members of the tenure committee be compelled to disclose their votes inasmuch as the committee did not disclose the substantive basis for the result.

Admittedly, this case involves a claim of racial discrimination, and much of the court's opinion relates to the manner in which a professor making such a claim can inquire into the tenure process to discover evidence favorable to his or her position. As the court noted, "Academic freedom is illusory when it does not protect faculty from censorious practices but rather serves as a veil for those who might act as censors." The ruling clearly signals that courts will not look favorably on tenure decisions that deny the candidate the due process of knowing the reasons for the rejection. It is possible that the Dinnan case would have been resolved differently if the University of Georgia procedures included currently recognized elements of fair process instead of relying on unqualified secrecy and non-disclosure.

To provide perspective, the American Association of University Professors (AAUP) governing council issued a *Preliminary Statement on Judicially Compelled Disclosure in the Nonrenewal of Faculty Appointments* (1980). The statement addresses the necessity of using proper procedures for rectifying discrimination and the proper scope of judicial compulsion. Faculty have a right to evaluations free of "impermissible considerations, violative of academic freedom, or prejudice as to race, sex, religion, or national origin." They should be advised of reasons for denial and the right to a review if there is reason to believe impermissible considerations contributed. In appropriate circumstances, "participants in the decision-making process may permissibly be called upon to account for their actions."

Courts usually review whether impermissible considerations may have affected the decision before requiring committee members to disclose votes. There must be a strong inference of impropriety to overcome the claim of academic privilege. Factors the court may consider are the adequacy of the review procedures and the reasons given for the decision, statistical evidence of discrimination, and factual assertions of bias. Courts are loathe to substitute their judgment for a legitimate peer-review determination. The courts may direct that a university turning over a personnel file to the Equal Employment Opportunity Commission (EEOC) eliminate the name, address, affiliation, and other identifying features of the scholar who gave the tenure evaluation. The judge may issue a protective order to assure that the privileged materials are not disclosed to the public. The Supreme Court has acted on a case-by-case basis in deciding when and whether procedures for silent peer review will be upheld.

Institutional Considerations

In addition to the customary academic measures, general concerns of the college or university must be applied to individual promotion and tenure decisions. Disputes involving institutional considerations usually arise at the campus-wide level when the provost or president overturns a positive peer-review decision. Grievants often base claims on the application or interpretation of institutional policies concerning the proportion of tenured faculty, class size, departmental enrollment, and financial considerations, including retrenchment and the realignment of academic programs. Frequently, these policies are ambiguous or contradictory. For instance, a statement concerning the discontinuation of programs may be at odds with policies regarding seniority, tenure, and affirmative action.

Some institutions limit the percentage of faculty that can achieve tenured status. They should clearly articulate these policies so that tenure-track faculty understand that institutional constraints may affect tenure decisions. For instance, Pittsburgh Theological Seminary policies state that "no more than two thirds of the faculty [may be] tenured. When a faculty member becomes eligible for consideration, this factor may be important to those who participate in the decision on whether or not tenure will be awarded." But, no matter how clearly stated, institutional tenure provisions may still give rise to disputes. At the C. W. Post Center of Long Island University, a professor of English was found qualified by the trustees but was not granted tenure because the university had reduced the number of tenure positions. When a tenured member of the English department died shortly thereafter, the qualified but untenured faculty member claimed she was entitled to the vacant slot. The administration argued that the death of the tenured faculty member did not automatically create an open tenure slot. The arbitrator agreed with the grievant's position and awarded her tenure.

Declining departmental enrollment is sometimes the basis for the denial of tenure to faculty who are favorably reviewed at the peer level. However, stating declining enrollment as the reason for denial of tenure can lead to a legal challenge. For example, at a university in the Northeast, a faculty member was denied tenure on the basis that the department did not need courses in the faculty member's discipline. After being denied tenure, however, the faculty member accepted year-to-year contracts to teach the same courses he taught before coming up for tenure; in effect, his line was converted to nontenure track. This arrangement was acceptable to both parties until the university implemented an early-retirement program that applied only to tenured faculty. The faculty member grieved that he had de facto tenure because the reasons for denying tenure were not legitimate: He was currently teaching the very courses the department had said were not needed. Undoubtedly, this type of case occurs with some frequency, and it points up an irony that should not be overlooked. Given the requirement of stating reasons for rejection, it is usually prudent for the institution to sever the relationship with the professor involved rather than risk a later charge that the reasons given were merely a pretext. Thus, it can be argued that an advance in fair play for the general academic community carries with it the closing off of employment opportunities in individual cases.

The most far-reaching institutional considerations that affect faculty are those that relate to financial difficulties and retrenchment. At Goucher College in Baltimore a tenured professor of German who taught advanced literature brought suit when she was not reappointed because of the elimination of her position. A federal appeals court upheld the lower court decision that Goucher had acted in good faith to improve the school's financial condition by reducing the German department to one instructor for nonmajors. Similarly, a federal district court ruled that Odessa Junior College in Texas did not improperly dismiss a tenured professor of foreign languages when student demand dropped. The court held that the two-year notice given was adequate.

Disputes may also arise when faculty question the reasonableness or application of imposed or negotiated principles for dismissal. In a case before the New Jersey Supreme Court in August 1982, unions representing the state colleges brought suit against the State Board of Higher Education contending that the board must consult with union officials before adopting layoff rules. The court rejected this contention, ruling that layoff rules were "clearly nonnegotiable as matters of managerial prerogative pertaining to the determination of governmental policy." Nevertheless, it directed the board to negotiate the manner in which the procedures were implemented. For example, the union could bargain for longer periods of notice than provided in the rules and could also negotiate specific recall criteria.

Two contrasting policies for handling retrenchment issues have emerged. Either the institution is given broad latitude in coping with financial difficulty, or the institution is limited to clearly declaring financial exigency on the basis of specified conditions. The AAUP *Recommended Institutional Regulations on Academic Freedom and Tenure* (1976) stipulates a declared, bona fide financial exigency as the only basis for reductions in tenured staff. Many college presidents and trustees strongly oppose this position. For instance, in South Dakota the Board of Regents and the statewide faculty organization agreed to allow terminations for a series of conditions. This 1982 agreement between the South Dakota regents and the statewide Council on Higher Education permits termination of faculty members' contracts on the basis of legislative or gubernatorial action, significant loss of enrollment, consolidation of departments or other reorganization, dropping of courses or activities, or financial exigency. Reduction is to be accomplished mainly through attrition. The agreement lists retention priorities for cases where attrition does not suffice: permanently funded, full-time staff; tenure-track over term contractees; and seniority where there is equal retention status. Institutions cannot fill a place within two years unless the faculty member has been offered reappointment.

In contrast, the AAUP statement specifies early termination of tenured or probationary or special appointments only in extraordinary circumstances of demonstrable financial exigency —that is, "an imminent financial crisis which threatens the institution as a whole and which cannot be alleviated by less drastic means." The AAUP requires faculty participation in the decision, and, under the guidelines, the burden of proving the extent of exigency rests with the administration. Institutions cannot fill posts within three years without reappointment offers. The AAUP statement also proposes standards and procedures for formal discontinuance of a department or program. Discontinuance must be based on long-range educational considerations, not cyclical or temporary variations in enrollment. Affected faculty members have a right to a hearing before a faculty committee that considers the pertinent conditions and the basis for identifying those marked for termination.

Even the AAUP definition of a bona fide financial exigency is not foolproof, for it leaves open to interpretation the nature of the financial threat to an institution under particular circumstances. For example, Sonoma State University (California) laid off twenty-four professors because of low enrollment and shifts in course preferences. At the same time, professors, including three football coaches, were hired in other departments; the administration argued that the athletic program would save the university. Fired professors in liberal arts and the humanities filed grievances to review the decisions and to obtain faculty participation in these determinations. In this case and in others, what remains to be determined is whether, in the context of AAUP policy, programs, and therefore faculty, must be discontinued when financial difficulties arise or whether financial difficulties caused by slack in one area can be offset by expansion in another without the preservation of positions in the areas where enrollment has declined. At this time, unions are submitting specific requirements that faculty participate in declarations of financial difficulty and in the identification of faculty members affected by reductions. The courts are reluctant to substitute their judgment for academic and administrative decisions but will do so in the absence of clear principles and procedures.

Discrimination, Ideology, and Political Orientation

Claims of discrimination and violations of the right to free expression are argued in many tenure and promotion grievances. In form, grievants allege that inappropriate or extraneous considerations such as sex, age, or race adversely affected their positions or opportunities. Other claims allege improper or unfair consideration of a faculty member's ideology or union activity.

Discrimination. When promotion, tenure, or reappointment is denied, the faculty member may allege discrimination as the main or sole reason for the adverse decision. If a candidate is, for example, rejected on the basis of poor performance or lack of required qualifications, he or she may claim that in fact gender, age, race, or political or ideological orientation was the critical factor rather than academic achievement. In such cases the burden is on the grievant to demonstrate improper consideration either by direct evidence of bias by committee members or through an analysis of institutional personnel patterns. The institution seeks to refute the claim or justify the past and current situation in the context of civil rights law.

There have been several sex discrimination cases with different pretexts for denial of tenure. One of the best-known tenure-denial cases hinging on gender discrimination was that of the Harvard sociologist Theda Skocpol. Following a split departmental vote, which denied her early request for tenure, she charged bias, noting there were no female tenured professors in a department of eleven and a tiny percentage of tenured women in Harvard generally (12 of 353, or 3.4 percent compared with about 10 percent nationwide). A three-member faculty grievance committee upheld the professor's charges and said that no woman had been seriously considered for tenure in the last decade. An internal committee created by the president following the furor found no bias but concluded she had not been given a fair hearing and recommended that her name be sent to an ad hoc committee, the next step in the tenure process. Later, another committee, composed of peers from other departments and schools, reconsidered her qualifications, but again there was a split decision, leaving the matter to the president for final disposition. The president announced he would request reconsideration in a few years. Meanwhile, Skocpol moved to a tenured post at the University of Chicago. The dean of the Harvard faculty of arts and sciences has since appointed an advisory committee of distinguished scholars from within and outside Harvard to aid the sociology department in filling tenured posts. The Harvard affirmative action office will also review the policies and procedures of the department.

At Keene State College (New Hampshire), a female faculty member, Christine Sweeney, charged that the faculty-evaluation process was inherently discriminatory and resulted in less-qualified male faculty being promoted ahead of her. The Supreme Court, in a 5-4 decision, ordered the court of appeals to reconsider its ruling that the college had discriminated against the faculty member by failing to promote her to full professor. The Supreme Court stated that the appeals court placed too heavy a burden of proof on the college by requiring the institution to prove the absence of a discriminatory motive. After the Supreme Court order, the lower court upheld its earlier ruling of discrimination, finding that the decision not to promote was pretextual and that Sweeney, but for her sex, would have been promoted earlier.

In another significant sex-discrimination case, a federal district court in Pennsylvania ordered Muhlenberg College to grant tenure to a physical education instructor, Connie Rae Kunda, who had been denied tenure on the basis that she did not hold a master's degree, which was a requirement. The instructor persuaded the court that the college had failed to inform her of the need for the advanced degree. Three national education organizations criticized the court action as an inappropriate remedy and a substantial departure from other rulings that remanded such matters for proper consideration. They argued it would be more appropriate to restore her lost opportunity for tenure reconsideration than to automatically grant tenure status.

Claims of sex bias and violation of academic freedom are sometimes joined. In 1974, a female professor of educational policy studies was denied tenure by an all-male panel of peers at the University of Wisconsin. She filed complaints with both federal and state agencies claiming that her activity in women's causes rather than insufficient scholarly research was the basis for the denial. Her case drew publicity and support from students, faculty, and the Wisconsin affiliate of the National Education Association (NEA), and in December 1975, almost two years later, the Wisconsin Industry, Labor and Human Relations Board found probable cause for her claim. The university made an out-of-court settlement for $30 thousand rather than incur litigation.

In another suit involving promotion, a tenured associate professor at the University of California (Irvine), Alice Laborde, appealed to the Supreme Court to obtain records that were used as the basis for a decision by the chancellor to deny her promotion. She claimed that a committee of outside scholars, in a 7–1 vote, supported her promotion and that a federal district court uncritically accepted the decision of the chancellor, who denied promotion on the basis of inadequate scholarship. In her argument, she cited supporting statistics showing that ninety-nine men and only two women were promoted at the university in the ten-year period since 1966. She further claimed that the district court imposed too great a burden of proof—namely, that she had to show that the chancellor's decision was unreasonable rather than that, on balance, she had more persuasive statistical evidence. The Supreme Court refused to review the court of appeals ruling that the university procedures provided adequate protection against bias and that the professor had failed to show that the denial of promotion was unreasonable.

Discrimination disputes cut several ways. When a federal court held that a predominantly black university in Alabama had engaged in a pattern and practice of racial discrimination against white people following dismissal of a white professor of English, white faculty filed several suits based on denial of promotion and unfair work conditions. At Coppin State College, in Baltimore, a white political scientist claimed he was unfairly denied promotion to full professor while less qualified blacks were elevated. With a Korean colleague, he also maintained that their salaries were lower than those of blacks with similar experience, that they had inferior office space, and that they were denied travel expenses.

A federal district court found both race and age discrimination and ordered rehiring of a former faculty member in a case involving Harris-Stowe State College in St. Louis. The college decided to cut costs by reducing the number of tenured positions and hired a less-qualified sixty-two-year-old black assistant professor instead of the former chair, a forty-seven-year-old white professor. The black teacher had been intentionally selected, on the recommendation of a consultant, as a better role model for the students than the white teacher, in violation of Title VII of the Civil Rights Act of 1964. Thus, although budget cutting is justified, it may not create discriminatory patterns in faculty retention or hiring.

In a remarkable suit charging both sex discrimination and disparate treatment, the chair of the general studies faculty at the Atlanta College of Arts contended she was denied tenure because she dabbled in the occult and reportedly was an astrologer with an interest in the mystic arts. Her claim of discrimination was based on the awarding of tenure to a male faculty member who was a warlock at the time and a member of a witchcraft organization. She claimed she was "certainly no witch." The college denied that sex differences influenced the deliberations.

Ideology and Political Orientation. Challenges based on ideology arise when a faculty member claims that political beliefs or activities rather than academic achievements were the basis for rejection. The institution may take the position that commitment to an ideology prevents objectivity or neutrality in teaching or that other instructors of the same persuasion adequately represent a particular political viewpoint.

The intrusion of political and ideological considerations was recognized by arbitrators in cases involving the City University of New York (CUNY). In two instances, they ordered reinstatement and compensation for loss of income where there was convincing evidence that internal differences based on ideology were the critical reasons for denial of professional advancement. One arbitrator noted, "Where testimony from both sides confirms the existence of schism in the faculty and other evidence reveals a political cesspool, the neutral observer would be compelled to believe the nonreappointment of grievant had to be colored by intradepartment political discrimination."

The issue of political ideology as the basis for negative peer-review determinations also arose in two cases involving the University of Maryland. In refusing to grant tenure to self-described "radical decentralist" David H. DeLeon, the faculty committee in the department of history judged his teaching above average, his service to the school adequate, but found his latest work, *The American as Anarchist,* ambitious but not of the expected scholarly standards, despite favorable reviews by prominent historians outside the university. The same institution decided not to hire Eugene Genovese, a historian with a Marxist approach. Although a subcommittee of the department recommended him, the full departmental committee tied, failing to provide the required majority vote. The university thus had guidance but not a mandate. The vote could have reflected disapproval of his views or an assessment that there were enough instructors in his specialty.

A particularly well-publicized case involved Bertell Ollman, a professor at New York University who was selected by the faculty and chancellor of the University of Maryland to be the chair of the political science department. When his appointment was not approved by the university president, Ollman claimed he was rejected because of his Marxist orientation. The university asserted that although his credentials were satisfactory, a more qualified candidate than he could be found. The Ollman case resulted in censure of the university by the AAUP. And the censure action itself, on a 143–101 vote, was controversial because the AAUP Committee A had recommended against censure. A suit by Ollman was rebuffed by a federal court, which found that the university's decision not to hire was made "honestly and conscientiously" and was not based on Ollman's political beliefs.

A different conclusion was reached in an Oregon State University case where the state court of appeals ruled that a mathematics professor was improperly denied tenure on the basis of his political activities. The university was ordered to pay a year's back salary to the activist, who led antiwar vigils, picketed Dow Chemical Company, and organized an antimilitary ball to compete with the Reserve Officers Training Corps ball. The court found that, but for these extracurricular activities, the administration would have granted the professor tenure as recommended by the department.

In a case that bears indirectly on political ideology, a Brooklyn College faculty member alleged he was denied tenure because he agreed to be debriefed by the Central Intelligence Agency after conducting research in Europe. He filed suit when the political science department reversed its original favorable decision, claiming that the action violated his First Amendment rights. A federal district court jury agreed with the faculty member, but the court of appeals returned the case on the basis that the jury instructions were incorrect. The Supreme Court declined further review.

Issues of ideology can arise also in connection with union activity. An arbitrator held that a Kansas school district violated the union agreement when it did not renew a probationer's contract and thereby denied tenure. The candidate was active in union affairs and had a grievance in litigation to compel processing at the time of the evaluation. The arbitrator ruled that the board would not have made the decision not to renew if the candidate had not filed the grievance. Although cases of this type have been critical in testing the limits of academic freedom, with the decreasing emphasis on union-organizing activity these issues arise less frequently.

Issues regarding free speech and possible violations of the First Amendment also arise when a faculty member claims tenure was denied because of his or her criticism of departmental matters. In a case involving East Carolina University, the Supreme Court refused to review a court of appeals ruling that Robert Mayberry, a former professor of romance languages, was not entitled to tenure on the grounds that the denial was in retaliation for his critical comments. The court of appeals had ruled the evidence "simply too thin." Similarly, the Supreme Court let stand a court of appeals decision concerning a professor at Michigan State University who charged he was denied tenure because of critical statements concerning the curriculum. The appeals panel found the university's action constitutionally permissible and, as in the Mayberry case, set aside an earlier jury verdict in the professor's favor.

An admission by a university officer or even a faculty review committee that promotion or tenure has been denied be-

cause of extreme political views, expressed or taught, is unlikely. But few would deny that these considerations are given some weight. How much, how valid or justified, and with what effect are questions that will doubtlessly be raised for a long time by those rejected because of alleged political coloration.

Procedural Aspects

Procedural defects involve violations of due process. Distinctions between procedural and substantive elements, however, are not always clear. To overturn a decision on procedural grounds, the defect must be sufficiently serious to have affected the outcome, and it must be based on specific policy statements or on contract provisions or, more generally, on the absence of fundamental due process. In grievances filed because of denial of promotion, tenure, or reappointment, asserted violations often relate to the application of criteria at the peer or administrative level and to the interpretation of procedural provisions. Examples of these provisions are entitlement to a hearing, compliance with procedural sequence and form, and adequate notice and documentation.

The right to due process depends on the faculty member's status or rank. At Arizona State University, a novelist and director of creative writing sued the university after getting a one-year terminal contract despite the fact that he had a written promise of tenure from the dean. A federal district court enjoined the university from terminating him without providing the due process accorded tenured faculty members.

Two celebrated cases involving specific due-process rights of faculty members in public institutions rose to the Supreme Court. In *Perry* v. *Sinderman,* where the faculty guide explained de facto tenure, the court ruled in favor of Robert Sinderman, a faculty member at Odessa Junior College in Texas. As a teacher for ten years in the Texas state college system, he had the right to a hearing at which he could challenge the grounds for nonretention. The professor had been denied the chance to argue that his criticism of the Board of Regents was the grounds for nonrenewal of his contract, in violation of the First Amendment.

But, in *Board of Regents* v. *Roth,* David Roth, a non-tenured faculty member at Wisconsin State University at Oshkosh, was not entitled to a statement of reasons for nonreappointment because he was hired for a fixed term of one academic year. He had no basis for expecting reemployment or the protections of the Fourteenth Amendment such as accorded to regular tenured professors. There must be a legitimate claim of entitlement to such protections, not solely an abstract need or desire.

A similar issue arose at East Carolina University, where a professor was rehired after his probationary period. He claimed de facto tenure because he was not notified to the contrary after his third year, as required by the faculty manual. The federal district court dismissed his plea without trial and the appeals court said that tenure can be granted only by official university decision, not through reappointment.

In cases such as these, the procedural error must be damaging to require another review. Technical insufficiency is not enough. In a dispute at the University of Connecticut involving a faculty member's eligibility for a satisfactory-performance raise, a procedural error of failure to notify was cited. The university had failed to include in the personnel file a memorandum criticizing the instructor's performance but referred to it later. Although the document was not entered within the time required, other documents on file justified the decision to deny the extra pay. Thus, no remand was indicated because the outcome would not have been different if the procedural error had not occurred.

Procedural errors, as a rule, cannot be disregarded or corrected at a later stage, as the president of Rutgers University found out. When a promotion-review committee recommended reevaluation of an assistant professor's bid for promotion because of inadequacies in the department review process, the president could not exercise his managerial prerogative to decide unilaterally on the promotion. The arbitrator ruled that "the evidence available to the promotion-review committee had been tainted by defects in the procedure," and thus a reevaluation was essential.

At Lake Superior State College (Michigan), an arbitrator

found a violation of the union-contract promotion clause when several department heads recommended five additional candidates beyond those proposed by the promotion committee. The arbitrator ruled that the committee had sole authority to consider candidates who met minimum eligibility requirements. Two of the five candidates recommended independently were selected along with seven on the committee list. The college was not required to rescind the two questioned appointments and promote others because the action was taken in good faith, but it was limited to the correct procedure in the future. Thus, the procedural error was not considered damaging enough to require a complete reconsideration.

A review of the CUNY grievance experience, as reflected in arbitration cases, provides a host of examples of procedural defects serious enough to require a reconsideration of adverse decisions. A procedural violation was found when a dean failed to inform a faculty member of the negative import of the dean's observations and significant criticism of the faculty member's performance. This omission was tantamount to failure to provide timely, adequate notice. In a grievance over an initial appointment, procedural defects (called an "arbitrary administrative exercise of authority") were confirmed when a dean of the faculty denied appointment to a candidate who had been approved through all subordinate channels. The procedural irregularity was based on the finding that the dean did not have a full record on the proposed faculty member and that the dean's denial occurred within twenty-four hours after he received the recommendation. Obviously, the required consideration at this level was omitted or avoided. Similarly, in another case, the failure of the college to make required formal observations and to hold required evaluation conferences resulted in an order to reinstate the grievant so that the observations and evaluations could be made.

Procedural flaws can sometimes create unusual problems of remedy or enforcement. Thus, CUNY found it difficult to comply with an order issued in the middle of an academic term to reinstate a faculty member so that proper procedures could be followed. In this case, the arbitrator remanded the case to the parties for further negotiations concerning the manner in which the reinstatement would take place.

Problems associated with restricting review to procedural elements are illustrated by a case that arose at Quinnipiac College in Connecticut, where the college-wide review committee was limited originally to reviewing procedural aspects. This limitation led to so many difficulties in interpretation that the contract was changed so that the committee could ensure that evaluations were made "equitably and dispassionately" and that recommendations were adequately documented and consistent with appropriate and uniformly applied criteria. But even this revised responsibility was questioned in arbitration when the committee and provost concluded that publication of one article and one book was not sufficient to meet one of the standards for promotion to full professor. The arbitrator ruled that the committee's and provost's evaluation of the candidate's publications was justified because they were not judging the intellectual worth of the publications but rather the professor's record when they determined that he had not achieved sufficient external recognition to warrant promotion. Thus, the issue, as viewed by the arbitrator, focused not on academic judgment but on the application of generally accepted criteria.

Hence, distinctions between form and substance and rights to certain procedural protections often make the critical difference. Much as merit should be the measure, process often prevails. In light of this reality, grievants as well as administrators will continue to claim possible procedural defects to advance their positions.

CHAPTER 2

Disciplinary Action: Dismissal, Sanctions, and Penalties

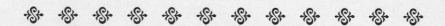

Actions taken by a college or university to dismiss or otherwise discipline faculty are among the most serious incidents that occur on campus. A faculty member who is asked to leave because of misconduct or incompetence will usually have problems continuing his or her academic career. This chapter deals with discipline and dismissal for cause—for specific acts or allegations of misconduct or inappropriate behavior. Generally, the institution initiates the case by taking or proposing an adverse action, such as resignation, retirement, or even dismissal. If the faculty member contests this action, the institution may use special internal procedure for managing such problems. In all cases, the institution asserts that the faculty member is unable to carry out his or her responsibilities; the university must then demonstrate that the discharge or suspension is justified. In response, the faculty member denies the charges, objects to the penalty, or both. In our discussion, we first consider the grounds for discipline or dismissal, then the basis for challenging the in-

24

stitution's actions, and finally the kind of penalties that are imposed.

Basis for Disciplinary Actions

The basis for disciplinary action is usually found in the faculty handbook or other governance documents. Institutional statements defining cause for initiating disciplinary sanctions vary widely. A few institutions continue to cling to ambiguous terms such as *moral turpitude*; most, however, express grounds for discipline in readily accessible, although not definitive, language. Many institutions incorporate by reference the American Association of University Professors/Association of American Colleges (AAUP/AAC) 1958 *Statement on Procedural Standards in Faculty Dismissal Proceedings* and follow the procedural steps described. The AAUP/AAC statement was developed as a guide for formulating dismissal procedures and does not attempt to define adequate cause for dismissal.

Incidents that provoke discipline and dismissal include personal misconduct, professional incompetence, certain political and religious beliefs and activities, and medical disability. The spectrum of acceptable or permissible activities depends on the nature of the institution and the types of students served. A professor of theology at the Moody Bible Institute of Chicago claimed he was dismissed because his wife wrote a book that advocated equality for women in the church. This alleged retaliatory action would be unthinkable on most campuses.

Policy statements that define the grounds for discipline and dismissal include these examples from Columbia University, Drew University, and Princeton University (in that order).

No dismissal shall be effected by the university except for adequate cause. By "adequate" cause is meant the clear manifestation by an academic staff member of his or her professional unfitness for the position. Evidence to demonstrate professional unfitness, under the above standard, may include, but is not limited to, evidence of gross inefficiency, habitual and intentional neglect of duty, or serious personal misconduct.

The definition of adequate cause for dismissal cannot be made precise. The general areas of concern that obviously may generate charges of misconduct sufficient for dismissal—or other forms of action, such as reprimand or suspension—are professional incompetence, unprofessional actions, and unethical or immoral conduct.

A member of the faculty may be suspended, dismissed, involuntarily retired early, or subject to discriminatory reduction in salary for cause only on the basis of (a) substantial and manifest incompetence, (b) substantial and manifest neglect of duty, or (c) conduct which is shown to violate the university rules and procedures applicable to a member of the faculty or substantially to impair the individual's performance of the full range of his or her responsibilities as a member of the faculty.

These policy statements illustrate the difficulty of describing with particularity the conditions or actions that may result in discipline. This lack of specificity presents problems when an academic institution is required to defend a disciplinary action in court For example, in a case at Northern Kentucky University, the district court ruled in favor of a dismissed faculty member on the basis that the university policies regarding unprofessional behavior were vague and overly broad.

Personal Misconduct and Professional Incompetence. Many disciplinary actions result from long-standing disagreements between individual faculty members and their departmental colleagues. Two widely publicized disputes, one at the University of Wisconsin and the other at Central Washington University, illustrate the controversial, impassioned atmosphere these cases can create. Walter J. Blaedel, a tenured chemistry professor at the University of Wisconsin at Madison for more than thirty years, refused in 1979 to teach a chemistry course, claiming unsafe conditions in the laboratory. In response, the university reduced his salary on a proportional basis. An exchange of charges ensued, with Blaedel alleging that his mail was censored, that courses were assigned to him without consultation, and that the department meeting where his termination was recommended was illegally called and conducted. The chemistry department charged that Blaedel refused to teach, that he refused to accept majority rule within the department, and that by bringing a bullhorn to a faculty meeting he was disruptive. When the dean of the college suspended Blaedel, he attempted to register students; for a time he was barred from the registration room by campus security officers. The departmental recommendation to force Blaedel into early retirement was endorsed by a faculty committee; the chancellor accepted the committee recommendation, which was subsequently approved by the regents. According to university officials, the heart of the matter was the professor's unwillingness to accept departmental decisions.

At Central Washington University, Charles I. Stastny, a tenured associate professor of political science, was accused of gross misconduct, insubordination, and violation of rules because of repeated unauthorized absences from class, including a four-day absence to conduct a criminology seminar at Hebrew University in Jerusalem. The professor claimed the charges were a result of personal animosity on the part of the administration and were an attempt to stifle his professional activities. The faculty grievance committee upheld the charges of insubordination and violation of rules but made no recommendation regarding dismissal. The university-appointed hearing officer, a lawyer from outside the institution, recommended dismissal. The university president then recommended to the trustees that Stastny be dismissed, and the board accepted the recommendation.

Conduct in the classroom is the subject of many disciplinary actions. Alleged infractions involve novel approaches to instruction, including the use of profanity and other devices to gain the attention of students. At Bowling Green State University (Ohio), an instructor of creative writing was stripped of his teaching duties when he played Russian roulette in class in an attempt to heighten the students' sense of literary feeling. Western State College in Colorado suspended an associate professor of history charged with physically and verbally abusing students in an extracurricular program in Oriental self-discipline. Following a ten-month investigation, the professor was reinstated, although the course was discontinued.

A professor of psychology of human relations at a junior college in Florida was suspended when he was accused of violating a college policy prohibiting the use of hypnosis in the classroom, despite the fact that the demonstration did not involve a student as subject. The professor noted that he had used hypnosis for many years to help students who came to him requesting his help to overcome their inability to concentrate, their fear of exams, and their failure to retain subject matter.

The use of profanity resulted in dismissal of a professor of social science at Shaw University in Raleigh, North Carolina. The professor filed a $250 thousand lawsuit against the university, claiming that he used language to show how the meaning of words depends on the context within which they are used.

Rarely are alleged personal and professional misconduct publicly joined as they were at Long Beach State University (California) in a case involving a controversial tenured associate professor of psychology who was suspended after admitting he had been "romantically involved" with students. In connection with a course in the psychology of sex, the professor was reported to have given course credit for homosexual and extramarital sexual encounters. The case took a bizarre turn when the professor acknowledged being intimately involved with students; he then went even further by releasing a letter written to colleagues two years before that outlined the benefits of dating students. After the university imposed a thirty-day suspension, he resigned his teaching post. In another example of alleged combined personal and professional misconduct, a tenured professor at the University of Arizona was disciplined with a six-month suspension by the Board of Regents after allegedly providing marijuana-laced cookies to students on a field trip.

Criticism of institutional management has occasionally prompted disciplinary action. At Philander Smith College in

Arkansas, faculty members were dismissed for insubordination when they complained about campus conditions to the Board of Trustees. The administration asserted that it was improper for faculty, in their role as managers, to make an end run around the administration. The National Labor Relations Board (NLRB) disagreed and ordered reinstatement with full back pay. In a case at Troy State University in Alabama, a circuit court of appeals upheld a lower court ruling that forbade the dismissal of a faculty member who reported rumors to a state legislative committee concerning financial irregularities in the investment of school funds by officials of the university. The courts accepted the claim that the faculty member's statements were protected under the First Amendment despite the fact that he told investigators he did not know whether the rumors were true.

Conviction on criminal charges related to campus activity may also result in dismissal, although in many cases the faculty member will resign before formal dismissal action is taken. At the University of Washington, a professor resigned after pleading guilty to a charge of misspending research funds; he had been convicted of a similar offense earlier at another university. A former faculty member at Northeastern University (Boston) was sentenced to prison after pleading guilty to stealing funds that had been allocated for a particular program. And, at New York University, the chair of the anthropology department was suspended and barred from campus after being convicted of producing and distributing illegal drugs.

At unionized institutions the right of the president to discipline or dismiss a faculty member may be limited by the terms of the collective bargaining agreement. Thus, at the University of British Columbia, the president was blocked in his efforts to fire a professor who was convicted of theft when he used grant funds to pay students for work unrelated to his research projects. The agreement between the faculty and the university vested final authority for faculty discipline in a three-member committee. The committee found the professor guilty of gross misconduct but ruled he be suspended for eighteen months without pay rather than dismissed.

Charges of forgery, fraudulent research, and plagiarism are among the most serious that can be brought against a faculty member. Because all academic endeavors rest on credibility, a substantiated charge of this kind usually destroys the faculty member's professional career. In highly publicized cases where fraudulent research was based on falsified data, faculty have resigned during the investigation rather than wait for formal findings. At Wake Forest University (North Carolina), a researcher on the medical school faculty resigned when the dean of the medical school recommended his dismissal; an investigative report stated that, in "at least one project, experiments were not performed as described in a manuscript prepared for publication."

Among forgery and plagiarism cases, one of the most sensational—because of press coverage and the prestige of the people involved—occurred at the Yale School of Medicine. After an outside auditor recognized irregularities and flaws in data presented in a study of insulin binding in anorexic patients, the researcher who conducted the study admitted falsifying results. This incident was particularly alarming because the research results were coauthored with a nationally renowned endocrinologist. The plagiarism came to light when Yale researchers critiqued the manuscript of an endocrinologist at the National Institute of Health as part of the prepublication review procedure for *The New England Journal of Medicine*.

Issues involving professional competence usually arise during the peer-evaluation process, before tenure is conferred. In conferring tenure, the institution, in effect, certifies a professor's professional competence. Unless a university has substantial and verifiable evidence that a tenured professor's teaching has deteriorated, it usually cannot justify termination for incompetence.

This issue was raised at Northern Michigan University when it terminated a tenured associate professor in the department of education principally because of incompetent teaching. Responding to complaints from students, the dean asked an evaluation committee to review the professor's teaching effectiveness, and, with the committee, he developed a survey to be completed by students; the data indicated that students were dissatisfied. When the professor failed to respond to the negative survey results, the dean concurred with the evaluation-committee recommendation that the professor be terminated for "incompetence in teaching performance as indicated by repeated student complaints, . . . intransigency in addressing the issues regarding teaching performance, . . . uncooperative attitude, . . . and unprofessional conduct toward students." The provost then advised the professor by letter that unless significant improvement occurred, he would be terminated at the end of that academic year. The professor claimed the administration should provide specific criteria to measure teaching effectiveness, and he questioned the validity of student opinion as a measure.

These issues were presented in a six-day arbitration hearing that produced more than 1,000 transcript pages. The arbitrator noted deficiencies in the professor's teaching of undergraduates, his refusal to meet with the dean, and his uncooperative attitude and approach to the evaluation committee. The arbitrator, however, ordered reinstatement of the professor (without back pay) on the basis that the termination was arbitrary and abrupt in not providing sufficient time for the professor to improve. He noted that "once tenure is granted and a problem is discovered, a reasonable time must be afforded to the individual to correct the problem." He further noted that reinstatement put the burden on the professor "to make the necessary changes to improve his teaching performance."

The broad category of insubordination is a catchall that covers misconduct, impropriety, dereliction and neglect of duty, and other such forms of personal or professional misbehavior. The charge of insubordination as grounds for dismissal was made in two arbitration cases involving the State University of New York (SUNY) when faculty members challenged SUNY actions. The university moved to dismiss a tenured professor of statistics for refusing to comply with a directive to undergo a complete physical examination in connection with a fractured toe and related problems resulting from a fall in the shower. SUNY cited two previous incidents of insubordination and an unsatisfactory work record to support the penalty. The grievant claimed he was willing to take an appropriate examination but that a complete physical was not warranted and constituted a humiliating, degrading, and dehumanizing invasion of privacy. The arbitrator, noting that the professor submitted unclear and conflicting medical diagnoses regarding the extent of the injuries, ruled that it was not unreasonable for the university to require a complete physical and rejected the contention that such an examination would be dehumanizing. He sustained the university's claim of insubordination, based on the current incident as well as the two previous incidents, stating that these incidents "reinforce an impression of continuing truculence, . . . an attitude that does not contribute to a fruitful academic relationship." A $1 thousand fine was imposed.

Another SUNY case involved a coach of intercollegiate athletics charged with insubordination on several grounds: permitting students to participate in athletic events when he knew they were ineligible under college and athletic-association regulations; billing the university for unauthorized travel expenses; refusing to comply with requests for information about possible violations in accepting reimbursement of funds from the booster club; and violating purchasing procedures, including collusion with a vendor and maintenance of false inventory. The arbitrator ruled that the coach committed disciplinable misconduct on each of the charges, ordered a six-month suspension, and denied the grievant's request for reinstatement as coach.

A simple recitation of the outcome in this case, however, is not particularly instructive by itself. Because of the multiple charges and the complexity of the issues, it took twelve days to complete the testimony. Many of the events involving student eligibility were untimely under the grievance procedure and thus were outside the purview of the arbitrator. The arbitrator was not convinced that the proven acts of misconduct in their totality warranted discharge; he concluded that although "SUNY has provided proof of acts of grievant demonstrating dereliction of duty, administrative irresponsibility and incompetence, and repeated insubordination, none of those acts were directly connected with grievant's duty as an assistant professor of physical education. In fact, no evidence or testimony was presented that grievant committed misconduct in the course of fulfilling his duties as assistant professor." In another section of the opinion, the arbitrator concluded that although "grievant is competent in the area of teaching, . . . he has demonstrated woeful incompetence and laxity in the related areas of administration." On this basis, the arbitrator did not require SUNY to reappoint him to the post of coach.

Impairment. There are shadings rather than sharp distinctions between inability to perform because of objectionable conduct and inability to perform because of recognized mental illness. It is also difficult to distinguish between lateness and absence caused by irresponsibility and lateness and absence caused by alcoholism. Clearly, profanity in the classroom is at some distance from a heart attack or weakness due to cancer. But there is real question whether an unconventional life-style, use of drugs, or belligerency are manifestations of willful disobedience that call for disciplinary penalties or whether they are symptoms of a medical or psychological condition. Whereas medical impairments are excused and often evoke official sympathy, even though they may be grounds for termination, misconduct and manifest neglect of duty do not allow for mitigation. The difference is significant in relation to the future career of the faculty member, who may have to explain the reason for termination.

Increasingly, colleges and universities face the problem of appropriate termination of faculty members whose conditions or capabilities do not permit them to carry out their responsibilities. The problem has been heightened because of budgetary restrictions, reorganizations, and changes in student preference in fields of study. Academic institutions, perhaps to a greater degree than other institutions, have been able to absorb the impaired faculty member or hidden pensioner because the work is not physically arduous, the range or scope of activity is wide, and teaching can easily shade into research, study, and preceptorships.

To a large extent, these cases do not appear as reported grievances because they are handled through informal negotiation. Some result in a transitional solution that respects the contribution and dignity of the professor and permits the university to exercise its managerial prerogatives. In a typical case, the department chair, speaking for the administration and other colleagues, suggests that the faculty member leave. If the benefit program permits it, the department chair proposes disability or other form of compensation. Such an arrangement is possible only when a faculty member is eligible for such benefits because of age, years of service, or degree of physical or mental impairment. Many institutions in financial difficulty have expanded fringe benefits temporarily or permanently to permit retirement under liberal conditions.

Impairment as a result of alcoholism is increasingly common. The issue is whether there is cause for requesting a voluntary departure or imposing a dismissal. How matters such as benefits, possible rehabilitation, opportunity for restoration, and suspension versus termination are handled depends on the situation and school policy. There is growing acceptance of alcoholism as a disease covered under federal laws dealing with the handicapped; therefore, an institution faced with the problem must act carefully to avoid potential lawsuits.

Cases involving life-styles, including sexual orientation and preference, have arisen at several institutions. At Georgetown University, a Catholic institution, an avowed homosexual was dismissed. The university argued that it could not countenance such an open sexual preference in light of its religious foundation. The case became prominent because it raised the question of the prerogatives of private religious institutions. Georgetown is located in the District of Columbia, which protects homosexuals against discrimination. A somewhat similar issue was raised at Long Beach State University (California) where an instructor in a course on women and their bodies was suspended when members of an evangelical Christian group complained that her teaching promoted lesbianism. The instructor was reinstated after an investigation determined that her presentation of the subject matter was appropriately balanced.

Sexual Harassment. Clearly one of the most sensitive areas is termination of faculty members based on charges by students. These cases raise difficult questions of fact, evidence, and proof, especially when an individual charges sexual harassment. In several cases involving sexual harassment, the courts sustained dismissal or suspension of teachers where established procedures were followed and fairness and due process were observed.

In the past, colleges and universities handled allegations of sexual harassment informally if at all. At most, these institutions sent a letter of reprimand to the faculty member charged with the offense. In 1980, these informal arrangements were challenged when the EEOC issued guidelines stating that sexual harassment is a violation of Title VII of the Civil Rights Act of 1964. Under the guidelines, a student can hold the administration responsible for incidents of sexual harassment if it fails to act when it knows or should know that an incident occurred. This provision makes it likely that an institution will take disciplinary action against an alleged offender to protect against a potential lawsuit from a harassed student. The threat of legal action is sufficiently serious that even in situations where the administration has doubts about the legitimacy of the complaint, it may feel pressured to instigate disciplinary charges.

Cases involving sexual harassment at academic institutions are somewhat different from those encountered in industry. The teacher is a mature authority figure who has substantial influence over impressionable and frequently immature students. Faculty members bear a special responsibility because of their role in stimulating intellectual growth; the collegial nature of the learning experience may foster an atmosphere of informality that encourages impulsive behavior.

In specific allegations of sexual harassment, problems arise concerning credibility or the interpretation of events that almost always occur in private. Jesse Simons, a distinguished arbitrator who has handled a number of cases involving charges of sexual harassment within the SUNY system, notes that female students are not necessarily immune to fantasy on the one hand or vengeance on the other. He also notes wide variation in the level of sophistication of students and the need to consider the context within which these complaints are presented.

In considering the appropriateness of a disciplinary action based on charges of sexual harassment, the arbitrator must determine whether the faculty member's sexually aggressive behavior is compulsive. If so, the faculty member may be considered to have an illness, and disciplinary action can then be similar to that in cases involving alcohol or drug abuse. Under such circumstances, an arbitrator may require the offending faculty member to participate in a treatment program.

Perhaps the most significant lawsuit involving sexual harassment is *Alexander* v. *Yale,* which established the right of students to sue under Title IX of the Education Amendments of 1972 if the institution has no procedure for handling sexual-harassment complaints. The court, however, dismissed the students' claims on the grounds that they were moot and that they had failed to meet the burden of proof. As a result of this decision, most institutions have developed procedures.

One of the first formally presented cases was a 1978 lawsuit involving a tenured professor at Whitman College in Washington state. He brought a $2 million libel action against the college, claiming damage to his professional reputation when he was dismissed on the recommendation of the faculty academic council. The council determined there was evidence the professor had made sexual advances toward staff, wives of faculty, and students. The court dismissed the professor's claim on the basis that the college had followed proper dismissal procedures.

The most widely publicized case involved two lawsuits arising from alleged incidents at Clark University in Massachusetts. Responding to complaints of sexual harassment, the university imposed disciplinary sanctions against an associate professor of sociology. The professor brought a $23 million lawsuit against the complainants on the basis that their false charges injured his reputation. Two female faculty members who brought the complaint against him subsequently brought suit against Clark University, charging that the university had retaliated against them for filing the complaint. The suit requested $1.3 million in damages and an injunction ordering the university to stop permitting or condoning sexual harassment. A settlement was reached under which the university agreed to take no further action against the professor and he agreed not to serve as department chair, not to participate in decisions regarding the status of the complainants, and to take a leave of absence and a sabbatical.

A sexual-harassment case at Harvard University was settled when its administrative board, which handles academic and disciplinary issues involving students, changed the grade of a female student in a poetry workshop from C to Pass after she charged the visiting professor from Boston University with sexually harassing her. The student, whose identity was not revealed, claimed her mediocre grade was influenced by her failure to respond to the professor's sexual advances. After an investigation, the student was told that formal action had been taken against the professor. The action consisted of a letter of reproach sent by Harvard to Boston University. This fairly mild response drew attention to the need for Harvard to devise effective procedures to deal with sexual-harassment complaints and specifically to inform the victim of the action taken against the harasser. Students had complained also that there were no time limits on the investigation, no forum for appeal, and no process of reviewing students' grades when complaints were made. At the time the case was settled, Harvard announced that strict procedures would be developed for handling sexual-harassment complaints in the future.

Challenging Disciplinary Actions

Within an industrial setting, employees frequently challenge disciplinary actions on the basis that the punishment is overly severe or inappropriate or that the employee should not be held accountable because of extenuating circumstances such as alcoholism or drug abuse. Faculty members can challenge disciplinary actions also as violations of academic freedom and as retaliation for activities objected to by the institution.

Violations of Academic Freedom. The academic freedom challenge may be based on substantive issues such as espousing an unpopular ideology. Disputes of this type were frequent in the 1950s, at the height and in the aftermath of Senator Joseph

McCarthy's investigations into Communist infiltration of American society, and again in the 1960s and early 1970s in the context of protests against the war in Vietnam. Recent challenges are based on union activism and Marxist ideology. In its *Special Report on Labor Relations in Higher Education, 1981,* the Bureau of National Affairs noted a dramatic increase in major cases involving First Amendment rights of faculty. The report stated that there were probably more of these cases in 1981 than at any time since the McCarthy era.

For more than forty years, the AAUP has been a potent force for the protection of academic freedom. Its well-known and widely accepted 1940 *Statement of Principles on Academic Freedom and Tenure,* developed jointly with the AAC, is the standard by which allegations of the abridgment of academic freedom are judged. The AAUP receives more than 1,000 complaints each year from faculty who believe they were dismissed without the protection of academic due process. According to Jordan E. Kurland, associate general secretary of the AAUP, most of the complaints are resolved informally. The association formally intervenes in approximately 150 cases each year and about a dozen cases result in a full investigation, which sometimes leads to AAUP censure of institutions when breaches of academic freedom are verified. Improper dismissal of tenured faculty is the most frequent cause for AAUP censure. In recent years the basis for alleging violations of academic freedom has shifted away from retaliation for political activities to personal issues involving life-styles, such as cohabitation and sexual preferences.

Although AAUP censure imposes no obligation on AAUP members to turn down employment at censured institutions, censure is imposed only after a highly visible vote of the full AAUP membership, which highlights the possibility that a candidate for a faculty position may not receive the protection he or she deems important. Probably the most salutary aspect of the AAUP investigatory process, however, is the fact that, in negotiating with an institution, the association can exert pressure, either informally or through its investigatory process, to gain improvements in protections of academic freedom.

The issue of academic freedom was raised at the University of Texas, where an instructor in the government department was relieved of her teaching duties and reassigned to a nonteaching faculty position because the department chair believed her commitment to a left-wing ideology would prevent her from providing quality instruction. This action was taken despite a grievance committee report that the instructor's right to free expression under the First Amendment had been infringed.

Receiving justice can be a lengthy process when the issue of academic freedom is raised during a period of political turmoil. It took thirty years for a group of professors who were dismissed in 1952 by Hunter and Queens colleges in New York City to obtain compensation for unjust dismissals based on their refusal to state whether they had been members of the Communist Party. The ten former professors shared in a $935 thousand settlement.

In a case reminiscent of the 1950s, an assistant professor of history who lost his position when he announced communist sympathies was reinstated at the University of Arkansas by a federal district court on the grounds that his political beliefs were protected by the First and Fourteenth amendments. The University of Nevada at Reno, however, was upheld in dismissing an assistant professor of English who violated a university code requiring faculty members to show respect for the opinions of others when he participated in an antiwar demonstration in 1970.

Retaliation. Faculty may challenge the imposition of discipline on the basis that the institution retaliated for an activity objected to by the administration or a department. It is difficult to demonstrate that a disciplinary decision was based on spite or revenge because the faculty member must present evidence and credible testimony regarding the existence of invidious motivation. Faculty have had some success, however, in both arbitration and the courts in overturning disciplinary actions on this basis. In 1981, a jury found Wayne State University (Michigan) guilty of illegally discharging a faculty member in retaliation for her advocacy of civil rights for women and blacks. She was awarded $85 thousand in damages.

The retaliation defense was successful in a federal lawsuit involving an athletic scandal at the University of New Mexico. The plaintiff, an untenured faculty member and head of the Afro-American studies program, claimed the university used the scandal, which involved transcript forgeries and the awarding of academic credit to athletes who did not do the work, as an excuse to sever the professor's employment. The professor, who was awarded $147 thousand in damages, claimed his dismissal was in retaliation for his criticism of university policies, his advocacy of the rights of athletes and their need for academic counseling, and his push for the hiring of minorities and the designation of his Afro-American studies program as a department.

A tenured associate professor of economics at Bloomsbury State College (Pennsylvania) successfully challenged his dismissal on the grounds that it was in retaliation for his failure to support the department chair for election to a position in the faculty association. The dismissal was based on the professor's breach of a written contract, signed at the time tenure was awarded, that he would take a leave of absence to pursue graduate work in quantitative economics to prepare him to teach mathematics and statistics. He contended in arbitration that he was hired as an economic historian and that his contract renewal and tenure in the fourth year of employment were not conditional on taking further graduate work. The college tenure-committee recommendation to award tenure stated that it was "strictly on the ground that during his three-year period of probation . . . he has demonstrated overall strength in teaching, scholarship, and college service." The arbitrator stated that the professor, "through no fault of his own, was placed in the position after the election of having his academic qualifications denigrated and his job security jeopardized despite satisfactory performance as a member of the economics department. As a result, he was compelled to sign the agreement in order to obtain tenure and save his position at the college. For these reasons, his repudiation of the agreement . . . may not be found to be just cause for the termination of his employment."

Another claim of retaliation occurred at Stephen F. Austin State University in Texas when a former art professor claimed he was dismissed for refusing to participate in a grading scheme to inflate student attendance in order to obtain additional state revenue. The professor, contending that his First Amendment rights were violated, was upheld in the federal trial court but was unpersuasive in the circuit court of appeals. The appellate court ruled that he was dismissed for "his continual lack of cooperation and unacceptable conduct, of which the grading incident was just one example." The Supreme Court declined review.

Sanctions and Penalties

Unlike penal codes, institutional policies do not prescribe the sanctions for misconduct. The circumstances are too varied and the problems too complex to be anticipated through some type of parallel listing of crime and punishment. Because of institutional obligations to students and the way academic life is arranged (semesters, projects, tutorials, thesis committees, collegial relationships), the imposition of disciplinary penalties presents unusual difficulties. Progressive discipline, as exercised in industry, through warning, suspension, transfer, discharge, or loss of benefits, is hardly applicable when students in the classroom depend on continuing competent instruction to meet requirements for advancement, graduation, and professional examinations. Thus, for example, it may be unreasonable, if not impossible, to remove a professor temporarily during a semester or to assign a faculty member to a lower position. Harsh penalties are rarely inflicted, not only because they cripple career development but because they critically affect students, colleagues, and programs. Penalties not only must match the infraction or violation at the base of the disciplinary decision but must fit the school structure and the expectations of academic life. Although it is usually unstated, it is hoped that the faculty member will resign at an appropriate juncture, saving face (no recorded penalty) and avoiding embarrassment for the institution.

What are the options? Impairment, disability, or habits

affecting ability to teach may be penalized by the imposition of early retirement or the allowance of sickness benefits. Immediate dismissal is reserved for the most objectionable conduct or incompetence. Termination for insubordination may be made effective at the end of a term rather than in the middle, unless the conduct interferes significantly with teaching.

Lighter penalties than termination include suspension between semesters, with the resulting loss of pay or benefits. This penalty affects the faculty member but not the students. Or there may be a salary reduction. Frequently this option is ordered when termination or suspension, including removal from campus, is deemed too severe. A light penalty is usually based on the otherwise good record of the faculty member or the disparity between the offense and the penalty. In arbitration proceedings, the arbitrator may reduce the penalty imposed by the administration; thus, a harsh penalty may be imposed by the institution with the expectation that it will be ameliorated by an outsider.

When grievants successfully challenge disciplinary decisions, institutions must act to repair, correct, or compensate. Such action may be difficult. Reparation through reinstatement may not be feasible if, for instance, the dismissed faculty member has been replaced. In such situations, a wronged faculty member may never be made whole, even with back pay and interest and the restoration of benefits and perquisites. The most common sanction, by court order, consent agreement, or internal ruling, is a monetary settlement to cover salary loss and injury to status or reputation. In discrimination cases, an individual case is usually closed in this way, with the college or university being required to revise personnel programs or practices to prevent similar claims. For the institution, such an internal system must surely be preferable to the penalties that administrative agencies and courts can inflict.

CHAPTER 3

Faculty Rights:
Academic Affairs,
Collective Bargaining,
and Employment Conditions

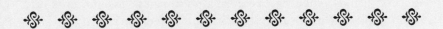

As members of the academic community, faculty members enjoy rights deriving from both their professional calling and their relationship with the institution. In the broadest sense, faculty rights conceivably encompass a role in the management of an institution, including a possible part in the selection of the president and other officers, relationships with the board of trustees and alumni, and a voice in the funding decisions of the institution. These are not entitlements; they are based on a sense of collegiality, the intensity of which is unique to each institution. Here the concern is only with rights individual faculty members may claim through grievances or appeals procedures. One set of rights concerns governance—that is, participation in the academic affairs of the institution. These rights include involvement in the formulation of academic policy and participation on governance committees. A second set of rights is entitlements of faculty members as professionals and as employees to specified conditions of work, privileges, and benefits. Both sets

43

of rights are frequently set forth either in institution-wide policy statements or in individual agreements.

By tradition, faculty in many institutions serve as both managers and teachers and are regularly called on for opinion and advice, particularly on academic matters. At issue in recent years, however, is the demand of faculty members for protection as employees under labor laws designed to assure workers the right to organize and be represented. Precisely because faculty members in many institutions are seen as engaging in many essential aspects of governance, they have sometimes been denied the rights of employees under statute.

In general, faculty members as employees have the same rights as other employees: a term of employment or understood commitment; the perquisites of employment, including salary and other compensation and fringe benefits; and specific working conditions, such as those related to class assignments and opportunities for advancement within the department and professional community. University employment also provides certain professional rights, such as the right to engage in independent research and protection of intellectual activity.

The preceding chapters discussed issues involving faculty members' claims for status through promotion and tenure and their objections to actual or proposed discipline or discharge. Here the focus is primarily on problems and issues customarily associated with employment conditions and participation in academic affairs, usually through an established faculty senate or union. In recent years, special issues have arisen involving part-time faculty. Problems associated with the increasing use of part-timers will undoubtedly grow as colleges are attracted to this more flexible and often less permanent employment relationship.

Participation in Governance

Unlike contracts in business or industry, those in academic life, whether negotiated or not, accept the principle and practice of collegial participation in governance. Obviously, the degree of participation varies depending on the mission and history of an institution. Traditional rights and privileges of faculty have for years been taken for granted because neither faculty nor administrators see an advantage in precisely defining respective territories. Indeed, as long as no element in the institutional community (faculty, administration, or students) insists on a clear definition of its turf, there is no need to disturb the somewhat amorphous but nonetheless workable relationship that developed over many decades.

In the late 1960s and early 1970s, student demands for clearly delineated rights forced other segments of this triangle to define more precisely than before their respective areas of authority. On some campuses, this development coincided with the unionization of faculty. These changes have tested the degree to which decision making is shared by the various groups in the academic community. For example, controversies have arisen because some universities have refused to consider a significant role for the faculty in such matters as budgeting and retrenchment. Conversely, in some institutions, faculty have pulled back from shared responsibility, hesitating to identify faculty members to be terminated in fiscal crises, for example.

The scope or area of faculty involvement is by no means the same in all institutions nor does it necessarily remain constant at the same institution. For example, when a faculty union renegotiates a contract, the area of faculty participation is often subject to review and change. Similarly, with or without a union contract, economic circumstances and student preferences, among other factors, may extend or limit faculty influence in management. Moreover, the faculty itself is a mix of interests, and departments and units within the university do not all have the same influence.

The issues at stake in disputes concerning governance run the gamut from strictly parochial matters, such as the selection of department chairs, to major commitments of institutional and financial support for new educational and research activities. At unionized institutions, the faculty's role and that of deans and department chairs is generally described in the collective bargaining agreement and in the by-laws of the college. Disputes arise when there is ambiguity between these documents.

At colleges where the relationship between faculty and administration is less formally articulated than at unionized institutions, administrators have greater room for exercising authority.

In a dispute involving the appointment of a department chair, an arbitrator ruled that Onondaga Community College (New York) violated the union contract by failing to appoint one of the two candidates for the position nominated by the department in accordance with accepted procedures. The issue arose when the president requested that the nominees report on their plans for the department and one of the nominees did not comply. The college contended that this refusal reduced the field to only one candidate. The arbitrator disagreed and directed the college to appoint retroactively the other nominee.

At the University of Colorado, a professor in the medical school brought suit charging that he had been improperly removed as chair of the anesthesiology department. In settling the suit, the university agreed to pay the professor $73 thousand plus legal expenses.

Collective Bargaining

Faculty rights in a collectively organized institution stem from two sources: the existing personnel policies and statutes and the collectively bargained agreement. Usually specific provisions in an agreement supersede an inconsistent policy statement. In a dispute over the relationship between the union contract and documents dealing with institutional governance at the University of New Haven, however, a faculty member protested the dean's nonrenewal of his position as head of the fine arts department. He claimed that this matter was subject to negotiation with the union. The arbitrator, however, ruled that the faculty-senate document covering department-head vacancies limited department members to making recommendations; thus, the dean had the final authority to renew department heads.

Although the day-to-day situation of the faculty in a unionized institution may not seem to differ from their situation before the advent of the union, proponents of collective bargaining perceive that the difference is the contractually required participation of the union in important decisions affecting the faculty. For example, the union agreement may require consultation or negotiations over specific personnel to be retrenched and may even contain a specified procedure for reducing the number of faculty positions.

At the more prestigious institutions, faculty have traditionally participated to a great extent in decision making. It follows that they are less likely than faculty at less prestigious institutions to seek collective agreements to establish their rights. Faculty at prestigious institutions play prominent roles in making decisions about almost all aspects of professional affairs and employment, including admission standards, curriculum, course requirements, degree requirements, and the selection, promotion, and retention of colleagues. In these institutions, faculty senates, departmental committees, and other structures provide for joint decision making by faculty and the administration.

Faculty rights in public institutions have been determined as much by legislation as by policies and practices. Legislation permitting public employees to join unions was stimulated in large part by the growth of state university systems, including the remarkable expansion of the community colleges. This growth greatly expanded the number of public employees and exerted pressure on state legislatures to pass laws permitting collective bargaining. A secondary effect has been an upgrading of the status of community college professors, who, prior to collective bargaining, were viewed by many as second-class teachers more closely aligned to the high schools than to higher education. Because legislation extending the right to organize does not distinguish between instruction in the four-year and two-year colleges, many state universities and junior colleges became unionized. In the 1970s, an increasing number of faculty in independent institutions also organized and achieved collective bargaining status. In 1982, the National Center for the Study of Collective Bargaining in Higher Education and the Professions identified 382 contracts, of which 313 were in public institutions.

The basis for recognition of collective bargaining agents in independent institutions is the National Labor Relations Act (the Wagner Act as amended by the Taft-Hartley Act). To be afforded the protection of the act, faculty must be employees as opposed to managers, for both the act and numerous NLRB and federal court decisions have sharply differentiated these two statuses. Generally speaking, employees who fit under the definition of the act are entitled to the protection of the act when it comes to union activity or individual rights developed under collective bargaining. In contrast, there is no legal requirement that employers bargain with managers.

In 1980, a Supreme Court decision in a case involving Yeshiva University in New York dealt with the conditions under which faculty can expect statutory protection for their organizing and bargaining efforts. The court held that institutions of higher learning are not required to bargain with faculty unions whose members play a significant role in institutional affairs. In effect, the court deemed these faculty members to be officials and managers rather than employees entitled to protection under the National Labor Relations Act. Both the circuit court of appeals and the Supreme Court determined, for example, that, under the act, faculty participation in screening candidates for positions and in tenure decisions made faculty members supervisors rather than employees.

Many see the Yeshiva decision as a misreading by the court of the managerial role of the faculty. To illustrate, in many independent institutions, the board of trustees can grant tenure despite unanimous rejection of the candidate by colleagues in the department. Moreover, faculty consultations with administration range from the merely perfunctory to a serious exchange of views. It would be hard to convince faculty who have a perfunctory role that they are indeed managers.

Because the degree of participation of faculty in such managerial activities differs widely from institution to institution, the applicability of the Yeshiva decision must be decided on a case-by-case basis. For example, the Supreme Court decision was ruled by the NLRB to be inapplicable to the medical faculty at Yeshiva University. In analyzing the composition of the faculty-senate steering committee and the governance structure, the NLRB determined that college officials control recruitment and hiring of physicians and that the principal committees of the senate, which handle matters of student admissions, curriculum, and faculty status, are dominated by administrative staff. In fact, the grievance committee is the only committee on which there are no administrators, and the existing grievance procedure does not require the college to consider the recommendations of the committee.

Nevertheless, the presence of any significant degree of managerial participation by the faculty raises the possibility either that the National Labor Relations Act cannot be invoked to achieve union recognition or that recognition of an existing union may be withdrawn. Of course, the Yeshiva case does not prevent institutions from continuing a collective bargaining relationship with faculty unions if they so desire. Faculty, however, cannot charge the institution with an unfair labor practice if it does not choose to do so or if a provision of the volunteered agreement is alleged to have been violated.

It is too early to fully evaluate the complete impact of the Yeshiva decision. So far it has had a chilling effect on further unionization of independent institutions. The NLRB upheld a number of institutions in their refusal to recognize new unions. These institutions include Ithaca College in New York and Duquesne University Law School and Thiel College in Pennsylvania. The Yeshiva decision was applied to an existing union for the first time in 1982 at the University of New Haven. Here, faculty unionized for most of the previous decade were declared managerial employees, barred from protection by the federal labor law. The NLRB administrative law judge ruled that New Haven faculty effectively determine course offerings, teaching loads, graduation standards, and student-body size, and have substantial control over tenure, hiring, and promotion decisions.

Nevertheless, it can be argued that the existence of a faculty union, even though it is not protected by the National Labor Relations Act, makes life easier for the administration than it is without a union. Once the process of defining respective turf begins in earnest, it becomes beneficial for the administration to establish the scope of the area it alone controls. On those campuses where faculty unions are recognized, this differentiation is accelerated through the negotiation process. As administrations become concerned with their role as employers, they focus on defining and articulating management rights. As a result, the dichotomy between employer and employees becomes sharply etched. Withdrawal of union recognition brings a return to the untidy old days when the respective jurisdictions of faculty and administration were fuzzy and often amorphous. Having experienced the benefits of clearly defined managerial prerogatives, a board of trustees might be expected to think twice before determining to withdraw recognition from an existing union. Moreover, the circumstances are favorable for the trustees in another way. By continuing to recognize the union, they retain their clearly defined managerial position and remain immune from the strictures of the National Labor Relations Act. This is a rare case of having it both ways.

Collective bargaining agreements may not establish new rights, but they often establish clear definitions and methods for resolving differences and ambiguities. The collective bargaining agreement, for example, may stipulate conditions for promotion or tenure and specify how such decisions will be made. In addition, the collective agreement may indicate whether the president, the board, or a faculty committee has final authority in such decisions. Thus, although the provisions in personnel policies and collective agreements may be substantively the same, the means for interpreting them may be markedly different. The collective bargaining agreement gives the union an opportunity to represent its members and present its case when a problem of entitlement or discipline arises. In other words, an appeal is more likely to be an accepted part of the process than it is without a collective bargaining agreement.

What is lost to the individual faculty member is the ability to bargain individually because, under union provisions, the institution is bound to treat all similarly situated faculty members in the same way. However, at least one institution, CUNY, provides a special category to attract nationally prominent scholars. These distinguished professors are covered by compensation arrangements outside the bargaining process.

Compensation, Benefits, and Conditions of Employment

In the broadest sense, a professor is an employee with the same basic rights afforded to all other employees at the institution. In addition, however, the academic relationship carries with it both traditional and negotiated rights. Understandably, most claims and grievances arising out of this relationship concern requests for benefits, perquisites, and privileges to which faculty members believe they are entitled by specific contract provisions, personnel policies, or university tradition. These claims run the gamut from retirement provisions to such relatively minor concerns as the appropriateness of deducting unpaid parking fines from the compensation of faculty members. Almost all university or college grievance officers would agree that the number of grievable topics is virtually infinite. This section covers some of the common and important issues raised in connection with entitlements.

For descriptive purposes, faculty members' professional and employment entitlements can be separated into salary and other benefits and questions of professional independence, such as the right to free expression and the nature of the professional contribution. Allegations of discrimination on the basis of either sex or race have been grounds for many disputes over employment entitlements. Frequently, the issue is one of disparate salaries or other benefits. For example, in a lawsuit involving the University of the District of Columbia, a predominantly black university, a white accounting professor reached a $45 thousand out-of-court settlement after claiming he was denied salary increases because of discrimination.

In a case involving physical education faculty at Western Oregon State College, a federal district court ruled that six women faculty members in the departments of physical education and elementary education were victims of intentional sex bias on the basis that they received lower starting salaries than their male counterparts. They were awarded $244 thousand in back pay and damages. The judge declared that a comparison of the salary levels of women physical education faculty and male coaches was valid because teaching is the primary duty for both groups. Similarly, a federal district judge awarded $1 million in back pay to 117 female faculty members and administrators at the University of South Alabama in one of the largest sex-discrimination suits brought against a university. The suit was based on payroll data that showed discrepancies between male and female faculty in compensation and promotion.

Pension and salary inequities were also the issues in a 1975 case in federal district court brought on behalf of 250 women physicians at Yeshiva University's Albert Einstein College of Medicine. The physicians alleged sex discrimination based on wide discrepancies in pension benefits and salaries for male and female faculty. The university countered that salaries were set by the going rate and were tied to performance and the budget and further asserted that the analysis presented by the women omitted such variables as experience and credentials, which accounted for the discrepancies. In the area of pensions, a comprehensive claim was brought by women faculty who alleged that the Teachers Insurance Annuity Association-College Retirement Equities Fund (TIAA-CREF) discriminated against them in that they paid the same premiums as male faculty but received lower annual payments when they retired based on their longer life expectancy.

Salary discrepancies are receiving growing attention as colleges seek to reward professors in popular academic disciplines so that they will not be tempted to accept lucrative offers from industry or from other campuses. Historically, colleges have established across-the-board pay levels for professors of equal rank and experience on the basis that each academic discipline is of equal merit. In the past, exceptions to this norm were limited to law and medicine. The trend, however, is toward providing sweeteners for professors of finance, accounting, computer science, and engineering. A 1982 survey of thirty-two engineering schools, conducted by the American Association for Engineering Education, found that in the previous year more than half provided additional compensation for engineering faculty. At Princeton University, the difference in starting salaries for junior professors in engineering and in the humanities can run as high as $10 thousand.

The use of selective salary increases in the California state university system was challenged after the chancellor ordered extra pay for faculty in the fields of engineering and computer science as a means of aiding recruitment and retention of faculty. The union filed a complaint of unfair labor practice that included a charge that the chancellor failed to consult with either the faculty senate or the union before issuing her executive order. The faculty union at Arizona State University raised a somewhat similar issue. The union filed a lawsuit claiming a violation of due-process guarantees when the university distributed funds allocated by the state legislature for merit raises without first establishing guidelines for the distribution.

Eligibility for a salary bonus based on merit was the subject of a lawsuit involving the president of the University of Texas and a professor who claimed his bonus was rescinded because his lobbying activities angered members of the state legislature. The federal appeals court agreed that the bonus was withheld illegally because the professor's political activities were a factor in the president's decision to retract the bonus.

Discrimination on religious grounds was the subject of an entitlement case at Baylor College of Medicine (Texas). Baylor was sued for $500 thousand in damages by two Jewish physicians who claimed restraint of trade when they were denied rotation assignments to the Saudi Arabia Medical Center. The doctors claimed the center offered special medical experience not otherwise available, as well as high pay and family benefits. Baylor, which has an antidiscrimination policy, denied that it violated this policy.

In an issue involving retirement, a Nobel laureate in chemistry instituted a grievance at the University of Houston when he was being forced to retire at age sixty-nine. He charged that he had made an agreement with the university when he came from Sussex University in England that he could retire when he chose, despite university policy that faculty members over sixty-five would remain on a year-to-year basis only on request from the department that they be retained.

The assignment of office and laboratory space can also be

a cause for dispute. At the University of Texas at Austin, a tenured zoology professor sued the university and his department chair when his laboratory facilities were reduced from 1,000 to 300 square feet. The professor charged that the decision was made without proper notice or a hearing. The department chair defended the action on the basis of an overwhelming faculty vote in favor of the change.

Cases that focus on the employment relationship also include disputes over work load. This was a long-standing issue at CUNY, where it took six years for an arbitration award to be issued. The complicated award distinguished, for purposes of computing contact hours, between courses requiring sizable amounts of outside preparation, such as large lectures and laboratory courses, and those requiring minimal preparation, such as physical education courses. In computing work load, the arbitrator also considered student-faculty ratios per program, split schedules, and the number of graduate students in the program. The award, which dealt only with contact hours for full-time teaching faculty, stated that it was not the intent to increase the work load of faculty currently employed. The arbitrator's award, however, did not put these issues to rest. Because it involved so many factors that have broad implications for the operation of the system, the CUNY administration and the Professional Staff Congress, which represents the faculty, entered into negotiations after the award was issued to come up with specific approaches for implementing the intent of award.

External factors unrelated to college or university programs or activities may also affect the status of faculty members within their institutions. Public institutions that are governed or whose budgets are controlled by a state legislature or executive department are particularly vulnerable. For example, under a law that bars any legislator from holding an executive or judicial appointment, a geography professor at Southern Connecticut State College was forced to give up his position when he was elected to the state legislature. The state supreme court held that his faculty post was an appointive job in the executive branch.

Another example of external factors influencing faculty

entitlements involves disclosure. In California, the Fair Political Practices Commission ruled that faculty at the University of California are required to disclose their financial stake in privately sponsored research. Until the ruling, faculty were exempt from the financial-disclosure requirements imposed on other state employees. This new requirement may be attributed to the widening scope of industrial-research activity by faculty and concern over potential conflicts of interest.

No discussion of the problems arising from professional entitlements would be complete without reference to the rapidly growing number of faculty who supplement their salaries with consulting assignments and, with increasing frequency, formal affiliation with the new university institutes that have corporate sponsors. The faculty problems that may be anticipated in these new consortia are described in detail in Chapter Four, but the issue of compensation should not be overlooked. According to Robert Linnell, director of institutional studies at the University of Southern California, more than half the faculty members in the United States conduct research or consult for business or government. Many educators are concerned that multiple allegiances may endanger objectivity in research, dampen enthusiasm for open access to research results, and even alter a basic mission of the institution.

Part-Time Faculty

Problems relating to part-time and adjunct faculty are expected to grow as their use becomes widespread and as they constitute an increasing proportion of the teaching staff at many institutions. Retrenchment and belt tightening have made part-time faculty attractive. The National Center for the Study of Collective Bargaining in Higher Education and the Professions notes that in the 1981–82 academic year almost 40 percent of classes in unionized institutions were taught by adjuncts. The National Center for Education Statistics reports that, in the period from 1972 to 1977, the rate of growth for part-time faculty was 50 percent compared with 9 percent for full-time staff. The expanding use of other than regular, full-time faculty, such as adjuncts and special lecturers, will exacerbate disputes concerning academic advancement and will introduce special problems of faculty participation and union organization and protections.

Part-time faculty have diverse career objectives. They may be semiretired, using part-time employment to sustain academic interests, or they may be full-time professionals, such as accountants, lawyers, and engineers, who offer special expertise and perspective, or they may be fully committed academicians who desire full-time status. Their needs may not be similar, and their interest in institutional activity may vary widely. Thus tenure, promotion, and benefits may be of concern to some but not others.

Part-timers are both vulnerable and valuable. On the one hand, they are the first to be dismissed, and, on the other, their use provides flexibility during periods of financial difficulty. The following contract language from Harper College (Illinois) was apparently intended to give retention preference to full-timers: "Full-time faculty shall not be dismissed as part of a reduction in force and systematically replaced with part-time faculty except as required by changes in enrollment or program(s) or as the needs of the college clearly require." Under this provision, an arbitrator held that the college did not violate the contract by using part-time replacements after 8 percent (16) of the full-time faculty were dismissed including two who were tenured; more than half the dismissed faculty were later recalled. The problematical nature of part-time status is illustrated by the Massachusetts case involving Tufts University. A federal district court ruled that a lecturer (a part-time designation), even with a full work load and prior full-time service, was not entitled to tenure. She claimed de facto tenure based on more than seven years of full-time employment.

In many institutions, part-time faculty are organizing either in unions or in associations. Their primary goal is job security, which in some instances conflicts with the goals of full-time and tenured staff. Other issues are the part-time/full-time ratio, schedules, salaries, fringe benefits, and rules regarding layoff and rehire. Part-time faculty usually do not participate in governance and decision-making activities. With respect to fringe benefits, however, part-time and full-time faculty may be entitled to the same treatment when the contract does not distinguish between them. So ruled an arbitrator who determined that nontenured teachers at San Francisco Community College with term-to-term appointments are covered for dental benefits during the summer recess if they are rehired for the fall semester.

As academic institutions face increasing financial pressures, they naturally tend to cut the costs of faculty. One obvious direction, adopted by a good number of institutions, is the gradual replacement of full-time faculty with part-timers. This process of substitution can occur by replacing a newly retired professor with part-timers and by denying tenure to erstwhile full-time teachers and replacing them with part-time staff. However, a number of considerations pull in the opposite direction. Part-time faculty, by tradition, rarely participate in the selection, promotion, or granting of tenure to other faculty members. They are often the last to be consulted, if they are consulted at all, about curriculum, textbooks, and programs. They are, in other words, employees, closer in nature to the private-sector workers covered by the National Labor Relations Act than to Yeshiva-type managers. Thus, a prime consideration in moving toward an increased percentage of part-time faculty may be the likelihood that they will form a bargaining unit recognized by and covered under the National Labor Relations Act. In the same vein, where part-time faculty are already included within a recognized bargaining unit, they have an increasing opportunity, if they so desire, to sever ties with the larger unit and form a separate unit. The case can be made, therefore, that an institution that tends to emphasize part-time over full-time faculty should be prepared to deal with two bargaining units rather than one.

Another dimension to be considered is the impact of part-timers on academic quality. All accrediting agencies place great emphasis on the part-time/full-time ratio; institutions, schools, and departments seeking the imprimaturs of accrediting agencies frequently must forgo all but the minimal use of part-timers to gain and retain accredited status. Another measure of academic quality subject to intense scrutiny by the accreditation teams is the proportion of an institution's budget committed to academic compensation; when many part-timers are used, this proportion decreases.

A more profound issue, however, is the image the institution desires to project to both the academic community at large and to prospective applicants. As serious financial pressures mount at private institutions and even at some public universities, product differentiation in higher education must be given full consideration. In a region where a handful of small colleges and universities compete for a limited number of potential students, each institution must determine what type of school it is either to remain or to become.

Some institutions have chosen quality as their defining element, arguing that in a buyers' market prospective students will become increasingly discriminating and will choose schools with high academic standing and research capabilities. They argue that their status will be an attraction for the better students. Obviously, the matter of quality in higher education, as in business, is a function of costs. At some point, preferably at an early date, the institution must come to grips with determining the appropriate balance of full-timers to part-timers. To the extent that specialized accreditation and top-notch full-time faculty become the drawing cards of the future, the use of part-timers will create problems. This is not to say that a full-time faculty, accredited by the relevant agency, must, of necessity, furnish better teaching and instruction than one that is non-accredited or consists of a substantial number of part-timers. In particular instances, the reverse may indeed be the case. The thing to keep in mind is that to some degree, as Detroit used to demonstrate, image plays a role in product differentiation, and to many people accreditation provides the proper image.

Another consideration of obvious concern to students and often voiced as a major drawback to the extensive utilization of part-time faculty is the restricted availability of part-time faculty outside regularly scheduled class meetings. This problem can be serious, and all institutions should clearly state to part-time faculty the extent of this obligation and provide an effective way to make sure students obtain their due. In a buyers' market, among cost-conscious students, faculty availability can make a difference.

Some assert that a full-time professor is more readily able to keep up with the literature and research in the field than a person who teaches a single course, whether on a regular or occasional basis. An extension of this position is that students who take courses with part-time teachers may have less rigorous course requirements and examinations and fewer and less extensive outside readings, assignments, and papers. As a generality this view may have some validity, although it depends on the institution. As an offset, instructors who participate full time in a particular field often bring to the classroom practical expertise, invaluable hands-on experience, and a realistic perspective as to how the course material fits daily life; an academic, by virtue of his or her relative isolation, often cannot provide these advantages.

If an institution determines to increase utilization of part-time faculty, a series of issues inevitably arises. One issue is how much use should be made of a particular part-time faculty member. Is a faculty member who consistently carries a three-quarter load, semester after semester, really not a full-time faculty member?

Other issues involve renewal and promotion. An examination of the considerations that touch on the promotion process will illuminate the issues involved. Most schools have some ladder or ranks through which adjunct faculty progress—adjunct assistant professor, adjunct associate professor, and so forth. In some institutions lecturers are categorized A, B, and C, and there are even such designations as star lecturer. Aside from the amount of time in the classroom, should the criteria for promotion to adjunct associate professor be precisely the same as the criteria for promotion to associate professor? In some institutions, the criteria are so generally stated that administrators seeking to enhance the quality of the teaching staff may seek to impose the same criteria on adjuncts. An example is whether an adjunct need have a terminal degree (a frequent requirement for a full-timer's tenure and promotion). When the faculty statutes require the terminal degree or equivalent, it may be difficult to evaluate the practical experience of the adjunct, even though the teaching excellence of the part-timer is unquestioned.

Another problem causing difficulty is the part-timer who is given an academic title but is in fact a type of clinician attached, for instance, to a reading or speech program. On the one hand, accredited programs often require a practicum for students in particular disciplines to provide them with experience in a teaching or laboratory situation. On the other hand, the clinic is often thought of as merely ancillary to the academic department to which it is attached. A similar situation is presented by an adjunct professor whose forte is teaching lighting to students in the drama department and whose responsibilities include teaching students to create and use lighting effects for the student productions regularly put on by the department. Are these technicians or teachers? In the sciences, part-time instructors with different levels and titles have as a primary responsibility overseeing and assisting students in laboratory work. In the narrowest sense, they are not classroom teachers. Are they members of the academic faculty or are they technicians? In defining a bargaining unit for collective negotiations, these questions may sometimes be resolved, although not in a foolproof manner. For example, referring to a clinician or a technician as a faculty member for purposes of collective bargaining may cause ambiguity as to the criteria to be applied for renewal, promotion, and tenure.

Indeed, the institution may be required to apply faculty standards for promotion and tenure where they in fact do not sensibly apply in order to avoid violating the contract. If it seems unreasonable in the absence of specific contract language to apply the general faculty criteria, an ad hoc set of standards needs to be formulated. Who should formulate such a standard? For the administration to do so unilaterally when clinicians and technicians are covered by the contract would probably raise the specter of an unfair labor practice. The most salutary route is to have standards mutually determined by all parties involved. This solution, however, may lead to another dispute if the parties cannot mutually agree on the standards.

A related problem may be the status of a term employee who is on a nontenured track. Here the most important document is not faculty statute or policy but the individual contract negotiated by the faculty member and the institution. Especially where market forces run in favor of the institution, the individual faculty member would be wise to obtain legal counsel in developing the contract.

CHAPTER 4

Collaborative Research Between Universities and Industry

Collaborative relationships between academic institutions and corporate sponsors have clearly become a significant and growing force in leading academic institutions. Jointly sponsored research institutes are new legal structures that accommodate industry goals and traditional academic rights. The institutes engage in basic and applied research in many fields including genetics, molecular biology and the creation of new life forms, drug and pharmaceutical development, computer science, and petroleum and energy research. The continuing efforts of administrators, attorneys, and enterprising faculty have already produced over a hundred of these arrangements, predominantly at large, prestigious institutions. The varied arrangements range from small projects to multimillion-dollar research centers. These collaborative ventures can cause a number of troublesome faculty problems. The creators of these centers have had to deal with the inevitable conflict between open exchange of scientific information among the members of the academic and research community and industry's need for secrecy; between the spirit of inquiry and applied, sponsor-related research; between pure research and commercialization. And, on a practical level, conflicts can come about through the intervention of industry in academic affairs.

Despite the contrasting interests of the parties involved, the mutual advantages of such relationships are readily apparent: Universities receive money and other resources, while industry gains access to established scientists, research facilities, and academic investigation; universities find opportunities for placement of graduate students, while industry draws from a pool of trained, promising employees; universities expand their programs and research potential, while industry gains some influence in devising academic curricula; finally, both gain prestige and the chance to contribute to education and to productive research. Because the agreements are generally for specified periods, both interests have an opportunity to assess the relationship and to propose changes as needed.

New Collaborative Arrangements

Public attention has been drawn to the more dramatic and exciting of these partnerships—for example, the Whitehead Center at the Massachusetts Institute of Technology (MIT), which will conduct research in the field of biomedicine. Although the most revolutionary areas for collaboration are genetics, molecular science, and biotechnology, joint arrangements have been made in many fields outside the natural sciences. For instance, North Carolina State University has a cooperative program with an industry group concerned with the development and testing of furniture. These research coalitions are pioneering new formats and systems for the sharing of financial and scientific benefits.

Washington University in St. Louis and Monsanto established a five-year renewable agreement under which the university holds patents and receives royalties in biomedicine; Monsanto has exclusive licensing rights. Researchers may publish their results; the chemical firm retains the right to review potentially patentable developments and to delay publication. The partnership is financed by a $23.5 million fund. Industry scientists work with university investigators, who contribute research expertise and findings. Individual investigators do not personally profit from their discoveries, which is not the case in some consulting arrangements. This provision was included because of the criticism of the "entrepreneurial activities" of faculty members at other institutions where corporations have been established by groups of faculty members who contract with industrial firms.

University/industry collaborations, however, may take various forms depending on the research area, the corporate interest in a single or consortium relationship, and the pattern preferred by the university. This representative list indicates some of the possibilities:

Single-Entity Partnership

Carnegie-Mellon University and Westinghouse
Harvard University Medical School and DuPont
Harvard University Medical School and Monsanto
Massachusetts General Hospital (Harvard) and Hoechst
    Pharmaceuticals (in planning stage)
Massachusetts Institute of Technology and Exxon
Massachusetts Institute of Technology and Whitehead
    Center for Biomedical Research (in planning stage)
Rensselaer Polytechnic Institute and International Business Machines
Washington University and Mallinkrodt
Washington University and Monsanto
Yale University and Celanese (in planning stage)

Partnership of a University and a Multiple-Industry Sponsor

California Institute of Technology Silicon Structures
    Project
Carnegie-Mellon Processing Research Institute
Cornell University Injection Molding Project

Dartmouth College Innovations and Ventures in Technology

Massachusetts Institute of Technology Polymer Processing Program

North Carolina State University Furniture Institute

Stanford University Center for Biotechnology Research (in planning stage)

Stanford University Center for Integrated Systems

University of Delaware Catalysis Center

University of Minnesota Center for Micro Electronics and Information Resources

Partnership of an Industry Consortium and a University Consortium

Case Western Reserve Center for Applied Polymer Research

Engenics (chiefly Stanford University and University of California at Berkeley)

North Carolina State University Cooperative Center for Communications and Signal Processing

Ohio State University Center for Welding Research

Rensselaer Polytechnic Institute Center for Interactive Computer Graphics

Rutgers University Ceramics Cooperative Research Center

University of Massachusetts Center for Research on Polymers

In these research centers the tendency is for industry to be attracted by the superstars and Nobel laureates among the faculty because these individuals have received credit and publicity for having made the seminal scientific breakthroughs. Frequently these individuals have already established some type of commercial entity, with or without university involvement, to explore and exploit commercial applications of their findings. However, these nationally recognized, charismatic researchers are but a small fraction of the total faculty involved in such activities and enterprises. Because of their prominence, their faculty status is usually secure and their professional options almost limitless.

In contrast, support faculty, whether already in the university or recruited for these projects, depend on two sets of institutional policies for their protection, the policies of the center and those of the university. Although they may expect the same rights and privileges in the new entity as they enjoy as faculty members, they may encounter special limitations in such areas as the choice of research topic and methodology, accountability, and recognition. Although these new arrangements encourage glowing expectations of commercial success, faculty may be disappointed by the practical realities of a business-oriented venture.

Roots of Conflict

Problems for faculty members in joint research relationships arise from differences in goals, methods, and attitudes. Some of these are differences in principles rather than in methods of management. Therefore, in the operation of these partnerships, fundamental differences in approach should be recognized. The following list contrasts the interests of corporate and academic participants in values and principles and in administration.

University Interests	*Industry Interests*

Values and Principles

Freedom of expression	Limited expression
Right to publish, share scientific findings, and critique research of others	Obligation to consider commercial and competitive concerns by withholding information or delaying publication
Freedom to pursue scientific interests	Goal-oriented research
Latitude in selecting re-	Scope governed by predetermined interests and objec-

University Interests	Industry Interests
search areas and methodology	tives; applied rather than basic research
Responsibility to educate Research designed in part to train students and advance academic interests	Emphasis on product development Research subjects and methods directed toward devising marketable products
Research timetable Methodology and processes suited to evaluation, replication, and other research requirements	Results schedule Research plan and scientific steps oriented toward obtaining results within competitive deadlines

Administration and Management

Peer review of proposals and achievements Evaluation by and recommendations from colleagues in institution or profession	Review by joint committee Evaluation and approval based on corporate interests
Research reporting Interim and final reports based on research findings	Contractual accountability Reports based on corporate needs
Academic advancement Research and educational activity directed to promotion, tenure, and higher academic status	Entrepreneurial rewards Achievements and progress directed to commercial or proprietary interests
Dedication to research Applications offered for professional or public use	Interest in results Patent and license arrangements requested

Many faculty express concern that the new research arrangements will affect existing research programs, particularly those funded by unrestricted grants, which are especially attractive to university scientists. Another concern is that the joint venture will focus on applied, product-oriented research rather than on basic research, which universities consider a prime academic mission. This issue of academic mission is so typically an obstacle that some recent agreements specify only the general character of research and provide funds for unrestricted investigation. A typical agreement of this sort states that 20 percent of the industry contributions will be made available for basic research that need not be reported to the industry sponsor. However, all projects including the unreported basic-research portion must still be in a mutually agreed-on area of research. Government grants usually permit greater scientific latitude for the faculty who participate than do these collaborative arrangements.

Status, Selection, and Compensation of Faculty. A major impetus for collaboration from the point of view of industry is the availability of faculty with specific training or expertise. The staff of the centers is generally drawn from the existing faculty and may be augmented by new faculty recruited for specific programs. Some agreements specify that participating industry scientists be given faculty status as lecturers, preceptors, or adjuncts—a hotly debated feature. A provision in the Whitehead Center contract requires MIT to provide faculty status to a limited number of scientists assigned by the industrial sponsor. Although it is expected that all such scientists will meet academic and professional standards, the university evidently must accept a certain number. Even though administrative arrangements are specified, the effect this provision will have on the morale of the regular faculty is yet to be seen.

Participating faculty usually remain subject to departmental rules. In contrast, project colleagues drawn from outside the university may be governed by different constraints. Indeed, permanent faculty will view the relationship to the center in general differently from scientists who participate under term contracts. This two-tiered system can present administrative problems when scientists of comparable status have primary employment through different entities and are treated differently.

Another problem that confronts the university in these

arrangements is the potential for conflict between faculty who participate and those who do not. The conflict cuts two ways. Participating faculty may have opportunities for recognition and commercial success not available to their departmental colleagues. Yet they may not be able to offer their research achievements as justification for academic promotion. In addition, the heightened prospects for substantial economic reward may prove a sore point among colleagues in other disciplines whose commercial opportunities are severely limited. Thus, the manner in which faculty are selected to participate can cause conflict.

In the traditional academic system, faculty members are selected through departmental screening and institutional approval. Now, however, a dispute may arise between two faculty members in the same department competing for a position in the new venture. Most probably the selection will be made not on the basis of peer judgment but by the project director and an industry committee. At first, it may not be widely recognized that this system for selection is markedly different from the usual academic system. This shift in decision-making authority may lead to conflicts involving a fundamental principle of governance: that those making such decisions be solely within the university, not quasi outsiders.

Questions of compensation may also arise. Are the participants to be salaried? If so, by whom? Or are they to receive some form of stipend? If so, will the amount of the stipend be subjected to joint faculty negotiations or be negotiated independently? If the new institute does not adopt the university compensation levels and time periods for review and advancement, there may be conflict between institute participants and other faculty, particularly when participating faculty are not working longer hours but enjoy a change in the composition of their duties, perhaps less time teaching and more time supervising graduate students.

Management and Control of Research. In theory, the new environment should enhance opportunities for the instructor and students by broadening the scope of their research activities and offering facilities that the university would not otherwise

have. This is not necessarily the case. At one university, graduate students claimed that the department chair's relationship
with a company affected the research in which they were engaged. They contended that the program was commercially ori-
ented and that they were not permitted the latitude they had
been promised when recruited. By the same token, faculty
members may find that research assignments are not self-selected.
In many centers, joint committees review and approve individual applications for research studies; with this system, faculty
may believe that rejections of their proposals are based on industry interests rather than on scientific criteria. To avoid such
claims, some agreements, as previously noted, allocate funds for
unrestricted, university-controlled basic research. However, as
most collaborative arrangements are for a specified period only,
after which they are reviewed for renewal, faculty, even under
conditions that allow for basic research, are aware that continuation of the center depends in a broad sense on their cooperation with the interests of the sponsor.

Government and foundation grants generally do not require researchers to account strictly for time and productivity.
Although university faculty involved in collaborative projects
may accept the concept of accountability to the sponsor, the
norms of academic behavior in this area may not easily apply
in the new research enterprise. Practices such as the independent right to publish may not be acceptable in a quasi-industrial
setting. Similarly, specific work assignments and reporting requirements, common in industry, have only limited parallels in
an academic setting.

The university scientist is responsible only for explaining
the purpose and methodology of a project and reporting the results in a professional publication or forum. A privately employed scientist, with similar training and interests, recognizes a
responsibility to report to superiors on the project and to publish or withhold publication in accordance with the needs of the
employer. Although the university professor may see an expression of individual disagreement as a duty to the academic community, the industrial scientist may temper or withhold views
to enhance the progress of his or her career. A professor may

not feel constrained in making public a dispute with a colleague over a matter in his or her professional field even to the point of aborting an experiment, whereas the industrial scientist may feel constrained because of the likely consequences of such a bold step. These differences reflect the fact that academic freedom and individual expression are protected by the tenure system.

From a different perspective, it may very well be the faculty member whose activities are questionable. Faculty who consult as independent contractors may have clients whose business interests overlap. There seems to be no requirement that a faculty member disclose potential conflicts of interest in these situations. When the faculty member now becomes an employee of a collaborative enterprise, disclosure frequently becomes a necessity. For example, Yale University, on the recommendation of its committee on cooperative research, patents, and licenses, requires annual reporting of consulting arrangements and other substantial financial interests. The rules do not in themselves limit time or compensation or force relinquishment of business equities, but they allow for an inquiry that may reveal conflict. Other schools, notably Harvard University and the University of California system, have similar disclosure provisions. Traditional arrangements permitting unaccounted-for off-campus activity may yield to formal requirements as growing interest in commercial ventures highlights the need for strict enforcement.

Disputes may also arise when the research venture is reorganized or terminated. Experience demonstrates that when soft-money projects are terminated, the right to transfer back to the university may have to be extended to project professors. During World War II, when many universities expanded research efforts to serve government, many faculty members were given full-time or part-time assignments supported by special funds. When these projects were completed, fierce competition erupted for the few permanent positions at the universities. Many colleges were unprepared for this contingency, especially when projects had been in existence for as long as a decade. With the new industry/university ventures, similar project terminations appear likely. The 1982 report of the National Science Foundation, *University-Industry Research Relationships,* relates, for example, that "in the biotechnology field events have been moving so fast that some major arrangements have been announced and then canceled during the period of writing this report."

Conversely, problems will also arise when success exceeds expectations. At this point, original profit-sharing arrangements or other distributions may have to be renegotiated if participating professors feel they are entitled to an increased share. Furthermore, the university as an institution may insist on its fair share. The University of Wisconsin took this position with regard to the well-known Alumni Research Foundation. The university believed it was entitled to an increased return because the foundation was established not only to benefit the participating professors but to benefit the entire university.

Faculty Problems as Perceived by Participants. To identify the problems that may arise in these collaborative research ventures, the Center for Mediation in Higher Education conducted a survey in 1983 of program directors and participating faculty. This work, sponsored by the Schering Plough Foundation, was designed to provide guidance in the operation of research centers. The twenty-three research centers participating in the survey were diversified in geographic location, maturity, and size of program. Responses to questionnaires were obtained from nineteen program directors and forty-one research faculty.

Faculty and program directors were asked to note complaints, expressed or anticipated, in these twelve areas: restrictions on publication, limits in choice of research topic, insufficient personal financial reward, inadequate recognition for research, disagreement over research methodology, academic advancement impeded, undue industry involvement in establishing research priorities, patents or licenses not properly shared, misallocation of space and equipment, excessive time demands of the project, lack of staff to assist research, and excessive reporting requirements.

The most frequent complaint was restrictions on publication, mentioned by seventeen faculty and seven directors.

Thirteen faculty also noted undue industry involvement in establishing research priorities and limits in choice of research topic, and twelve complained of insufficient staff support. The ranking of complaints by the directors differed somewhat from that of faculty, with six directors noting insufficient personal financial reward, lack of staff support, and excessive reporting requirements.

Faculty and directors were also asked to note which of the twelve potential problem areas were of critical concern. The survey results parallel the data on complaints: Six directors and ten faculty considered restrictions on publication as critical, with eight faculty noting lack of staff support and five expressing critical concern over limits in the choice of research topic.

The faculty were asked, "Would you be likely to join industry if you could continue to work on research that interests you?" Sixteen (or 42 percent of those responding) answered in the affirmative. The amount of time these faculty members devote to teaching and to collaborative research was compared with that of faculty who responded that they were not attracted to an industry affiliation. Not surprisingly, faculty researchers who are most likely to consider a direct affiliation with industry devote proportionately larger amounts of time to collaborative research and less to teaching. The nine research faculty who taught less than 25 percent of the time and spent 25 percent or more time on collaborative research were far more likely to be interested in joining industry; 78 percent of this group expressed such an interest.

Program directors were queried with regard to program management and design and the factors that attracted industry participation. They generally agreed that major attractions were specific research expertise of the faculty (noted by eighteen), overall reputation of the faculty (sixteen), and an existing faculty/industry contact (fifteen). Directors of sixteen programs stated that the university made the initial contact with the industry sponsor. The attraction for the university was overwhelmingly research opportunities for current faculty (nineteen) and immediate financial support (sixteen). In most of the programs surveyed, the position of program director was a part-time one (thirteen), and most directors (sixteen) participated directly in research. All but one program director held a faculty position. In every program, faculty were permitted to seek grants outside the project, and all but one permitted faculty to engage in outside consulting activities. Most programs (seventeen) received financial support from multiple sources. Students participated in all programs surveyed.

The research faculty were asked to assess the impact of the collaborative program on the allocation of time committed to teaching, graduate supervision, and other activities. Most stated that there were no changes in the allocation of time, although 40 percent noted less time for teaching and 22 percent committed more time to graduate supervision.

However, when research faculty were asked directly, "Do faculty have sufficient role in selecting research topics?" 97 percent responded in the affirmative—a finding at odds with the previous data.

Participants agreed that the collaborative program did not impair opportunities for academic advancement; 79 percent of the respondents believed it does not. However, responses on whether participation enhances academic advancement were mixed, with 54 percent stating the affirmative. Responses to other issues relating to the academic relationship were also mixed but generally positive; 59 percent believed confidentiality requirements did not impair the academic exchange of ideas, and the same percentage believed that industry needs for tangible results did not conflict with academic responsibilities. A surprising finding was that only 19 percent of the faculty respondents believed participation in the collaborative program would bring substantial future financial rewards.

Although this sample of research centers is only a small cross section, the complaints expressed may indicate the areas in which disputes will arise in the future. Although all participating program directors stated that complaints, which are predominantly handled through informal resolution, are currently managed in a satisfactory manner, the issues that have arisen, particularly restrictions on publication, need periodic review to assess the need for revisions in policy or procedure.

Dispute Management

Clearly, the fundamental differences in the traditions and the missions of industry and universities present a distinct set of problems. Although many universities that join as partners with industry insist on clearly delineated boundaries to avoid improper or undue influence, it is unlikely that the management structure will completely insulate the university and its faculty. Methods for managing disputes in these new arrangements will probably differ from those established to address issues of faculty performance within the university.

At this early stage, these new organizations seem ready to accommodate faculty needs. As the centers mature and are more rigidly managed, however, research options may narrow, and the direction of the research effort may be based on the needs of the corporate sponsor. Faculty researchers may then be forced to choose whether to continue to participate. At this juncture, avenues of appeal may be needed.

In order to examine the range of possible approaches for responding to conflict, it may be instructive to describe a situation that could occur. A scientist in a collaborative project may become convinced the research is not likely to produce meaningful results. In a complaint that eventually reaches the center director, the scientist seeks to alter the direction of the research, despite a decision by the joint research committee that this component of research is vital to the whole effort. The researcher may assert that industry representatives on the joint committee were unduly influenced by considerations not directly related to the project. The company, for example, may need the work completed for purposes of comparison with in-house research.

Under the terms of the joint operating agreement, the center director could require the scientist to continue to pursue research along the lines agreed to earlier. This fiat would probably not be a useful response. Resentment could affect not only the researcher's work but that of colleagues, who may feel that responses will affect them in the future.

A variety of other responses could be considered for handling the complaint. The director could ask the scientist to prepare a statement documenting the scientific evidence of a dead end and offer to submit this statement to the joint research committee for reconsideration and a written response if such a response has not already been provided. Or the director could request that the company representatives explain the basis for the decision to continue this line of inquiry. The director could also seek the views of university participants concerning the value of the research in question.

The director could also seek approval from the joint research committee to establish a small, perhaps three-person, committee to take a fresh look at the problem. Committee members could be selected as representatives of specific interests—the grieving scientist, the center, the university, the sponsor—or they could be drawn from a preselected panel composed of individuals acknowledged to be fair minded. The degree of formality of the committee procedures and tasks would depend on the size of the center and its management style. If a committee is selected, participants should understand in advance the weight that will be given to the committee findings; if findings are advisory only, this provision should be clearly understood.

A variation is the appointment of a respected, knowledgeable neutral who would work with the parties who had a stake in the outcome to fashion a voluntary settlement. The selected neutral would serve as a mediator, encouraging each of the interests to specify common and opposing positions with a view to achieving a mutually satisfactory solution. It would be understood that the mediator had no authority to impose a solution; however, it might be decided in advance that, in the absence of a voluntary resolution, the mediator would submit recommendations to the joint research committee. This provision might stimulate the parties to reach their own agreement. If the mediation approach were used, time limits on the negotiating period would need to be established to avoid unnecessarily prolonged discussion.

It must be recognized that approaches that depend on reconsideration and negotiations may not produce a solution. In establishing a joint venture, the parties should clearly state in the implementing agreement that unsettled complaints will be resolved by the governing board or a designated official or committee.

When efforts at accommodation fail, those making the final decision should consider a number of factors including the importance of the particular project to the overall research effort, the value of the individual scientist, and the possible effect of the controversy on the future creativity of other participants. A principal concern is the relevance of the dispute in the sometimes fragile link of academic and commercial interests. Serious consequences may ensue if the researcher has a proprietary interest or ownership in the joint venture or is the leader of a team that would move with the scientist. The situation has further ramifications if the researcher and the team have access to industrial data that should not be released. The center may also need to reach agreement with the departing scientist on the use of patentable material. To ensure the stability of the center, these situations should be managed in a way that minimizes fragmentation and dilution of the research effort.

In general, sensible management practices suggest that although there may be no legal or administrative right to appeal, the texture of researchers' relationships to the joint enterprise is so crucial to its prosperity that efforts must be made to respond to the legitimate needs of the participants. Clarification of a center policy is especially critical when the interests of the university, the sponsor, and the research center conflict. Policies concerning research direction and control should be articulated with precision. For example, the policy on disclosure of research results should be specified and well understood; it should indicate not only the constraints on freedom of expression but also the possible use of data in connection with peer review for promotion and tenure. Likewise, policies on compensation should specify the relationship to general faculty salaries.

In clarifying policy, it is also important to distinguish between issues of administrative and professional judgment. Administrative matters, such as salary, fringe benefits, and support staff, can be handled through the use of well-recognized management principles and procedures. Professional issues, such as intellectual differences, cannot be handled through the usual university channels because these issues almost always involve both academic and commercial interests. Thus, a new policy for resolving professional problems should be formulated to meet the interests of all the parties.

Center directors should try to anticipate the types of disputes they expect to arise. The nature of the research effort may determine many of the issues; in biotechnology, where patents are important, the need for interpretations of the agreements and ownership rights may be frequent and significant, while in the communications industry developments are so rapid and products rely on so many patents and licenses that individual patentable discoveries may be relatively unimportant. Certain types of research rely on teams, whereas others rely on individual scientists with support staffs. In a team project, administrators and policy makers should examine the potential for rivalry among members and the possibility of competition for both professional credit and advancement.

Whether university professors will be subject to all the center controls or whether they will continue to retain rights and responsibilities within the university is a fundamental concern in devising an approach for responding to conflict. It may be that almost all problems can be referred to the department or the university. For instance, the research results obtained in connection with a center project may be submitted for departmental peer evaluation for advancement. Objections to such an evaluation would then be considered under university procedures. In contrast, infractions calling for discipline under the center personnel regulations could be handled without reference to the university. Although it may be unnecessary to devise a system in advance for each type of potential infraction, it may be useful to set forth guidelines that establish when the university is to be involved and when it is not. Guidelines would help both the institution and the faculty to know the appropriate course to pursue in any given situation.

PART II

Procedures for Resolving
Recurring Disputes

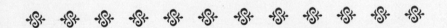

The two chapters in this part discuss elements and principles in the design of grievance structures and present examples of procedures that are working well at three distinctly different institutions. The discussion of design elements is drawn in part from the regional workshops on procedural design run by the Center for Mediation in Higher Education and from a review of descriptions of more than sixty grievance procedures submitted in response to a questionnaire. The questionnaire was developed to identify both the types of procedures currently being used and the problems academic administrators see as critical. For the most part, the descriptions of procedures came from nonunionized, independent colleges because this was the group that sought the Center's assistance. Grievance procedures at unionized institutions are developed through collective bargaining negotiations. Although the sample is far from representative, the study does provide insight into the issues of greatest concern.

The survey asked administrators to identify the issues they view as most critical. The first of these questions asked what was the main issue or problem in employment: promotion, tenure, discipline, dismissal, salary, and so forth. Fifty-nine institutions responded. Of the large institutions (those with over 100 faculty members), 45 percent checked tenure; 13 percent, promotion; 13 percent, retrenchment; 10 percent, salary; 7 percent, work load; with 3 percent each for discipline, discrimination, assignment, and contract renewal. The responses from the small institutions differed with respect to their principal concern: 27 percent indicated tenure; 12 percent, promotion; 32 percent, retrenchment; 16 percent, work load; 6 percent, appointment; and 3 percent each for discipline and assignment. (The fact that after retrenchment and tenure, work load is the principal source of grievances at the small institutions no doubt reflects the long-term pattern of greater teaching contact in those schools than in larger schools, coupled with the limited funds for teaching assistants.)

Another question asked was "What specific issues for faculty complaints do you expect will be prominent or likely to emerge? (For example, discipline, tenure, retrenchment, teaching assignment, work load)." Of the large institutions, 39 percent checked tenure; 13 percent, retrenchment; 8 percent each indicated promotion, discipline, selection/appointment, salary, and work load; and 4 percent each noted dismissal/severance and contract renewal. The responses from the small institutions showed differences in emphasis with regard to principal concerns: 26 percent checked retrenchment; 25 percent, tenure; 15 percent, work load; 9 percent, promotion; 5 percent each for dismissal/severance and assignment; and 2.5 percent each for discipline, selection/appointment, contract renewal, rank, retirement, and competence.

In response to another question, "Was sex or race discrimination raised as an issue?" only a few large institutions indicated that discrimination complaints were being filed. This response appears to be somewhat puzzling in light of the vast publicity such complaints have received. The fact that none of the smaller institutions responding to the survey indicated discrimination as a current issue deepens the puzzle. Either these types of claims have peaked or the number of responses was not truly representative. Support for the conclusion that these claims have peaked can be found in the responses to the question concerning expected issues. Neither large nor small institutions saw discrimination as a potentially critical issue.

Interestingly, collective bargaining was not listed by a single respondent as a current or expected issue. According to the survey, formal grievance procedures were used relatively infrequently; only the large institutions reported substantial activity. Most of the institutions, however, were nonunionized, and there are traditionally fewer formal claims in nonunionized schools than in those with collective bargaining. When collective bargaining is used in the institutions surveyed, it appears that resolution can frequently be achieved at the first level of appeal.

Almost every institution has in place some form of complaint procedure; only four respondents stated that their institutions did not have a mechanism for handling faculty complaints, and three of these colleges were currently designing procedures. Most institutions adopted their procedures in the early to mid 1970s. The impetus for this activity was concern for individual faculty rights highlighted by lawsuits and regulatory action in discrimination cases. An additional factor was the increase in collective bargaining; some internal review system was a standard union demand. At some institutions, grievance procedures were adopted because faculty distrusted or lacked confidence in the administrative leadership. Procedural reforms initiated by faculty came about either because the administration was perceived as weak and incapable of resolving faculty problems in an expeditious, decisive, and fair manner, or as a reaction to an autocratic leadership that made unilateral, some say arbitrary, decisions that failed to command support from the faculty at large.

Institutions use an extremely broad spectrum of approaches in detailing procedural steps for complaints. In a few institutions, these procedures take up one paragraph in the faculty handbook; some take as many as sixteen pages. The typical procedure is described in three pages. Most cover a narrow range of issues with separate procedures for faculty-status complaints and those involving discipline and dismissal for cause. As might be expected given the current economic difficulties, recently revised faculty handbooks include specific provisions for retrenchment and fiscal exigency. These provisions are remarkably similar and reflect the 1972 AAUP guidelines, *Institutional Problems Resulting from Financial Exigency.* The statements in many instances refer to dismissal appeals procedures as the mechanism for filing a grievance based on an improper application of a retrenchment policy to an individual faculty member. Although there is a big difference in tone and perhaps in import between dismissal for cause and dismissal due to retrenchment, a single appeals forum can appropriately address both issues. The most important requirement in both cases is that the institution demonstrate the reasonableness of its action.

In designing complaint procedures, most institutions appear to have considered the recommendations of the AAUP, which has for many years advocated the use of specified principles. The AAUP encourages colleges to design their own procedures tailored to their own needs but to take into account the standards enunciated in AAUP policy documents. Essentially these documents set out the tenet that academic freedom is the basis for both institutional operation and for individual faculty rights. The AAUP provisions use the term *should,* reflecting a moral or ethical condition rather than a legal right. Thus, in effect, the AAUP suggests appropriate procedures but obviously does not impose specific requirements. For example, with respect to tenure, the AAUP document states that "after the expiration of a probationary period, teachers or investigators should have permanent or continuous tenure, and their service should be terminated only for adequate cause, except in the case of retirement for age or under extraordinary circumstances because of financial exigencies."

For both dismissal and tenure cases, the AAUP has played a major role in assisting colleges and universities to design grievance procedures; its impact in defining due process has been widely felt. The AAUP recommendations for grievance procedures in connection with dismissal, either for cause or as a result of financial exigency, describe the way the hearing should be conducted and provide for appeal to the board of trustees. In recognition of the variations in governance styles and in the levels of faculty participation in the peer-review process as it relates to tenure decisions, the AAUP sets forth the requirement that faculty are entitled to reasons for decisions with the expectation that each institution will determine the elements and considerations on which these judgments will be based. The AAUP recommends standards for achieving adequate consideration of merit in procedural terms, thus leaving it to each institution to spell out the substantive elements.

All procedures reviewed in the grievance-procedure study provide for faculty involvement in the hearing of complaints, either through an ad hoc committee or a standing committee elected by the faculty senate. If an ad hoc committee is used, the procedure typically calls for a three-member review panel that includes a designee of either the faculty or the grievant, a designee of the president, and a third member selected by the other two designees. The committee is usually required to prepare a report and recommendations for the president. Most procedures dealing with dismissals provide an opportunity for appeal to the board of trustees. The appeal to the board does not usually involve a hearing but simply a review of the file. Many procedures have a provision for the committee to reconsider its recommendation if it is at variance with the president's decision.

Procedures at most institutions are written clearly in unambiguous language and are usually free of legalisms. The procedures rarely include a rationale for the steps that follow. Almost all procedures, however, stress the desire to settle problems in an informal manner, although the importance of the informal stage and the extent of it vary. The informal stage is usually completed before the grievance is submitted in written form.

For unionized faculty, arbitration is a standard feature of the procedures. These procedures also generally specify in greater detail the definition of a grievance, the jurisdiction of the grievance committee, the deadlines for filing, and the manner in which the hearing will be conducted. This specificity reflects the more formal relationship between the administration and faculty expressed in the collectively bargained agreement and the need for greater precision in the event that the grievance is not settled in the earlier steps and is submitted to an arbitrator for final resolution. This opportunity for external review is the primary and basic difference between procedures used at union and nonunion institutions. Northeastern University in Boston is the only nonunion institution responding to the survey that includes arbitration as a step in the procedure. Chapter Six includes a description of the Northeastern approach.

During the late 1970s, institutions had a chance to realistically test their grievance systems and often carefully scrutinized their efficacy and identified any impediments. The survey results reflect this review activity. Ten responding institutions stated that their procedures were currently under review. Approximately one half of the procedures adopted in the 1970s were subsequently revised, many in 1981. Because it might be expected that procedures, once established, would stay in place for quite a long time, this spate of activity suggests that unanticipated events and circumstances require a periodic reconsideration of procedures. The move to review procedures also reflects the need to resolve new problems, particularly retrenchment.

CHAPTER 5

Elements
of Dispute Resolution
Procedures

The grievance process is a formal method for addressing individual faculty disputes. Although informal methods often achieve understanding and reconciliation, a formal grievance mechanism exists at virtually every academic institution and is used to resolve the bulk of the disputes that arise. Although faculty may appeal to public agencies and the courts, the grievance process is usually a necessary prelude to legal action. Unless the issue before the court involves a special statutory right, such as nondiscrimination, the courts require use of internal remedies.

Although the grievance process offers the same opportunity for due process provided by courts, the procedures may not be the same. Government agencies and the courts are designed to accommodate all types of cases within a set format and schedule. The courts have restrictive rules regarding the admissibility of evidence and testimony. In such a forum, a person may win or lose on technicalities or on the basis of delays. A claim justifiable on merit may be dismissed because it was untimely or presented improperly. In contrast, a grievance system established by the parties can allow for a degree of flexibility and latitude not possible under the rules of the court, where judgments are based on narrow legal principles.

A prominent advantage of an internal system is that it permits the parties to address the grievance on a timely basis. Unlike the courts, which cannot be expected to consider the institution's calendar or a faculty member's need to plan his or her future, a college or university can establish a process to accommodate these well-understood considerations. For example, the procedure can specify that a hearing must be scheduled within one month and may not be started during vacation periods or intersession.

The degree of formality of an internal system reflects an institution's preference for detailed procedures or for a loose format. Procedural elements such as time allowances and the availability of appeal can be described with precision and can be generally applicable, while evaluative factors may require flexible treatment. For example, the peer-review process usually involves evaluation of qualifications and performance and contribution to the institution. The emphasis programs and departments give to these factors, however, may vary. Thus, it may be inappropriate to detail in the procedures the weight or significance of each of these elements. The procedural features, however, such as time, notice, and hearing rules can be precisely described because they can be universally applied.

Defining the Grievance and the Decision-Making Authority

Basic to the entire process is the question What is a grievance? The way a grievance is defined is a key to the way the system is viewed by faculty members. An individual faculty member who does not have the opportunity to present a case may be dissatisfied not because the claim is rejected on the merits but because it has not been heard at all. No system, however, can be expected to cover every type of dispute. The degree of inclusivity depends on the needs of those using the process. Proponents of having scope for grievances narrowly defined argue that the system will not then be burdened with minor issues. Advocates for an expansive definition suggest that the relative formality of the process tends to discourage the filing of frivolous complaints.

Generally, the procedures indicate whether the faculty member can set forth only specific types of allegations or whether the review committee decides what claims merit consideration. The choice of approach depends on the structure of the college and the faculty members' relationships with each other and to the administration. If informality is highly valued, it may be appropriate to rely on the faculty review committee to determine whether the grievance is worthy of consideration. In this system, there is usually no appeal from the committee's decision.

At institutions where structure is important, the way a grievance is defined will determine when a faculty member has the right to be heard. In such systems, a distinction may be made between a grievance and a complaint, with more rigid applications of standards and procedures if the issue is a formal grievance rather than a complaint. Faculty procedures flowing from a collective bargaining contract frequently distinguish between complaints and grievances. Generally, complaints cover any number of issues but are subject to resolution only through informal discussion. In contrast, a grievance is a formal statement of alleged contract violations. The filing of a grievance triggers a clearly delineated step-by-step progression toward final resolution. In some instances, an unresolved complaint can be transformed into a formal grievance. In many instances the lodging of a complaint and its informal discussion are precedent conditions for access to the grievance mechanism.

The grievance procedure usually encourages informal settlement through direct negotiations between the parties. If these negotiations are unsuccessful, most procedures provide for a hearing, which typically results in a recommendation to the president or the board of trustees. There may be an appeal step between the president's decision and that of the board of trustees. Under some procedures, these final decisions may be limited by the recommendation of the hearing committee or the terms of a collective bargaining contract. For example, an institutional policy may state that the president may not override in whole or in part a determination by the tenure and promotion committee without stated reasons for disapproval and an opportunity for further review. Although no procedures place limits on the decision-making authority of the board of trustees, it is understood they will usually not contravene a presidential action without good cause. When an outside review through arbitration is provided as a last step for cases involving promotion and tenure, it is customary in matters of peer review for the arbitrator to issue an advisory award recommending a decision to the board. Usually the issue before the arbitrator in such cases is whether the proper procedures have been followed rather than a second guessing of academic judgment.

Arbitration is a standard feature of guidance procedures for unionized faculty. It is included as the final step on much the same basis as in other labor contracts. Arbitration reflects the formal relationship between the administration and faculty in these cases and the need for precision in interpreting collectively bargained contracts.

Although some procedures place final authority at the presidential level, it is questionable whether this solution is suitable for either the faculty member or the institution. In situations where a presidential determination creates controversy, it is useful to have the broad oversight of the board of trustees, who have the advantage of knowing the institution without day-to-day and possibly partisan involvements.

Outside agencies such as federal and state authorities that enforce civil rights laws and other statutes and the courts exert profound influence on institutional/faculty relationships. Recourse to such outside forums is, of course, not a part of internal faculty grievance procedures, but under the law, these agencies provide ultimate review. The extent to which the internal procedures furnish due process and unbiased consideration of the faculty member's claim generally determines whether outside forums will intrude.

Procedural Steps

Procedures for grievance management usually consist of three elements: informal negotiation, sometimes through mediation; the hearing or other formal review; and final resolution. Resource C at the end of the book outlines specific provisions for these steps.

Informal Negotiations. With rare exceptions, grievance procedures in higher education start with an informal process. This informal process can be recommended as the forum of first resort or it can be a mandatory first step. If it is mandatory, a potential grievant is required to attempt informal resolution through discussion with the department chair, dean, or administrator against whom the grievance will be lodged. To be eligible to file a grievance under this system, the grievant must be able to demonstrate that the informal steps have been completed. Although the imposition of informal negotiation as a requirement may present difficulties where there is hostility or a deteriorating relationship, the desire for informal settlement is a hallmark of academic life. The fact that formal procedures for handling complaints were not widely implemented until the 1970s is an indication that members of the academic community believed their interests were protected through informal lines of communication and that the formal systems routinely used in other sectors of the economy were inappropriate in a collegial setting. The continued emphasis on informal negotiations suggests that academics continue to value this traditional approach.

The desire to handle faculty problems informally is expressed within the procedures in a wide variety of ways. Here are several examples of ways this procedural element has been described.

At Heidelberg College (Ohio):

It is expected that all departmental problems will first be considered by the department involved and that most will be resolved within the department. The following procedure is suggested only after these resources have been utilized to the fullest extent.

At Pratt Institute (New York):

The administration and the union agree that they will use their best efforts to encourage the informal and prompt settlement of grievances which may arise under the terms and conditions of this agreement. In the informal settlement procedure, the employee and/or the union shall present and discuss his or her grievance with his or her immediate supervisor.

At Yale University, Faculty of Arts and Sciences:

A faculty member is encouraged to seek initially an equitable solution to the problem in direct discussion with the responsible persons. A faculty member may always seek assistance and advice from any administrator or any faculty member of any school.

Within the Faculty of Arts and Sciences five senior faculty members stand ready to advise any member of the faculty who believes that he or she may have cause for complaint. . . . Consultation with any advisor is confidential.

At Bethany College (Kansas):

The purpose of the grievance procedure is to secure, at the lowest possible level, equitable solutions to problems which may arise from time to time affecting regular and adjunct faculty members. Both faculty and administration agree that proceedings will be kept as informal and confidential as may be appropriate before continuing to formal stages of the grievance procedure.

These statements, and similar provisions in other procedures, reinforce the college's commitment to resolving problems outside a formal system. The success of this practice is difficult if not impossible to judge because there usually is no record; even the complaining faculty member may not remember the registered complaint if it has been resolved satisfactorily. On the basis of discussion with faculty members, it is clear that most complaints are settled without resort to a formal mechanism.

Mediation. When informal discussion between the immediate parties fails to bring about an acceptable solution, mediation can sometimes provide the framework for reaching a satisfactory outcome. The distinguishing feature of mediation, as contrasted with informal negotiations, is that it is conducted with the assistance of a neutral or panel of neutrals who work with and between the parties to bring about an acceptable settlement.

The mediation step can be described in detail, as in the DePauw University (Indiana) procedure quoted here, or it can be treated in general terms as in the procedures used at Barnard College (New York).

At DePauw University:

D. Review Committee—Selection of Mediation Panel and Review Panel

For each petition there shall be two panels: a three-member mediation panel whose function shall be to seek resolution, not necessarily by compromise, of the case and a five-member appeals panel whose function shall be to conduct a formal hearing, if required.

E. Procedure for Tenure Decisions and for Promotion or Salary Decisions

In cases involving promotion or salary, the mediation panel shall, within three days after receipt of the request for review, meet with the petitioner; on the basis of this meeting and the petitioner's written statement, the panel shall decide whether the review shall proceed. . . .

G. Mediation Panel—Procedures

Within three days of the meeting described . . . or, if there is no such meeting (as in cases involving tenure, terminal reappointment, or nonreappointment), within three days of the receipt of the request for review, the chairperson of the mediation panel shall meet with the petitioner for the purpose of facilitating the panel's understanding of the nature of the grievance as defined in the petitioner's written statement.

1. At the same meeting the petitioner shall provide the chairperson of the mediation panel with three copies of all the documents which the petitioner wishes to submit in support of his or her written statement defining the nature of the grievance.

2. The chairperson of the mediation panel shall promptly submit the petitioner's statement to the Committee on Faculty (COF), which shall, within three days after its next meeting, provide the panel with:

    a. a written response to the petitioner's definition of grievance (this will usually be approximately the same reply which the COF sent directly to the petitioner, . . .

    b. a copy of the written statement of reasons for the original decision (already sent to the petitioner), . . .

    c. a written statement detailing the procedure followed and listing the persons consulted in reaching the original decision, and

    d. copies of all documents* [used] in deliberations leading to the original decision. With the approval of the panel, the COF may provide access to these documents for panel members and shall then provide copies of only those documents specifically requested.

    e. At this point, the mediation panel shall not disclose these statements to anyone who is not a member of the panel.

H. Mediation Panel—Attempt at Resolution

After consideration of all written materials provided . . . , the mediation panel shall seek informally to bring about a resolution in the case, not necessarily by compromise. The mediation panel is not an advocate for any party to the dispute. The role of the mediation panel is to assist both the petitioner and the Committee on Faculty to discuss the case and reach some agreement.

1. In seeking a resolution, the mediation panel may meet with the petitioner . . . or with the COF (or its designated representative) . . . or both together. Individual members of the panel shall not meet with individual members of the COF unless they have been designated by their respective bodies for such a discussion. The panel shall not disclose confidential documents.

2. If the mediation panel decides early in its proceedings that mediation will not be effective, it will report its decision and the reasons for it to the petitioner, to the chairperson of the COF, and to the chairperson of the appeals panel.

3. The mediation period shall normally not exceed fourteen days from the time the mediation panel receives from the COF the documents described . . . above. The mediation period shall be extended by at most seven days by mutual agreement of the two parties. The mediation panel's success or failure at bringing about a resolution of the case shall be communicated in writing by its chairperson to the petitioner, to the chairperson of the COF, and to the chairperson of the appeals panel.

I. Mediation Panel—Conclusion

Whether resolution has been achieved or not, the mediation panel shall return all materials to the persons from whom they were received. If resolution has not been achieved, the mediation panel shall submit to the appeals panel (with a copy to the petitioner) a statement which defines the nature of the grievance which has been subject to mediation efforts.

*The Committee on Faculty shall provide, in place of those documents which it judges to be highly confidential, copies of the documents with all identifying material blocked out. The sources may remain confidential.

At Barnard College:

VI. Due Process
  A. Grievance Proceedings
  B. Rules of Procedure in Grievance Proceedings
    1. Informal resolution. An officer of instruction
        who feels aggrieved should initially seek to re-
        solve the problem informally. Such informal ef-
        forts may include a request to the vice-president
        for academic affairs and dean of the faculty to
        mediate or to refer the problem to the faculty
        executive committee for mediation. . . .
    2. Commencement of Proceeding
    3. Request for Hearing
    4. The Vice President for Academic Affairs and the
        Dean of the Faculty
    5. The Faculty Executive Committee
        a. The faculty executive committee (excluding
            the president, the vice president for aca-
            demic affairs, and dean of the faculty, as well
            as any committee member who is a party to
            the dispute) shall review the request for
            hearing and, before undertaking mediation,
            shall determine whether the subject matter
            of the request constitutes a grievance under
            the definitions provided. . . .
        b. The faculty executive committee is encour-
            aged to mediate the matter giving rise to the
            request for hearing. If mediation is success-
            ful, the party filing the request for hearing
            shall execute a statement withdrawing the
            request.
        c. If the matter is not resolved by mediation
            within fifteen academic days after the fac-
            ulty executive committee decides that the
            matter constitutes a grievance, the faculty
            executive committee shall select a hearing
            committee.

In some procedures, mediation is a required step before the parties have the right to request a hearing. Those who have designed such procedures explain that although mediation is essentially voluntary, the parties are expected to give bona fide consideration to reaching a settlement. The inclusion of a mandatory provision avoids the embarrassment or difficulty of a voluntary initiative but still permits the parties to reach the formal hearing stage if mediation is not successful.

However, it should be recognized that a willingness to negotiate is a precondition to mediation. Therefore, the parties should also have the right to bypass the mediation step if agreement seems unlikely or to terminate mediation early in the process if one or both parties sees no chance for settlement. Under some circumstances, the winner-take-all nature of the dispute will make a mediated agreement unlikely. For instance, if a faculty member who has been denied tenure asserts that the granting of tenure is the only acceptable outcome, mediation is fruitless. If the institution were prepared to grant tenure, the grievance would not have been filed.

Although disputes concerning tenure and many issues relating to reappointment and promotion may be nonnegotiable, a whole range of other disputes for which a number of solutions may be acceptable are amenable to this form of resolution. In a grievance over class assignments, a faculty member may grieve that he is consistently assigned introductory courses while other faculty in the department with less seniority than he teach challenging upper-level seminars on topics relating directly to their interests and expertise. Disputes of this kind often include an element of perceived hostility and a personality clash between the grievant and the chair or faculty committee members who determine class assignments. The mediator will discuss with the parties, in joint and separate meetings, the root causes of the dispute and provide a setting within which the important but tangential circumstances can be openly explored, permitting the free exchange necessary to develop a solution to the immediate problem.

In some cases, the filing of a grievance is the only way a faculty member can express exasperation over a series of actions

believed to be undermining his or her position in the institution. The grievant may have proposed a new course that was rejected by the department or may have been denied travel funds
to attend a conference. A neutral who is uninvolved with the
dispute and its genesis may be able not only to help the parties
resolve the dispute but also to promote understanding so that
collegial relationships are reestablished and destructive exchanges are eliminated. This aspect of mediation, as a process
that promotes collegiality, is perhaps its greatest potential benefit for academic institutions.

The grievance procedures will describe the way in which
mediators are selected, either on an ad hoc basis or from a prepared list. The mediators will generally be faculty members at
the institution and in all cases will have no stake in the outcome
or settlement. Acceptance of the mediator is crucial because
the process can be useful only if the parties are open and willing
to share with the mediator their views on possible areas of accommodation. Much as a doctor will have difficulty curing a patient without a truthful and complete description of symptoms,
a mediator will be helpful only to the extent the parties share
the information necessary to bring about agreement.

Hearing. If informal negotiations and structured mediation do not result in resolution, the hearing provides a forum
for formally presenting the issues and positions of the parties. It
is the central and most elaborate step in the grievance procedure; the respective arguments are heard, the merits decided,
and a remedy recommended to the president or board of trustees.

At this step, the grievant has the opportunity to express
fully and formally the basis and reason for the complaint. The
distinguishing features of the hearing are the elements of due
process—representation, introduction of evidence, cross examination, and balanced assessment of issues. Generally, the procedures include rules for the initiation and conduct of the hearing
and the issuance of a determination. These rules establish equality between the parties to the proceedings. The courts may
scrutinize the hearing process to judge whether due process and
a fair review were provided.

A variety of approaches is used in selecting hearing-com-

mittee members. In large institutions, the committee is frequently composed entirely of faculty, most often either three
or five tenured faculty members selected from a standing committee of the faculty. Committee members are usually elected
to serve for set periods of time, typically two years. At small
colleges, the review panel is most often a three-person ad hoc
committee, with one member selected by the president or dean,
one by the grievant, and the third chosen by the other two
members. A few institutions use both standing and ad hoc committees; the standing committee reviews the relevance of the
complaint and attempts informal resolution, and the ad hoc
committee is selected when informal negotiations do not produce an agreement.

Because the hearing is a formal inquiry and usually results in a fact-finding report and recommendations, the composition of the panel is critical. In many procedures, the grieving
faculty member may select one or more committee members.
This participation is recommended, for if faculty have little or
no say in the selection, they may regard the hearing as just another step in the imposition of a solution by the administration
or trustees.

The hearing typically results in findings of fact and recommendations. We quote here three approaches to the design
of the hearing step in the procedure. The description of the
hearing can be brief and fairly general, as is the case at Dominican College of San Rafael and Heidelberg College, or the hearing
can be described in great detail and in a legalistic format, as is
the case at the University of Pennsylvania. The AAUP is a valuable source of ideas for designing the hearing section of the
procedures. Here, as in the design of other procedural elements,
the specific procedures described in Chapter Six and included in
the Resources at the end of the book should also be useful.

At Dominican College of San Rafael (California):

> *Committee hearing.* The committee will con-
> duct a hearing of the grievance, which hearing shall
> be held in private unless the employee requests

otherwise. It will cause full minutes of the proceedings to be taken or, if requested by the employee
or the college and at the expense of the requesting
party, arrange for a full stenographic record of
such proceedings. Such minutes or stenographic
record shall be treated as confidential unless the
employee institutes litigation against the college or
unless the employee makes any public statement
concerning the proceedings or the subject matter
thereof.

At Heidelberg College (Ohio):

Procedures of the Hearing Committee
        A member of the faculty personnel board
shall serve on the hearing committee in any capacity that the committee chooses. The faculty personnel board member shall be present throughout
the formal hearing and shall ensure the confidentiality of all records of the hearing. Upon comple-
tion of this responsibility, the board member shall
not be involved in the deliberations of the committee.
        The involved parties have the right to select
a Heidelberg colleague as an adviser. If the grievance involves the dismissal of a person on continuous appointment (tenure), the grievant is permitted
to have an adviser of his/her own choosing who
may act as counsel.
        There shall be a single session in which all
parties involved shall make their statements before
the hearing committee. If the hearing committee
feels that it needs further information or clarification, the committee may call other sessions to
which both parties must be invited. From the time
of the original request for the hearing to the final
recommendations, the hearings should be completed as speedily as schedules and conditions will

allow, and, excluding vacation periods, this period
of time shall not exceed sixty days.

Testimony and all documents and information regarding the hearing are viewed as confidential. Any tapes or transcripts are the property of
the faculty personnel board and are not for dupli-
cation or distribution. However, either party may
have access to the records under the supervision
of the faculty personnel board.

At the University of Pennsylvania:

V.　Procedures
　　a.　The decision on the merits of a grievance will be made
　　　　by the panel after hearings in which the grievant and
　　　　the respondent have the opportunity to present their
　　　　cases. Hearings shall be chaired by the presiding offi-
　　　　cer, assisted by the legal officer. Arguments, oral and
　　　　documentary evidence, and witnesses will be pre-
　　　　sented first by the grievant and then by the respon-
　　　　dent. The presiding officer shall have the power to
　　　　call witnesses and to introduce documents and shall,
　　　　at the request of the panel, obtain expert opinion
　　　　from inside or outside the university. Each side shall
　　　　have the right to address questions through the pre-
　　　　siding officer to witnesses introduced by the other
　　　　side. If panel members then have questions, they
　　　　may submit them in writing to the presiding officer.
　　b.　A hearing will follow an agenda prepared by the legal
　　　　officer that is based on prior demonstration of rele-
　　　　vance by the grievant or the respondent. Such deter-
　　　　minations of the relevance of issues, oral statements,
　　　　or other evidence by the legal officer may be over-
　　　　ruled by the presiding officer on appeal by a party.
　　c.　The legal officer and the presiding officer shall have
　　　　access to all documentary evidence that is in the cus-
　　　　tody or under the control of the person or persons
　　　　who took the action complained of or of the griev-

ant and that is deemed by these officers to be relevant
to the grievance. If documentary evidence is needed
by the grievant or the respondent in the preparation
of his or her case, or by the panel in the course of its
deliberations, application for access to such evidence
shall be made to the legal officer, who shall determine, subject to appeal to the presiding officer,
whether the evidence requested is relevant and, under the authority of the commission, shall obtain evidence deemed relevant. All such evidence shall be
available to the panel, the respondent, the university
colleague(s), if any, and, subject to restrictions of
confidentiality, to the grievant.

Final Resolution by Board of Trustees or Arbitration. In
the absence of litigation, finality is customarily achieved when
the board of trustees or, at unionized institutions, the arbitrator
makes a determination. The courts are the only forum in which
this determination can be reviewed. The courts tend to dig less
deeply when they are satisfied that the internal procedures have
afforded the faculty member due process and a fair consideration of the merits. Courts usually defer to institutional judgments on the substance of a grievance and limit their inquiries
to procedural aspects. In any event, in most instances where
there is an established and detailed procedure, courts will decline to consider any aspect of the grievance until all procedural
steps have been exhausted.

Two different methods for appealing to the governing
board are described here.

At Keuka College (New York):

[For dismissal proceedings,] the president
should transmit to the Board of Trustees the full
report of the hearing committee, stating its action.
On the assumption that the Board of Trustees has
accepted the principle of the faculty hearing committee, acceptance of the committee's decision
would normally be expected. If the Board of

Trustees chooses to review the case, its review should be based on the record of the previous hearing, accompanied by opportunity for argument, oral or written or both, by the principals at the hearing or their representatives. The decision of the hearing committee should . . . be sustained or the proceeding be returned to the committee with objections specified. In such a case the committee should reconsider, taking account of the stated objections and receiving new evidence if necessary. It should frame its decision and communicate it in the same manner as before. Only after study of the committee's reconsideration should the Board of Trustees make a final decision overruling the committee.

At Medaille College (New York):

A party to the grievance may appeal the decision of the president to the Board of Trustees. Should the Board grant an appeal, it will determine its own procedures for reaching a decision and will inform the President, the parties to the grievance, and the grievance committee of its decision.

If a grievance is against the president of the college, as in dismissal or termination for cause, the grievance committee shall forward its recommendation to the president and, if the president does not follow the recommendation of the grievance committee, the committee shall forward its recommendation to the Board of Trustees for the final decision and to the parties to the grievance. The Board shall receive the grievance at its next regularly scheduled meeting. It shall transmit its decision to the grievance committee and the parties to the grievance.

Under most union contracts, arbitration is available for final resolution of specific issues, generally the tenure process, promotion, discipline, and discharge. In arbitration, the parties submit defined issues to an impartial individual or panel for final determination. The arbitration decision, called an award, is enforceable in court and is subject to judicial review only on specific grounds such as bias, failure to grant adjournment, or exceeding authority. We do not include examples of arbitration clauses here because they are the subject of a collectively bargained agreement and as such are not broadly applicable. The complete spectrum of higher education arbitration clauses at unionized institutions can be obtained from the Center for the Study of Collective Bargaining in Higher Education and the Professions at Baruch College in New York City. The single example of a nonunion arbitration clause is discussed in detail in the next chapter and the clause is included in Resource D.

Designing the Procedures

A critical question about the committee charged with responsibility for designing procedures is the extent of its authority. The committee is usually an advisory one, and its recommendations are subject to approval by the president or board of trustees. The committee may have broad authority, however, to detail the procedural approach and elements. If an existing structure for grievance procedures is expected to be retained, this expectation should be made clear. If final authority must be vested in the president or trustees, this requirement should also be known in advance. Within boundaries such as these, the committee will determine such elements as the scope of grievable issues, the individuals who can use the procedure, and whether a single system or separate procedures will be used for specific issues. At some colleges, tenure and promotion decisions go directly to the president; at others, all issues are handled in the same way.

Design Committee. The committee should include representatives of the constituent groups that will use the process, or at least there should be agreed-on steps for each group to review the draft procedures. If the president or the academic dean asks the faculty senate to appoint a design committee, this committee should gather informal comments and suggestions from appropriate administrators during the design process. In this way, the danger that a proposed faculty approach will be considered objectionable to the administration will be minimized. Another reason for having a broadly representative committee is that committee members will be the advocates for adopting the procedure. Particularly at a large university, these individuals will be asked to explain the rationale for the design, to provide assurances of its fairness, and to promote its use. A procedure designed by a cross section of the faculty has a greater likelihood of being approved and used than one developed by a less representative group. Broad representation is also important if the institution seeks to encourage use of the procedure for disputes that would otherwise end up in court, such as those involving sex, race, and age discrimination.

Setting Deadlines. The design committee should set deadlines for various aspects of the design process so that the committee does not become bogged down in endless discussion of various proposed approaches. If the design process is prolonged, initiative will be lost, attendance at meetings will seem less urgent, and, as sometimes happens, the committee will disband before completing its task. Some institutions review the procedures used at other institutions; this review may be useful, although such a thorough approach may not be needed. A comprehensive examination of available options may be unnecessary if the committee is considering only the section of the procedures dealing with external review or is only evaluating the inclusion of a mediation element.

At the outset, the committee should set a date for the final report to the president or faculty senate and interim deadlines for resolving basic issues. The schedule should not be so rigid that it precludes the raising of issues as they naturally arise. Shown here is a sample schedule for discussion and decision about the design aspects.

First Step: Three meetings, one month

                 Full critique of the current system and agreement on the negative and positive aspects; decision on the issues to be covered; determination of the basic administrative responsibilities for the procedure—that is, which administrator or faculty committee is to be responsible for handling grievances.

Second Step: Six meetings, two months

Decision on steps to be included in the procedure—informal resolution, mediation, formal hearing, external review; examination of the role of the president and the board of trustees in the review process; determination, in consultation with these groups, of their involvement in an appeal and final decision; preparation of first draft of the procedure and circulation of it for comment.

Third Step: One meeting, one month

Review and revision of draft procedure, including definitions of terms, preamble (if desirable), steps, and administrative mechanism.

Fourth Step: Two months

Meetings with the faculty senate, administration, and board of trustees to explain the procedure, its application, and the implications for the institution; approval of the procedure.

This six-month time frame is simply illustrative. If the procedures need only minor revisions, these can be accomplished in substantially less time. On approval of the procedure, the design committee should recommend administrative actions directed to wide dissemination of the procedures and information about how and where to file a grievance. The schedule does not include implementation of the process, which may involve printing forms, setting up an office, and publicizing the system. The complexity of this stage depends on the nature of the institution. For instance, implementation in a large university may be difficult because of the number of schools and departments and faculty members who need to be informed about the new or revised grievance mechanism.

Reviewing Existing Institutional Procedures and Policies. Institutional policy is the foundation for a complaint-handling system. At a nonunionized institution, these policies are the sole basis for judging the merits of a grievance. Thus, in the design and revision of complaint procedures, the importance of a concurrent review of institutional policy cannot be overstated. Certain policies are for all practical purposes set and immutable; these generally include the nature of the institution, the component schools, and the character of the faculty. Other policy elements in the form of bylaws or regulations are statements of operational needs and are meant to be revised periodically to reflect changing conditions. Faculty bylaws, for instance, may specify the number of student contact hours per semester, the composition of faculty committees, and provisions of benefit and retirement programs. These policy directives express the college's current expectations and are modified as needed. Policy provisions relevant to the design of a grievance procedure are those describing departmental structure and external relationships that bear on faculty obligations and contractual agreements made by or on behalf of the faculty. And, of course, faculty are subject to external statutes or regulations, such as those relating to equality of opportunity, that are incorporated directly or indirectly in institutional policy.

The committee review of relevant institutional policy should consider areas of potential conflict or friction. The effectiveness of the committee's work rests on its ability to predict trouble spots. The committee probably will find apparently contradictory, ambiguous, or even deficient provisions. Although it is not the responsibility of the committee to rewrite policy, these provisions can be flagged and brought to the attention of the appropriate policy-review committee. The design committee may also become aware of certain policies that are not always observed, and sometimes flouted. To the extent that these differences become important, they may arise as issues in specific grievances. A checklist that can be used to assess grievance systems is included as Resource A.

Procedures as an Aspect of Preventive Management

Paradoxically, institutions that have adopted an orderly and fair process for resolving disputes generally are not likely to have faculty members use the system. The existence of the grievance mechanism establishes or reinforces a collegial environment in which complaints are expected to be handled constructively, usually without recourse to the formal system. When the system is used, it presents an opportunity to fine tune or to develop policies and practices directed to improving the institution.

A primary institutional goal in establishing complaint procedures is to encourage constructive communications between faculty and administrators. The procedures serve to identify special problems. As such they are an important communications link that provides a regular and orderly way for the administration to anticipate and prevent needless misunderstandings or unrealistic expectations.

In some instances, the procedures are designed in response to what faculty view as tyrannical leadership. When faculty believe that presidential actions are based on whim or favoritism, faculty may seek to develop their own appeals processes, sometimes without official approval. This was the case at DePauw University in the mid 1970s, when the faculty implemented procedures to counter an administration they perceived to be hostile. When a new administration assumed leadership at DePauw in 1977, the faculty grievance procedure was adopted by the trustees as a formal element of institutional policy. At DePauw and other institutions, the spark for designing procedures was the need for protection from an administration seen as repressive. When a more responsive administration assumed control, the need for the procedures, as reflected in the number of grievances filed, was less apparent. The level of grievance activity is usually low at institutions where faculty play a major role in the design of grievance procedures.

To succeed, the system cannot rely on the good will of institutional leadership. The procedures must work effectively regardless of the quality of leadership. Because the procedures are intended to provide a self-correcting mechanism, faculty and management might well include a specific provision to stress this important objective. For instance, an annual report of the grievances handled could be submitted to the president and faculty representatives and perhaps the board of trustees. Such a report helps identify problems. Although the reporting function is usually not explicitly recognized in procedural design, it probably occurs at least informally at most institutions. The fact that the procedures on many campuses have been recently reviewed suggests that key administrators are aware of the need for policy clarifications.

CHAPTER 6

Designing and Applying Faculty Complaint Processes: Practices at Diverse Institutions

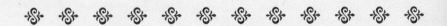

Growing interest in and use of grievance procedures in higher education since the early 1970s are at least in part a result of the trend toward unionization of faculty and the increasing tendency of faculty to go to court to secure due-process protections and redress for alleged violations of statutes prohibiting race and sex discrimination. Usually, the administration initiates the design of grievance procedures, although the faculty may propose procedural revisions when they feel their complaints are not being handled properly.

In view of the recognized need for procedures, a review of how three different institutions went about designing faculty complaint procedures may be instructive. These institutions vary dramatically in size: Northeastern University in Boston has a student body of 41,700 and 815 full-time and 2,000 part-time faculty; Pace University in New York enrolls 28,000 students, who are taught by 473 full-time and 944 adjunct faculty; Unity College in Maine has 340 students and 22 full-time and 13 part-time faculty members. Pace University and Northeastern University are both large, complex organizations that drew on substantial financial resources and management expertise in developing the conceptual framework for their grievance procedures. Differences in approach and in the outcome of the design processes reflect the distinctive management styles of the two universities and the fact that Northeastern serves a large urban constituency while Pace, as a multicampus institution, must consider the needs of both urban and suburban faculties. The Unity College experience demonstrates that a small college with limited legal resources can nonetheless design and implement a complaint system that fully serves its needs. It also illustrates how strong faculty participation can be incorporated in the grievance mechanism.

The objective of this chapter is to present useful suggestions based on these widely differing experiences. As has been emphasized throughout the book, procedures can be cut to the particular pattern of any institution. We are not suggesting that the examples can or should be replicated; they provide a spectrum of possibilities to consider. Similarly, the model procedures prepared by the Center for Mediation in Higher Education, which are included as Resource B at the end of the book, are not intended to be simply copied but should be seen as a point of departure for discussion purposes. Those designing grievance procedures can use the outline of provisions in Resource C as a guide.

An examination of grievance handling within a state system is not included because procedural design and implementation within these systems depend on many factors outside the control of the academic community. Grievance procedures may be set by the state board that regulates public higher education, by specific legislation, or, in some instances, by the governor. Wide variations in state systems and in the degree of autonomy in governance limit the applicability of an analysis of the ways these grievance systems are managed. Thus, the focus here is on independent institutions, where decisions are entirely self-contained.

The three procedures described were fashioned internally

without the presence of an outside legal entity such as a union. We focus on nonunion institutions because we believe that, in light of the Yeshiva decision and the generally slow progress of unionization in independent colleges, most of these institutions will not be unionized in the coming years. Nonetheless, the pressure from faculty for equitable procedures will remain intense whether or not they are formally represented by a collective bargaining agent.

The focus away from collectively bargained procedures does not, however, mean that techniques developed under collective bargaining should not be considered in drafting procedures in a nonunion setting. Designs for unionized institutions may still be useful in some form. For example, at Hofstra University (New York) a moderate-size private institution, the collective bargaining agreement created an appeals board, consisting of two representatives of the administration, two from the faculty, and one neutral, to make recommendations to the president when there is a dispute between the president and the provost or between the provost and the faculty personnel board over questions of renewal, promotion, tenure, and retirement. Similar boards could easily be created at other institutions.

Northeastern University Experience

Northeastern faculty have a more intense involvement in the development of university policy than is the case on many campuses. There is considerable emphasis on collegiality and wide faculty consideration of approaches for handling a variety of complaints and problems. This faculty involvement has led to the design and implementation of a number of complaint procedures for handling problems and issues as they arise. Resource D at the end of the book is the full text of the Northeastern grievance procedures.

Although the Northeastern grievance procedure was designed initially, at least in part, with an eye toward the possibility of unionization, the procedures are part of an extensive program of faculty evaluation and development. They represent a determined and successful internal effort to resolve faculty problems fairly and expeditiously. The administration, the university's legal counsel, and the faculty believe that the best way to maintain a harmonious atmosphere is to carefully develop and utilize avenues for redress. This belief is reflected in an extensive faculty handbook, which serves as a reference for almost every conceivable eventuality.

The initiative for the design of the Northeastern procedures came from the university's then president, Asa Knowles. He was probably persuaded, or at least encouraged, to begin the design process as a result of discussions with the university's legal counsel, Jerome Medalie, who described grievance procedures typically available through collective bargaining in the private sector. The president was interested to know whether similar procedures would be applicable to faculty.

Ultimately, through negotiations with members of the faculty senate, procedures were developed and implemented in the early 1970s. This was a time of great unrest on campus. The university was experiencing rapid growth in both enrollment and faculty. The faculty were drawn from all parts of the country, in contrast to the faculty at some other universities who are drawn from their own graduate schools, and who teach only there until retirement. The Northeastern faculty, with extensive experience on other campuses, were particularly attuned to the unrest that permeated the academic community nationwide in the early 1970s.

The combination of a somewhat peripatetic faculty and the political turmoil of the times led, in 1975, to an intensive attempt at unionization, which fell a few votes short of acceptance. Although Northeastern's previous adoption of a procedure with a broad definition of a grievance and a provision for binding arbitration was, as far as we know, unprecedented in the absence of a faculty union, the existence of this procedure did not guarantee that faculty would not be interested in unionization. The closeness of the vote, however, drove home to the administration the usefulness of having procedures and the need to develop and cultivate them in response to changing faculty needs. In 1975, the selection of a new president was based in part on his wide accessibility to faculty, resulting from his participation in the administrative aspects of the grievance procedures. After the close vote on unionization, the new president took the opportunity to involve faculty even more than previously in the grievance process.

Role of the Provost's Office and the Ombudsman. A demonstration of the university's broad concern for faculty is the existence of the high-level administrative position of special assistant for faculty relations and development within the office of the provost. Among other responsibilities, this administrator handles faculty grievances as part of his more encompassing concern for faculty development. In addition, the provost's office conducts workshops for the more than seventy department chairs, covering the substance of and changes in personnel law, procedures, and policies.

As experience with the procedures grew, an unusual aspect was the adoption of an ombudsman format. Although the procedures are detailed and contain a variety of steps, it is possible for a faculty member to involve the office of the provost early in the dispute and out of the regular sequence that would otherwise be followed. A representative of the provost's office, taking the role of an ombudsman, is available to meet with both parties in an attempt to resolve the dispute. Aside from the obvious fact that the provost's office may have a broader perspective than those immediately affected, it is reassuring for the faculty to know that, if they so desire, there can be an informal short cut to the highest levels. This system is in sharp contrast to many other academic grievance systems where the option to involve the provost is fenced in by protocol and sequential procedural steps. There is no requirement that a grievant select the accelerated procedure immediately. However, in those instances where resort to a mediation committee is appropriate, the mediation committee is not involved until the ombudsman approach is exhausted.

Resort to this ombudsman in the provost's office is without prejudice to the faculty member; if no resolution is achieved, the faculty member can reinstitute the formal grievance steps and proceed. Thus, the procedure actually provides two paths to mediation: one through the formal faculty mediation committee and the second through informal contacts with the provost's office. In the case of alleged sexual harassment, a separate procedure provides yet a third avenue for mediation.

Mediation Committee. With experience, it became clear that the mediation committee's effectiveness is determined to some extent by the nature of the issue; for grievances involving dismissal or tenure, mediation cannot bring about a solution. Generally, in disputes concerning the faculty member's continued employment, the only outcome acceptable to the faculty member is a full capitulation of the university position. Situations where there is an absolute winner and loser do not lend themselves to mediation because the process requires the parties to accommodate the interests of their adversaries. Thus, the procedures at Northeastern were revised to eliminate mediation in cases concerning dismissal and denial of tenure.

Those familiar with the Northeastern experience have suggested that wide participation of the faculty in the mediation process has served to dampen faculty enthusiasm for extended controversy. Faculty rotate as members of the mediation committee; 340 faculty served in the first ten years. These faculty have become familiar with the probing nature of mediation and the hard evaluation of positions that it entails. Thus, they are probably less likely than those who have not served on the mediation committee to file grievances of a frivolous nature. A concomitant pressure acting to reduce the number of grievances is that faculty who have served on the committee are sensitive to the manner in which disputes can develop a momentum of their own. As a result, many problems that surface are quickly settled by the informal involvement of the principals before they become full-blown disputes. Further, membership on the mediation committee allows faculty to become acquainted with informal techniques for dispute resolution and to develop the skills to settle their problems through available channels outside the formal mechanism. As a result, in the opinion of those working with the procedures, faculty have become increasingly tolerant of the decisions of their peers and the administration and have developed an impressive and rare ability to understand the merits of all sides of a dispute; they are aware of how painful it can be for a grievant to exhaust all remedies without coming to an acceptable solution.

Experience with the Grievance Process and Arbitration. From 1973 to 1983 there were 126 grievances, 18 of which went to arbitration. The most frequent grievance concerns merit raises; the second most frequent, faculty prerogatives; the third, denials of tenure. Grievances involving merit raises have increased slightly each year. There is a separate procedure for handling merit-salary issues, which includes a provision for accelerating the process so that matters can be resolved quickly. When the procedures were initially put into place, it was predicted that a large number of complaints would be filed, and they were. Paradoxically, increased confidence in the effectiveness of the procedures and the developing sophistication of the parties in handling grievances led to a decline in the total number of grievances filed annually. There was also a reduction in the number of cases going to arbitration.

As is true on many campuses, alleged abridgment of academic freedom is frequently the basis for the grievance. How far this concept is stretched can be seen from a case where a faculty member brought a grievance when one of his students asked to be assigned another professor in the same course. The grieving faculty member refused permission for the transfer, claiming this refusal to be within his rights under the principle of academic freedom. After considerable pressure from departmental colleagues, the professor was persuaded that important issues were not at stake.

Adherence to the procedural time limits is considered fundamental at Northeastern. The provost's office goes to some lengths to make sure the faculty are fully aware of time constraints. In particular the university is prepared to enforce the six-week initial filing deadline. If, however, a faculty member makes an issue of the deadline, the university will go through the grievance procedure and raise timeliness in arbitration. Experience shows that somewhere along the line the grievant will realize there is no point in pursuing the claim.

Another procedural variation is that if in going through the grievance procedure the university feels the grievance has merit, the grievance will be put on hold while efforts are directed to settling informally. If informal settlement is not reached, the university then waives further steps in the grievance procedure and goes directly to arbitration.

Technically, the university has never lost a substantive issue in arbitration, although several cases have been returned for reconsideration. Cases involving tenure are particularly troublesome because the university role is similar to that of a respondent in the appeal of a court decision. That is, the university is defending an adverse decision made by the grievant's peers. In one case where the arbitrator ordered a tenure review, the faculty member was in fact awarded tenure. In another, the new review did not reverse the original decision to deny tenure.

In 1979, the university's legal counsel prepared for the provost an evaluation of the use of arbitration in faculty disputes. He noted the importance of achieving, whenever possible, an internal solution: "To whatever extent alternative or remedial action can be taken before the matter reaches arbitration without the sacrifice of a fundamental principle or the incurring of a large expense, that action ought to be taken or, at least, thoroughly explored and evaluated." He also noted the somewhat ambiguous position of the university in arbitration because, as noted, many of the cases involved faculty who complained about faculty action in connection with the review process.

While arbitration may end a particular dispute, it also helps to refine and interpret contract clauses or procedural aspects. Although the question of whether a prior arbitration is precedent setting is not without its complexities, it is fair to observe that unless modified by a subsequent rewriting of the provision, the applicable procedure or standard consists of the clause in question plus the arbitrator's interpretation. Thus, it is incumbent on the parties involved to be aware not only of the clause but also of the award itself and, in dealing with future cases, to consider both the language of the procedure and the contents of the award.

Although the impetus for designing the Northeastern pro-

cedures came from the university's legal counsel, the early procedures reflected the nonlegal orientation of the faculty and administrators who developed them. Thus, the procedures included a number of general phrases that were open to varied
interpretation. Over time, procedural revisions tightened the
language to clearly express the intent of the designers. Furthermore, in revising procedures, the university notes the experience
in arbitration and in some instances incorporates the arbitrator's
perspective and decisions in the procedural revisions. One of the
early awards in arbitration dealt with the difficult problem of
handling the grievant's right to examine relevant documentation in a tenure dispute. The procedures were revised to reflect
the arbitrator's decision concerning privileged information.

  Grievance Procedures as a Preventive Strategy. The ombudsman and mediation processes have a by-product that tends
to dampen the possibility that a particular grievance will arise
in the future. The mediation committee is required to report
periodically to the faculty senate on the progress of a particular
dispute. As part of that report the mediation committee may
point to structural or procedural flaws or misconceptions in the
processes followed by departments or other university subdivi-
sions. This feedback provides the faculty senate with an opportunity to review the problem and to develop new or revised procedures to avoid this type of grievance in the future.

  In addition, the provost's office monitors the progress of
all tenure and merit-salary grievances for consistency with the
faculty handbook. There is also close contact with the university's legal counsel and the ombudsman from the outset so that
any issues that appear headed for arbitration can be given early
attention in an effort to aid in their resolution.

  It is the policy of the university that the many mediation
and grievance steps be followed with a view toward achieving a
fair and equitable result. In other words, the university wants
everything to be done on the procedural level that can be done
in order to bring about a solution. If the provost's office determines that the fault lies in the department, pressure will be
brought on the department to straighten out the matter. As a
result, grievances tend to become completely adversarial only

when there is resort to arbitration. At this point, after every avenue has been explored, the administration's position is that nothing more can be done for the faculty member. The university then takes the position that the burden of persuasion is squarely on the grievant.

The question arises as to whether these detailed procedures dissuade grievants from going to court. The answer is no. The university's experience in court, however, has been that judges tend to be satisfied that the detailed procedures provide substantive and procedural due process. They will therefore stay the court proceedings and retain jurisdiction, encouraging the parties to return to the internal processes.

Because of the extensive emphasis on developing specific and conscientiously followed procedures and the opportunity for many bites of the apple, Northeastern's legal counsel believes that, in Title VII (Civil Rights Act) complaints, there is no serious threat to the finality of any outcome resulting from the procedures. In other words, the federal courts will be satisfied with the outcome of the grievance procedure if it is shown that it has been carefully, regularly, and conscientiously followed and that all aspects of the dispute have been given full consideration.

One salient lesson to be learned here is that all levels of the university must be carefully respectful of the procedures. Northeastern goes to great effort to inculcate in the administrative staff, department chairs, and faculty committee members an understanding of the need for precision in all aspects of the review of faculty-status decisions. Department chairs are encouraged to contact the provost's office to make sure they are complying with university policy. Committee chairs are fully versed in the numerous detailed procedures for handling a variety of potential disputes. All parties involved agree that the possible disadvantages of having numerous procedures and high costs of administration are more than offset by the effectiveness of the procedures in resolving disputes.

This approach, demonstrably useful for Northeastern with its large faculty, many management divisions, and administrative sophistication, would obviously have to be custom cut to fit the needs of institutions that do not share these characteristics. The insistence on regularized procedures so that all faculty are treated in the same manner is surely a guiding conviction that serves the highest interests of all members of the academic community.

Pace University Experience

Pace University is one of the fastest expanding academic institutions in the country. It has grown from a limited, evening business and accounting school known as Pace Institute, organized in 1906, to a full-time business-administration institution that, in 1948, became Pace College with the authority to confer academic degrees. By 1973, when the New York Board of Regents conferred university status, Pace offered day and evening programs in the liberal arts and sciences as well as business. The principal campus is in downtown Manhattan. Other facilities include a New York City midtown center and two locations in Westchester County, White Plains and Pleasantville/Briarcliff. By 1982 the university was operating nine schools and colleges at these four campuses. The continuing and rapid expansion of the school and its use of a large number of adjunct professors and specialists, particularly for evening classes and for certain disciplines, have made it possible for Pace to avoid retrenchment.

In the late 1970s the administration asked the university counsel, Robert I. Ruback, to design a comprehensive faculty grievance procedure that would be uniform for all campuses. The project was undertaken because of the size and spread of the university and the recognized importance of internal procedures in the event of outside review by a government agency or a court. Further, because faculty fairly often move between campuses, it is important to have consistent application of procedures regardless of a faculty member's location.

In carrying out this mission, the counsel called on administrators, particularly the vice-president for academic affairs and the vice-president for human resources, and faculty leaders for advice and suggestions. No formal committee was established for this purpose, nor was the faculty council or university senate officially consulted. These groups were, however, advised periodically on progress, and they commented on drafts. Ruback drafted the procedures after a careful study of existing procedures on Pace campuses and the systems of other institutions. The procedures were fashioned in appreciation of the type of faculty and the conditions at Pace, reflecting its orientation toward preparing students for business. Resource E at the end of the book is the full text of the Pace grievance procedures.

Procedures. Faculty grievants are directed to one of three procedures, depending on whether the issue is promotion or tenure, salary review, or another matter. The procedure for issues other than promotion, tenure, or salary was put into place in late 1982. It is a comprehensive system for all faculty, including adjuncts. Formal procedures are provided for discrimination and contract claims, which are defined as allegations from a faculty member or group that a provision in the faculty handbook has been violated. Noncontract claims are handled informally.

Faculty members must first discuss problems informally with the department chair, the dean of the school, and the vice-president for academic affairs. If a contract claim remains unresolved, a hearing may be obtained via the appropriate faculty-council grievance committee. Under the procedure, the affirmative action officer assists the grievant in preparing a formal written complaint for both discrimination and contract claims. The final determination for all contract claims rests with the president, who issues decisions "as soon as practicable" after receiving the report from the faculty-council committee.

For claims of discrimination, the affirmative action officer convenes a three-member panel (each side selects one member and they jointly choose a neutral chair) from a pool composed of administrators, faculty, staff, and students selected by the all-campus university senate in consultation with the affirmative action officer. Final authority rests with the president, who discusses an appropriate remedy with the faculty member when it is determined the grievance has merit.

Noncontract claims relate to "allegations that any event or condition has adversely affected a faculty member regarding his/her welfare and/or terms and conditions of appointment not covered by the faculty handbook." Noncontract claims are not processed through the formal grievance procedure. Rather, they are resolved through communications with department chairs, deans, and the vice-president for academic affairs. The grievance procedure notes that "the faculty and the university recognize that the use of expert advisory opinions may assist in a fair and expeditious settlement of noncontractual disputes. ... The faculty member or the university may, if it deems necessary, introduce advisory opinions to support its position."

The procedure recognizes that, despite the review processes, faculty may opt to pursue a claim through an outside agency or in court. The final provision, therefore, states, "This procedure may not be used if a formal complaint has been filed with a governmental agency or a court action has been initiated based on substantially similar facts, in which event any investigation or hearing then in progress shall be terminated."

Procedures regarding promotion and tenure are issued annually. Faculty who seek promotion or tenure are reviewed by a university-wide council on promotion and tenure, which is composed of deans and faculty. If promotion or tenure is denied, faculty may appeal to the president and are advised by members of a university-wide appeals committee composed of faculty elected by the faculty councils for each campus as well as the liaison representatives of the university-wide council on promotion and tenure.

According to Joseph Pastore, vice-president for academic affairs, about a hundred individuals come up for tenure and promotion annually, twenty-five for tenure and seventy-five for promotion. Tenure candidates present few problems because the requirements are well understood and are generally met well in advance. But, some twenty promotion appeals are likely, most of which are resolved early by the local grievance committees. A few, perhaps five, proceed to the president. None has proceeded to an outside agency or to the courts. As noted, discrimination issues are referred to the comprehensive faculty grievance process, which provides for a formal hearing.

Salary issues, like others, are first discussed informally with the appropriate dean and vice-president for academic affairs. Thereafter, the grievant may appeal to the three-member salary review boards nominated by the faculty councils and appointed by the president. The provost serves as ex officio member of the boards. Final decisions, based on board recommendations, are made by the president. To date, few boards have been convened.

Comparison with Northeastern and Unionized Institutions. The Pace University system contrasts with the Northeastern University approach in several significant ways. Northeastern has found it preferable to have a series of grievance procedures and encourages the development of ad hoc processes when deemed suitable. Pace has sought comprehensiveness and consistency without imposing slavish uniformity so that faculty spread over many campuses may reasonably be entitled to the same review. Northeastern stresses informality and accommodation through the processes of mediation and arbitration; Pace favors a somewhat more formal structure. Northeastern, in keeping with its informality, is less impressed with timetables and deadlines once a complaint has been properly initiated. Pace stresses the importance of timely faculty and university responses, generally within relatively short periods. A major difference is in the degree of faculty participation in the development and management of the grievance apparatus. Both clearly express the availability of the procedures and open access to the various steps. Controversies at Northeastern, however, evidently raised the consciousness of the faculty to an insistence on active participation. At Pace, there seems to be no strong concern on the part of faculty for active involvement.

At both institutions, the grievance system is recognized as but one part of faculty governance. The complaint process is employed only when the positive aspects of governance do not prove satisfactory. This contrasts with experience in unionized institutions, where the contractual grievance procedure is clearly separated from statements of university policy. In those cases, it serves as the basis for enforcing and interpreting policy and is initiated by faculty through union representatives. It does not follow, however, that collectively bargained procedures are necessarily protective or democratic or, conversely, that university-initiated processes are biased toward the institution. The degree of protection afforded in unionized schools depends on the history of faculty participation in academic governance and on institutional structure as well as on the policies and attitudes of the university officers and trustees. It also depends on the extent to which the collective bargaining agent has been able to obtain a comprehensive grievance procedure through negotiations. The statement of the grievance procedure and its provisions for considering issues cannot merely claim that the procedure is adequate or that it is adaptable to all types of problems. As with any design for ending disputes, the belief and faith of faculty in actual performance remain the only test of efficacy.

Unity College Experience

Unity College is nestled in the gently rolling Maine mountains, approximately twenty miles from Waterville, in the middle of the state. Reflecting its rugged rural setting, the college offers a four-year natural-resource curriculum combined with more traditional general-education courses. Its concentration in the environmental sciences equips its graduates for environmental-management careers in such fields as fisheries, forestry, wildlife, and outdoor recreation. The college emphasizes intensive student and faculty interaction, small classes, and individual attention. Most of the students are drawn from small towns in New England and are attracted by Unity's strong environmental orientation.

It probably should be expected that a small college in a state that prides itself on Yankee thrift and ingenuity would develop faculty grievance procedures that are sparse in comparison with their counterparts at other colleges of similar size and that the procedural approach would be distinctive, would be clearly stated, and would reflect the specific needs of the faculty. Resource F at the end of the book is the full text of these procedures.

The college initiated the grievance-procedure design process in 1974 in connection with a comprehensive self-study directed to achieving accreditation for the college from the New England Association of Schools and Colleges. The three-member design committee was one of several committees appointed by the president to prepare the self-study report. This committee was chaired by Donald Mortland, a professor of English and one of the most highly respected members of the faculty.

The procedures are remarkable in the high degree of faculty involvement in grievance handling and in the availability of an appeal to the trustees. The procedures are faculty driven in the sense that the grievance committee, composed of three faculty members, decides whether the issues presented warrant investigation and a hearing. The committee is specifically charged with the responsibility to mediate in an attempt to bring about a settlement. If a settlement is not possible, the president chairs a hearing on the grievance. Following the hearing, the committee prepares a report with recommendations to the president. The president may ask the committee for clarification and revisions. The president then announces a decision. The grievant may appeal this decision directly to the board, which has access to the transcript from the hearing. The board decision is final. The availability of an appeal to the board is a particularly advantageous feature for the faculty member because the board may be expected to have a broader perspective on the issues than will those directly involved with the day-to-day management of the college. This feature provides some assurance that personal hostility or rancor will not be a factor in the decision.

Ironically, the procedures designed by the faculty at the request of the president became the source of controversy between the faculty and president two years after their adoption, when faculty displeasure with the president's performance became widespread. Faculty dissatisfaction was registered through the filing of many grievances, which the president rejected as lacking merit. A list of grievances submitted by the faculty during this period was summarily dismissed by the president, who told faculty that the issues presented were solely within his management prerogatives and not subject to review.

Throughout the 1976–77 academic year, faculty expressed

growing concern that the president's leadership style, which was characterized as authoritarian and inappropriate in a college where faculty were accustomed to taking an active participatory role in decision making. This displeasure came to a head when the president interrupted a faculty meeting with a request for a vote of confidence in his leadership. The faculty responded with a 25-1 no-confidence vote. Thereafter, the students responded in similar fashion at the student convocation with a vote by acclamation expressing no confidence. The combination of faculty and student pressure caused the president to resign the following year.

As a part of the president's legacy and a sign of the intense faculty feeling engendered during his term of office, two faculty members filed suit against the college claiming the grievance procedures did not protect their rights. The two faculty members were physical education professors whose appointments were not renewed when the college eliminated the traditional physical education courses in favor of an outdoor recreation program. The lawsuit against the college went to the Maine Supreme Court, where the judge ruled in favor of the college. This finding that the grievance process was without procedural flaw should be instructive for other small colleges that develop complaint procedures without tapping legal expertise. Faculty members are fully capable of designing appeals procedures that both reflect the college's management style and protect individual faculty.

In recent years, the procedures have not been used, and present members of the administrative staff and faculty do not expect grievances to be filed. With the appointment of a new president, Louis V. Wilcox, Jr., in 1980, the faculty are united in their efforts to sustain and strengthen the college. Although the faculty were not involved in the presidential selection process, they participated intensively in the selection of the dean for the college and wholeheartedly supported Wilcox's candidacy for this position, which he held until becoming president. Faculty at Unity characterize Wilcox's management style as responsible and collegial. The lack of grievances is attributed to his willingness to discuss faculty problems and to settle them informally. In commenting on grievance procedures, Wilcox noted that it is not so much the grievance procedures themselves that are important; the caliber and responsiveness of the staff who administer them set the tone and ensure the success of the appeals process.

Faculty unity and the lack of formal grievances are remarkable in this financially stressful period. An example of this cooperative spirit occurred in the spring of 1982, when the faculty unanimously agreed to a fourteen-week payless summer to assist the college in weathering a cash-flow problem. Under the deferred-compensation plan, faculty would be reimbursed retroactively for the summer throughout the following academic year. This action was taken with the understanding that the board of trustees would be reorganized with new members who would be active in securing financial support. The day after the faculty voted to defer summer salaries, the entire board of trustees resigned. The new board includes prominent local and statewide business and community leaders and respected educators. The college's emphasis on environmental sciences is reflected on the board by several trustees who have professional environmental-management experience.

This remarkable collegial relationship, which encompasses a strong consultative role for faculty and a willingness on the part of all members of the academic community to address problems and seek mutually agreed-on solutions, suggests the conditions that must be present if many financially beleaguered small colleges are to survive. Grievance procedures that are accepted by the faculty as a fair appeals process, combined with the willingness of the college leadership to seriously consider faculty complaints, can produce an environment that fosters joint problem solving and accommodation.

PART III

Special Issues
and Institutional Practices

Policy disputes focus on issues that fall outside the scope of the grievance procedures discussed in the previous chapters. These disputes arise out of demands by a group of faculty for specific actions or policy changes. Chapter Seven describes the variety of policy issues that have been the subject of controversy on many campuses. Chapter Eight suggests management styles and approaches for resolving them. Chapter Nine describes the way in which Hofstra University in New York handled retrenchment, one of the most frequent policy disputes.

    Disputes between the faculty and the institution over policy issues usually occur infrequently, and their timing and severity cannot be anticipated in advance. They are so diverse in content, complexity, and scope that a standardized framework for managing them would not be appropriate or useful. While grievance disputes involve the application and interpretation of institutional regulations to an individual or, in some cases, to a group of individuals, policy disputes concern the wisdom or ef-

127

ficacy of an existing or proposed policy or action of the institution. Rather than focusing on the claims and remedies sought by individual faculty members, these disputes involve the fundamental values of the institution.

The thesis of this part of the book is that techniques for managing these issues can be planned in advance by custom tailoring a framework for the response. Further, the procedures regularly utilized for recurring individual complaints can be part of an effective institutional strategy. For instance, mediation and ad hoc review panels, described as elements of procedural design in Chapter Five, can be adapted with appropriate modifications for use in these situations.

CHAPTER 7

Disputes
over Institutional Policies

Policy disputes have many different sources. Demands may relate to issues that are seemingly extraneous to the functioning of the institution, or they may relate directly to its management and operation. Demands about seemingly extraneous issues are usually matters of conviction or principle, such as the demands for divestiture of financial holdings in companies dealing with South Africa, the boycott of businesses involved in unfair labor practices, and agitation against the offer or denial of campus facilities to speakers taking bigoted or offensive positions. Demands about matters of institutional operation necessitate administrative action, such as initiating fair and equitable retention policies, allowing faculty participation in departmental or campus-wide reorganization, and reallocating resources. These internally based disputes may also arise when faculty claim that the customary grievance system is unfair or ineffective. An example of this kind of dispute is a claim of discrimination that results in litigation or in campus confrontation after internal procedures have failed to produce an acceptable remedy.

Issues of Principle and Politics

In the not too distant past, many people considered faculty members who engaged in political activity and espoused their views to students to be unprofessional. Since the late 1960s, however, many faculty have not hesitated to use the campus as a forum for urging their political preferences or points of view. In some instances, faculty are critical of a policy of the trustees with respect, for example, to the institution's endowment. Others express political opinions not specifically directed to their own institutions. The common denominator is the right to express individually held beliefs, commonly referred to as academic freedom.

There are similarities in the confrontations over loyalty oaths during the 1950s, the demonstrations against the Vietnam War, and the nuclear-freeze campaign. It is useful for administrators to recognize that although the specific content of these confrontations may be unpredictable, the general category can be anticipated. This understanding permits development of a reasonable response.

In exercising academic freedom, faculty members, often urged on by students, use the campus to draw attention to causes that promote civil rights, political democracy, humanism, or national or international justice. In addition, new issues such as cryptology involve faculty research and create conflicts between freedom of information and national security. Some of these issues seem central to the role of the institution in the community; others are clearly tangential. In all cases, however, participants justify the use of the campus as a forum on the grounds that some institutional action or statement, be it from trustees, the president, other faculty, students, or even alumni, is warranted.

Corporate Responsibility and National Policy. Issues of principle, usually accompanied by demands for corporate policy changes, may focus on individual companies—for example, protests against Dow Chemical and its production of toxic chemical agents and demonstrations against J. P. Stevens, the textile manufacturer, because of alleged unfair labor practices. Although some protestors limit the campus to being the stage for discussion and rallies, others may demand clear and rapid institutional response. In the campaign against J. P. Stevens, faculty members and committees of students petitioned universities and colleges to cancel contracts with that company and requested assurances that no further textile purchases would be made from its distributors. Many institutions acquiesced, some directly in open support and others indirectly by quietly curtailing purchases.

One of the most persistent on-campus protests is opposition to South African policies of apartheid. The faculty, often together with students, demand that universities sell their investments in companies dealing with that nation. This campaign, arising on a single campus, would have at best a marginal impact. By its very nature, however, it raises high feeling on many campuses, leading to the creation of networks and coalitions aimed at bringing the issue to national prominence. It is incumbent on university administrators to recognize from the outset that they are dealing with an issue of such magnitude.

Another set of issues involves governmental policy rather than an institutional decision. Examples of such issues are nuclear disarmament, intervention in El Salvador, and the government's relationships with undemocratic regimes. Two institutional responses are involved: the decision whether to make a statement for or against the governmental position in question and, because these issues tend to draw large numbers of protestors, the responsibility of keeping order on the campus. Academic institutions usually welcome free and divergent expression over issues of national policy. When opposing groups disrupt the campus or question the right of their opponents to use campus facilities, a response from the administration is required. The administration may feel it necessary to place limits on the use of certain facilities for demonstrations and rallies, to set the time for the events, and to restrict their duration. Thus, the nature as well as the substance of the protest must be examined.

Some policy disputes that develop between the government and a particular faculty member or department would seem to have no direct relation to the institution itself. Nevertheless, expressions of concern by academic institutions may influence such governmental policies. Although some institutions hesitate to become involved, others welcome the opportunity and, in some instances, are willing to act through education associations to achieve additional impact. An issue of this kind is the degree of control the federal government should exercise over independent university research when it impinges on national security. The American Council on Education, acting on behalf of professors engaged in cryptography and computer science, whose work has both civilian and military applications, argued successfully against strict controls sought by the National Security Agency (NSA). The compromise, based on voluntary participation, includes a provision for scientists to submit articles for review and comment; appeal is available to scientists who disagree with an NSA determination to bar or postpone publication. In this regard, the policy of the Massachusetts Institute of Technology for its Laboratory for Computer Science specifies that research papers be sent to NSA as progress reports rather than as requests for permission to publish. Apparently, NSA has not objected to the publication of papers so submitted. According to the laboratory director, if NSA does object, "it can join us in discussion toward informal resolution of the conflict." In the absence of resolution, "we may resort to existing laws on classification or adjudication by the courts." The control of cryptographic information illustrates the complexity of maintaining a balance between national security and academic freedom and, in addition, meeting private-sector commercial needs to employ cryptology to ensure electronic and computer security; research on codes for business use may lead to intrusions into governmental cryptosystems.

To protect against disclosure of patents that might be detrimental to national security, orders under the Invention Secrecy Act of 1951 may be issued to designate such inventions government secrets. One such order was issued on a patent developed by a University of Wisconsin professor and his graduate assistant who used advanced mathematics to design a cipher device that prevents unauthorized penetration of commercial computers. Because of local campus and community criticism and international publicity, the order was soon withdrawn. NSA explained that the order was issued in error because the basic mathematical theory had already appeared in the literature.

   Outside Financial Interests and Influences. Faculty have become embroiled in heated controversies over the acceptance by universities of politically sensitive contributions. Outside financial support has always been a matter of faculty concern because of the danger that a donor will influence the academic program or otherwise affect the educational mission and integrity of the school. Faculty members often express the view that it is impossible to have a no-strings-attached contribution and, thus, any donor's purposes and intentions should be scrutinized. Even governmental agencies are not exempt from such examination. When it was realized that the Central Intelligence Agency was covertly financing university research and publication, faculty objected strongly, even though the programs were justified as being in the national interest. When the extent of agency influence became known, faculty presented policy questions to the trustees: namely, should the institution allow secret research, and, if so, to what extent should this research be disclosed when challenged?

   In several highly publicized cases, outside financial interests contributed funds to major universities for Middle East studies. Even before large amounts of money were available from the Arab nations, many universities organized such programs, anticipating this new source of funds. As long as the funds for these programs came from the U.S. government and foundation grants, they seemed to arouse little controversy. Faculty bridled, however, when Arab nations became direct and substantial financial backers. Objections were raised at many universities, including Johns Hopkins (for accepting money from Oman and Saudi Arabia), the University of Michigan (for accepting funds from Libya for a summer institute), and the University of Utah (for accepting money from the Libyan Arab Development Institute).

   In 1976, wide press coverage was given to the University of Southern California when it was offered a million dollars by

Saudi Arabia to establish a King Faisal Chair of Islamic and Arab Studies. Although the university had long-standing relations with Saudi Arabia through the training of students, this was the first financial offer with conditions. Before the first appointment to the chair, the university president received a letter from the Saudi Arabian finance minister stating an understanding that the chair holder would be Willard A. Beling, who was closely associated with Arab governments and a former oil company official. Future appointees were to be selected by the university in consultation with the Saudi minister of education, "within the acceptable academic traditions of the university." Within these traditions, however, donors are not consulted on such questions except as a formal courtesy. In addition, the Saudis were to be involved with the establishment of the Middle East Center, also to be headed by Beling, which would provide research projects and related services for students and the nonacademic community and prepare students for careers relating to this region. The center was also to be given a voice "in the appointment and employment of . . . faculty teaching courses on the Middle East outside the center." Further, Beling was to head the Middle East Center Foundation, formed to raise money from businesses with Saudi connections. A principal fund raiser was J. Robert Fluor, chair of the university board of trustees and president of the Fluor Corporation, which had large construction contracts in Saudi Arabia.

Clearly, the independence of the center, and perhaps that of the university, was subject to challenge. Faculty opposition focused on the university's failure to consult in advance with the faculty, the potentially adverse effect on raising funds from other sources, the center's semiautonomous governance structure, and the danger that the center would be a target of investigations by federal agencies. Faculty pressure combined with wide public exposure prompted university trustees to set up a committee of faculty members, deans, and students to prepare recommendations on matters concerning the center and Middle East studies. By unanimous vote, the committee recommended voiding the agreement. It proposed creating a Middle East Center entirely under the academic and financial control of the university, with a new director chosen on merit, and refused support from the Middle East Center Foundation. With the acceptance of these recommendations, the center was established as a nonaligned university unit.

At Georgetown University (Washington, D.C.), a different set of circumstances arose in connection with the funding by foreign nations of an Arab studies program. In this case, nine Arab countries contributed approximately $4 million to the Center for Contemporary Arab Studies, established in 1975. Unlike the situation at the University of Southern California, no conditions were attached regarding the use of the funds. From the outset, however, university faculty and others criticized acceptance of these gifts because they believed that such large donations influenced the policies and teachings of the center.

Public controversy erupted in 1977, when the Libyan government made a grant of $750 thousand to establish a chair in Arab studies. Georgetown's president reluctantly accepted the gift in the belief that it represented a desire on the part of the Libyan head of state to move away from terrorist strategy. The gift was not so interpreted by the academic community, trustees, and friends of Georgetown. Because of continued criticism, the president returned the gift, explaining that "Libya's continued accent on violence as a normal method of international policy and its growing support of terrorism . . . made it increasingly impossible for Georgetown University to feel comfortable in having its name associated with the Libyan government." In a similar incident, Georgetown returned $50 thousand to Iraq in 1978 because, "between the time the gift was sought from the government of Iraq and the time it was received, the university received a gift from another source guaranteeing the presence of a renowned Islamic ethnician on its staff for the foreseeable future."

Another example of faculty objections to politically sensitive contributions was the furor over the Nixon Library at Duke University. The proposal to locate Richard M. Nixon's presidential library on campus sparked vehement faculty opposition and an initially negative recommendation from the faculty academic council. The controversy split the faculty and provided a rallying point for those who had been dissatisfied with other aspects of President Terry Sanford's administration. The issues were resolved when Sanford proposed that the academic council designate a committee to develop "an agenda of conditions" under which to conduct negotiations between Duke and Nixon's representatives. The subcommittee proposed conditions that were endorsed by both the academic council and the president. Thus, the faculty were able to gain a role in a decision regarding this politically charged proposal, which had been handled at first by only the president and the board. The conditions imposed apparently sidetracked the proposal. Nixon's aides were said to be considering a less controversial, probably nonacademic, setting for the archives.

Issues of Institutional Management

Unlike issues of national or corporate policy, which are often ephemeral, faculty views on important internal policies frequently generate sustained, campus-wide debate. A professor of physics may avoid taking sides on one or more of the hot national political issues of the day. There is little likelihood, however, that he or she will not have formed a strong and sometimes inflexible opinion on a proposed plan to reorganize the university.

Retrenchment and Reorganization. Many colleges have had to cope with fiscal problems and the resulting issue of faculty retrenchment. Although virtually every institution tries to save faculty positions, this course is not always possible. In some cases, campus-wide cutbacks are effected; often, a specified percentage of the total budget has to be cut, with belt tightening and retrenchment across the board. In other cases, institutions examine specific programs and departments with a view to selective reduction or elimination of academic disciplines based on such considerations as current and prospective enrollment and the availability of outside financial support. The challenge is to devise a retrenchment plan that is least damaging to the institution's basic educational mission.

Clearly, in the foreseeable future, the establishment of

policies and guidelines for faculty layoffs will have the highest priority. Under collective bargaining, these issues will supersede in importance negotiations on salary and work load. Institutional survival may demand general or departmental trimming, reorganization, changes in tenure policy, use of part-timers, modification of seniority rules, savings through normal attrition, early-retirement incentives, or other cost-cutting strategies.

Although financial problems can be anticipated, most institutions are not fully prepared for their impact and for the reaction of faculty, whether or not they are directly affected. In the deep recession of the early 1980s, most state institutions anticipated that state legislatures would cut, in some cases slash, higher education budgets. Until the cuts were actually effected, however, the academic community seemed unable to initiate specific contingency plans. Similarly, in the independent colleges, leadership and faculty often fully recognize the severity of a financial problem only after worst-case enrollment predictions are fulfilled. In other words, until the dimension of the crisis is presented in specific terms those affected seem unable to translate predicted financial constraints into program and personnel curtailment plans.

In addressing financial problems, institutions need first to assess whether in fact faculty retrenchment is necessary or whether cost savings in other areas can be substituted. Faculty may claim that academic positions should remain untouched until cuts have been made in the administrative staff, maintenance, materials, and auxiliary services. At Atlantic Community College in New Jersey, for example, eleven tenured faculty members persuaded a state administrative law judge that the college was not justified in declaring financial exigency because it had a special reserve fund.

Once faculty accept the necessity for retrenchment, controversy often centers on the trustees' plan for implementing the cuts proposed. Faculty may object to their lack of participation and influence in these decisions. In some cases, trustees may meet demands for participation because of a desire to foster collegiality during a period of inevitable strain. On some campuses, faculty dissatisfaction has the potential for eliciting

unfavorable publicity, which can lead in turn to further enrollment declines. At unionized institutions, the collective bargaining agreement increasingly includes a provision for faculty involvement in retrenchment decisions. For instance, the Wayne
State University (Michigan) contract approved in 1982 specifically provided for faculty input when programs were being considered for termination. For the 1982–83 academic year the
union granted wage concessions in return for assurances that
there would be no layoffs. Unfortunately, with continued financial problems, layoffs could not be avoided; in November 1982,
the newly inaugurated president, hard pressed to avoid a deficit
in excess of $5 million, announced that a number of nonten-
ured faculty would not have their contracts renewed, and the
following month he announced plans to eliminate ninety-nine
faculty and administrative positions.

The right of an institution to effect cuts in order to survive is unquestioned. Common sense dictates that these adjustments be undertaken in good faith, be rationally planned, and
be consistently executed. Typically, institutions offer furloughs,
reassignment or relocation, favorable early-retirement packages,
and reduced work load. Temple University (Pennsylvania), in
trying to overcome mounting deficits, sent dismissal notices in
May 1982 to fifty tenured professors, mostly in the colleges of
education and liberal arts. Under the union agreement, these
professors retained their positions for eighteen months and
could choose positions that opened in other departments or opt
for an early-retirement plan. Temple was obligated to pay a
third of their salaries for the next seven years, buy an annuity
for the lost Social Security contributions, and continue the
fringe benefits until normal retirement. For the next two-year
contract period, the faculty accepted small salary increases (3.5
percent and 6 percent) in return for an agreement that no new
layoffs would occur.

At Michigan State University, a group of faculty acting
on their own presented a particularly innovative plan for retrenchment and were successful in convincing the trustees, the
administration, and their fellow faculty members that the
counterproposal was workable. This aggressive faculty action

was sparked by anger with the president, who had assured faculty leaders that tenured faculty or those slated for tenure in 1981–82 would not be recommended for dismissal. At the same time, in the late winter of 1981, the president established an outplacement office to assist faculty, presumably nontenured faculty, to find new jobs and asked deans and vice-presidents to identify ways to achieve reductions in the coming year. The president also appointed eleven senior faculty to an advisory committee to evaluate programs for curtailment or elimination. This committee, which obtained its data from the administration and met in private, shocked faculty when its recommendations, which were approved by the trustees, included elimination of units not previously targeted. This surprise action ignited the faculty, which split between defending the retrenchment provisions and attacking them as undermining tenure and as overturning prior administrative assurances. In addition to the controversy on campus, there was public testimony in the state senate education committee, with pressure particularly keen in support of the nursing college, which had been targeted for elimination.

Recognizing that their plan was politically unacceptable, the trustees approved an alternate approach that called for the involuntary dismissal of 100 tenured and 8 tenure-track faculty. If the first plan angered segments of the faculty, the second drew fire from virtually every quarter and created the possibility that the university would be involved in grievances and legal action. Faculty response took the form of a counterplan, spearheaded by economics professor Mordechai E. Kreinin, who proposed a "buy out," in which faculty were offered a package of financial incentives to encourage early retirements, leaves of absence, and resignations. As a result of remarkable salesmanship, all segments of the academic community endorsed the plan. It achieved the necessary financial savings, did not require the layoff of faculty during the period, and established the basis for advanced planning.

Another approach to retrenchment of faculty was taken at the University of Washington in September 1981, when the governor ordered a 10 percent reduction ($33 million) in the uni-

versity budget. This order led the president to consider recommending the declaration of a state of financial emergency to the
board of regents. Before this declaration could be enacted, the
president was required to empanel the faculty financial-emer-
gency committee; the committee concurred with the president's
recommendation, and the regents declared an emergency. The
faculty emergency committee then set about to prepare the procedures for identifying programs for reduction. This committee
detailed the faculty and administrative process for pinpointing
cutbacks, including specific program terminations and reductions. Fortunately, however, the need for involuntary terminations of tenured faculty was averted when the state legislature
restored half the previous cut. Under these less restrictive measures, budget savings could be realized through attrition, a
hiring freeze, and nonrenewal of term appointments. The emergency was officially terminated in early December 1981. Subsequently, the president appointed a faculty/administrative task
force to review the process used to meet the financial crisis. The
task force endorsed the university's approach for declaring a financial emergency. It noted the importance of the role of the
faculty emergency committee and suggested that in the future
the committee consult with as many faculty groups as feasible
and expand its membership to make it more representative than
it had been.

Although mandatory retrenchment of tenured faculty
was avoided, the issue reappeared in November 1982, when the
university announced plans to eliminate twenty-four degree programs and reduce its enrollment by 5,000 over a three-year
period. Faculty reaction seemed restrained, perhaps reflecting
exhaustion after several years of increasingly stringent financial
conditions and the fact that the faculty's consultative role in
the process was well recognized. The university retrenchment
plan called for a further 7 percent budget cut in the 1983 academic year. Targeted programs and faculty positions were to be
terminated unless other savings could trim the budget by $21
million. In May 1983, the state legislature restored $8.5 million
to the university's 1983–85 budget. The final retrenchment
plan required the elimination of three departments and nine-

teen academic programs to effect a savings of $13 million over a two-year period. The university guaranteed jobs to tenured faculty in the terminated programs.

A somewhat different set of issues arises in disputes over the reorganization of a college or a redirection or shift in program emphasis. Although these are particularly sensitive issues when faculty believe the proposed rearrangements challenge traditional tenure and seniority rights, these disputes erupt even on campuses where faculty status is unquestionably secure. The Colorado School of Mines, which has a national reputation as a highly specialized engineering school, experienced a rift between a group of faculty and top administrators and department heads when a faculty panel recommended placing increased emphasis on science and humanities programs. The controversy focused on the degree to which the curriculum should be broadened to reflect the anticipated needs of society and industry.

More typical was the faculty reaction to a radical reorganization plan proposed by the president of Long Beach State University (California) in 1981. The president attempted to impose a plan to create teaching-service areas to replace standard academic departments. Under the plan, sixty departments were to be split into 200 areas, with faculty seniority based on positions in the small groups. Predictably, opposition was widespread, particularly among senior faculty, many of whom believed the plan would make them vulnerable to layoffs. Faculty countered the president's action with the filing of some 200 grievances, claiming that the president failed to consult faculty prior to enacting the plan, as required by law, and that he abrogated an agreement concerning departmental approval of the changes. Further, the faculty senate censured the president for his conduct. The breadth and bitterness of the controversy illustrate the reaction that can be anticipated in the absence of a program to include faculty in decision making.

Governance and Leadership. Issues of faculty participation in institutional governance are particularly divisive. Faculty frequently maintain they have the right to be consulted on executive performance as well as on the selection of the president and top-level administrators. Although the responsibility for appointment of a president and other principal officers rests with the board of trustees, faculty frequently serve in an advisory capacity on the search committees. The faculty senate may also feel entitled to express its view on procedure and nominations.

The process for selecting a new president and faculty influence in the search were the source of conflict when three colleges in the CUNY system (Brooklyn, City, and Hunter) conducted presidential searches. The faculty on each of these campuses demanded and won increased participation on the search committees after they threatened to sue or boycott the search process. A revised procedure increased the number of faculty on each search committee, eliminated the nonvoting status of faculty, and required that each member of the search committee submit a written evaluation of the candidates. The chancellor of the Board of Higher Education then selected one candidate to present to the board. This arrangement permitted active faculty participation and at the same time fulfilled the board's legal obligation and authority to select college presidents.

In contrast, the board of trustees of the University of Pennsylvania incurred vehement faculty opposition when, after a seven-month search, it proposed the appointment of F. Sheldon Hackney, president of Tulane University (Louisiana), as the new president. In so doing, the trustees passed over the university provost, Vartan Gregorian, whom many faculty members had considered a front runner. The faculty-senate vote to submit the provost's name to the trustees as a presidential candidate complicated the process because Hackney had already announced his resignation from Tulane. The chair of the faculty senate stated that Gregorian was supported by 90 percent of the faculty. Some faculty and students threatened a lawsuit, charging that the new president was selected at a closed session in violation of the state's open-meeting law. Unfortunately, the secrecy surrounding the search and the surprise selection resulted in the university's losing a popular administrator when Gregorian resigned his post.

Faculty also questioned the presidential search process at

Amherst College (Massachusetts). When Amherst was looking for new leadership, faculty chided the trustees for being too homogeneous a group to make this decision and not attuned to campus affairs. Some faculty claimed the trustees, predominantly corporate executives, did not understand how the college should be governed, preferring that it be run as a business. Dissatisfaction came to a head when the chair of the board appointed a presidential search committee consisting solely of trustees—all alumni, mostly graduates from the 1950s—with advisory votes for faculty and students. Faculty viewed this procedure as autocratic and condemned and resisted it. Faculty and students passed resolutions rejecting participation on the search committee except as equal partners, and the chair consented. One of the trustees, W. Willard Wirtz, former Secretary of Labor, resigned because he was concerned about underlying issues of college governance.

Dissatisfaction with the leadership of an institution can also be expressed in a faculty vote of no confidence in the president. No-confidence votes are typically preceded by displeasure with several management decisions and, in many cases, reflect the president's failure to consult appropriately with the faculty before announcing controversial or disturbing decisions. These votes, which have no legal authority, are designed to force the trustees to question the president's competence. In 1981, the Washington State University faculty council conducted a poll that disclosed widespread criticism of the president for supporting subsidies for athletic scholarships and for devoting state funds to intercollegiate athletics. According to many faculty, these funds should have been used for academic programs, particularly in engineering and architecture, where students were being turned away because of a shortage of teachers. The president's position was that funds for athletics were required to support women's sports so that the university would be in compliance with federal mandates to provide equal athletic opportunities.

Faculty disapproval of presidential action or inaction is rarely attributable to a single or even major cause. William McElroy, a well-known biochemist and chancellor of the Uni-

versity of California (San Diego), was given a no-confidence
citation in a faculty mail ballot for a "continuing pattern of not
consulting the faculty" on pertinent issues. The immediate
cause was McElroy's proposal in 1979 that a vice-chancellor for
research supervise all research deans. The vice-chancellor for
academic affairs, who objected that he would lose most of his
duties, was asked to resign. The real issue, critics of the president said, was the president's poor relationship with faculty,
which demonstrated "contempt" and "disdain." The president
of the University of California system responded to the no-
confidence resolution with assurances that McElroy would find
a solution. The reorganization was postponed until after consultation with faculty.

David Mathews, president of the University of Alabama
and former Secretary of Health, Education, and Welfare, was the
target of a faculty-senate request for his dismissal; the senate
charged him with underlying responsibility for poor salaries and
equipment when the state failed to increase funding. Disputes
of this type often divide the academic community, with the
various constituencies taking opposing positions. In this case,
alumni, students, and other interests supported the president.

Another example of disagreements over governance occurred at the Swain School of Design in New Bedford, Massachusetts. Faculty and students were outraged when the board
of trustees replaced the popular president of the school with an
interim president. The former president ran into difficulty when
he pleaded with the board to develop a long-range plan and to
become actively involved with fund raising so that the school
could become eligible for accreditation by the New England
Association of Schools and Colleges. The nineteen-member faculty, perceiving the board to be less than responsive to the needs
of the school, demanded the resignation of the entire board.

The consequences of faculty dissatisfaction with their
president are illustrated in a dispute at Auburn University (Alabama), a state-supported institution. President H. Hanly Fun-
derburk, Jr., appointed in 1980, almost immediately encountered faculty opposition, which focused on what his detractors
believed was overemphasis on the university's financial condi-

tion. Faced with a deficit brought about by state budget cuts, he postponed a 6 percent salary increase. In early 1981, nearly two thirds of the faculty on a senate committee that evaluated the president rated him "poor" in "overall effective leadership." Nevertheless, the board of trustees, chaired by the governor, endorsed his leadership. Faculty criticism persisted; as a result, in January 1983, the trustees announced that a chancellor would be hired to manage daily affairs at the main campus. The chancellor would report to the president, who would continue to handle fund raising and other external matters. In a not altogether successful effort to quell continued faculty objections, the trustees announced that the selection of the chancellor should involve "all segments of the Auburn family."

Class Actions

Colleges and universities also encounter allegations by a group of faculty that basic practices or policies are unfair or inequitable. These claims take the form of class action suits. The most notable are cases involving sex discrimination. Among the most significant of these were class action suits brought against Montana State University, Brown University, the University of Minnesota, and CUNY. The relief obtained in a class action is more effective in overcoming campus-wide discrimination than is relief to an individual plaintiff. However, the costs and complexity of mounting such cases, which often involve the subpoena and analysis of records and the development of statistical documentation, have deterred many potential litigants. Litigants must be prepared to raise substantial sums of money, maintain solidarity, and wait years for resolution. From the standpoint of the college or university, the class action immediately takes the issue away from possible internal resolution to a public forum, with its attendant publicity. Moreover, it places the institution in the unsettling position of contesting faculty complaints with legal force over a long period of time. In a few instances, universities have paid more than a million dollars in legal expenses, apart from the monetary settlements. Expensive and unsettling as class actions may be, they may create pressure for resolution that might not otherwise exist. At the same time, a class action, in wresting control from the collegial system, carries the danger that a solution will be imposed from the outside without an understanding of campus conditions.

The first publicized class action sex-discrimination case where female faculty prevailed was at Montana State University in 1976. The federal judge, acting under the 1964 Civil Rights Act, found that the university discriminated in pay and promotion of female faculty as a class. He further found that they were underrepresented in high positions, underutilized, and not represented at all in some academic fields. For the first time, the court order directed the parties to negotiate a settlement of the immediate problems and to provide a procedural base for any future complaint. In this case, women received salary adjustments and back pay, and the primary plaintiff was promoted. The judge's order recognized that only the university community could arrive at a fair and equitable agreement; less than nine months after the court order, the parties presented a settlement that the court approved.

In arriving at this solution, the parties first selected negotiators to represent them. They were aided in the settlement process by a neutral who was widely respected by the parties. To identify possible discrimination, faculty members were paired; female faculty were matched with male counterparts to uncover discrepancies in promotion and compensation. The report of the negotiating team was presented to the president as the basis for a recommended pay settlement and was eventually presented to the judge. Of the 138 women who were paired, 79 received recommended awards ranging from $126 to $14 thousand for a total of approximately $355 thousand in back pay and adjustments. The university also paid $50 thousand for legal fees and $30 thousand for administrative expenses. A special plan was developed for the nursing faculty because there were no male faculty members for pairing.

At Brown University, four female faculty members were successful in gaining class action status in a sex-bias case involving hiring, promotion, reappointment, and tenure. In an out-of-court settlement, Brown, while not acknowledging that it had been guilty of sex discrimination, agreed to procedural revisions, granted tenure to three plaintiffs (including anthropologist Louise Lamphere), and made a cash settlement to a fourth plaintiff who was not grieving. The settlement included a provision that Brown would establish a $400 thousand fund to pay damages to other women who had been discriminated against. Jennie Farley of Cornell University, in her book *Sex Discrimination in Higher Education,* notes that Brown's president stated that legal fees for the female faculty members' attorneys were twice the amount of the cash settlement.

In another widely publicized class action suit, Shyamala Rajender and five other female plaintiffs won a consent decree against the University of Minnesota in 1980. Rajender, denied tenure in the chemistry department, was awarded $100 thousand and legal fees, which the judge set just under $2 million (subsequently reduced to $1.5 million). As in the case at Brown University, the decree did not admit sex discrimination. It did, however, provide for an extensive and potentially costly affirmative action program. The court appointed a special master and a panel with broad powers to adjudicate university-wide sex-discrimination claims to supervise the settlement until 1989. The special master has authority to award back pay and other remedies including tenure and to hear complaints not resolved through the university's internal procedure. As of February 1983, 280 claims were brought under the procedure, and 52 claims had been settled. An attorney for the plaintiffs estimated that claims may be filed by as many as 1,600 women and that the cost to the university could reach $10 million.

The complexities of pursuing a class action are illustrated by a suit brought in 1973 that covered as many as 10,000 women who have held professional teaching and administrative posts at CUNY since 1968. A crucial factor in this case was the interpretation of statistical evidence. Women faculty and the university presented models, which, based on the data included in the model, differed greatly from each other. Conflict over data erupted even before the models were constructed. Both sides were dissatisfied with the incomplete data provided by the university on computer tapes. Because there were gaps in the data on rank, salary, and background, the statistician for the plaintiffs used only those faculty profiles that were complete. The data showed that on the average male faculty members earned approximately $2,680 more than females. The university's expert considered the data on the computer tape to be so unsatisfactory that he initiated his own survey. He then used his survey data to match similar male and female faculty and demonstrated that there had been no discrimination. These results were disputed in five days of testimony in federal court in November 1980. The judge, obviously not eager to announce a victor in the statistics game, asked the opposing lawyers to attempt an out-of-court settlement.

After eighteen months of sporadic negotiations, the plaintiffs' lawyer asked the judge to issue a ruling. In March 1983, the district court judge ruled that male professional staff earned on average $1 thousand more per year than females in the same positions. Judith P. Vladeck, the women's lawyer, estimated that the cost to the university's eighteen institutions could reach $60 million or more. This decision covered only salary practices. It did not address allegations against CUNY concerning discriminatory hiring, promotion, and fringe-benefit policies.

In view of the sacrifices that must be made when a case of this type is pursued, it is somewhat surprising that female faculty members do in fact undertake these legal actions. If they are successful, the monetary awards still do not compensate for the loss of professional status. The gains accrue largely to the plaintiffs' future female colleagues who seek fair and impartial reviews conducted with clearly defined criteria as the basis for their professional advancement.

CHAPTER 8

Responding to Demands
for Policy Changes

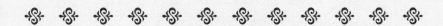

Policy disputes concern issues over which the president or the board of trustees clearly has authority. The faculty's role in such circumstances is generally limited to attempting to persuade the institution's leadership to consider alternatives. In other words, faculty at best are influential rather than codeterminative. Thus, both the objectives and the techniques of faculty will differ from those they have and use when they have a formal role in the process.

Another way to view the difference between, for example, disputes over tenure and those involving basic policy is to recognize that tenure involves the application of stated criteria to an individual faculty member; the questions are whether the criteria were properly applied and whether appropriate procedures were followed. Although the criteria are subject to interpretation and subjective judgment, they are the accepted bench marks in faculty-status decisions. In contrast, there are no generally accepted standards against which to judge policy decisions made by the trustees or president.

149

One policy dispute that arises with a fair degree of frequency is an impasse in labor negotiations between faculty and the administration—that is, a failure to achieve an initial or successor collective bargaining agreement. These impasses clearly involve policy issues; however, they fall within the general realm of labor disputes, for which there are a long history, machinery already in place, and accepted practices. For example, parties finding themselves at impasse commonly request the mediation services of a federal, state, or local agency. These agencies furnish such services in hundreds of thousands of disputes. Many other publications amply discuss the rhythm and mechanics of this process. Therefore, the emphasis in this chapter is on the unusual, occasional, and, for the parties involved, unprecedented issues for which collective bargaining was never intended.

Assessing Faculty Demands and
Selecting Management Responses

The nature of the institutional response to policy disputes depends not only on the issues in dispute and the level of authority for the decision but also on the president's leadership style and relationship with the faculty. In assessing appropriate responses to the disputes described in the previous chapter, the president should consider the reality of the demands and the image he or she desires to project. The seriousness with which demands are taken depends to some extent on the influence faculty members can exert; faculty in a single department who fail to create alliances with other faculty or student groups will be taken less seriously than faculty who represent a significant segment of the academic community. In the case of demands from a single department, an administrator or assistant to the president can respond that the president is aware of the issues, is carefully considering them, and will announce a decision in due course. Assuming the president gauges the political climate correctly, there should be no need for direct or immediate action. If, however, the faculty group raising demands is broadly representative, the president needs to fashion a timely response.

The president's response will also be determined to some extent by an evaluation of whether participating faculty are likely to rally students to their cause by transforming the problem into one that appears to affect students directly, either currently or after graduation. For example, students may sense that a change in the composition of faculty could decrease teaching effectiveness, leading to a decline in the reputation of the university in a particular field and hence a reluctance by employers to hire graduates. Here, as in many other disputes, the ultimate concern is the impact of the decision on enrollment. A local newspaper story describing a college's financial difficulties can dissuade parents from considering the school for their children. Or, because college freshmen usually maintain friendships at their high schools, dissatisfaction can easily spread back to students and guidance counselors and have an adverse effect on student recruitment. Thus, a small but vigorous faculty group capable of involving students and the press may well pose a greater threat to the leadership of a school than does a less focused sense of unease shared by a greater number of faculty members.

A corollary is that just a few faculty members who have informal access to individual trustees may be in a position to exert indirect pressure on the president by alerting the trustees to a potentially sensitive or controversial decision. Support from trustees may be difficult to obtain because boards frequently achieve a cohesive front through self-perpetuation. New members are selected by existing members; they are cast in the same mold and are related through business and alumni activities, but they tend to be of two distinct types—either they are active trustees or they have the sole purpose of capitalizing on the prestige and status membership on the board gives them in the community. Those who are there only for the prestige are not usually a factor in governance because they tend to ratify whatever the working group of trustees proposes. However, faculty seeking support from trustees are often aware of one crucial exception: Trustees who serve for the purpose of prestige and status will object to decisions by the president or the active trustees that have the potential for embarrassing them in the community. For example, a decision by the president, supported

by the trustees, not to pursue specialized accreditation or to re-
nege on a commitment to the local community or even to permit continuance of a particularly rancorous strike may embarrass heretofore inactive or placid trustees. They may be mo-
bilized when they believe a decision of the board will threaten
community interests or lose financial support from alumni.

An obvious element in this mix is the extent to which the
president feels secure in his or her position. However, even the
most secure executive, faced with widespread dissent, runs the
risk of being dispensable if the trustees determine that it is poli-
tic to turn a new page. Thus, disputes should be viewed within
the context of a political system. An important element in evaluating a dispute and appropriate responses is an assessment of
these political implications. Presidents rarely operate by fiat and
then only with the solid support of the board.

The president has at least three options in selecting a response to a policy dispute with faculty: to stonewall, to appear
conciliatory by permitting superficial faculty participation
through an advisory mechanism or to see faculty involvement
as a way to improve the quality of key decisions. The stonewalling or imperial president takes this position with the clear conviction that leadership requires strong unilateral action. This
management style always presents the risk of ultimate isolation
and an accompanying vulnerability.

A management style that seeks to create the appearance
of conciliation through advisory groups, with only illusory
participation in decision making, is a transparent tactic that
sooner or later will be seen for what it is. However, if faculty
are naively compliant, this approach can be used with devastat-
ing impact because at a later date, the administration can point
out that the decision was reached after "full faculty consideration." Another variation of this approach is to have the president assume the role of seminar leader, creating the impression
that proposals are being generated by the faculty. The apparent justification for assuming such a role is found in old-fash-
ioned notions of collegiality where, to all outward appearances,
the chair of a department, the dean of a college, or the president is but first among equals. This approach is not without its

dangers, for the president may ultimately be seen as a non-leader. A further danger is that the more issues that are handled in this way, the more likely it is that presidential authority will be eroded.

The style that we propose is based on the conviction that faculty suggestions may be useful in improving management decisions. It permits consideration of the appropriate means for incorporating a faculty dimension. Included among these methods are ways to share information and exchange viewpoints in order to enable faculty to influence such decisions.

Sharing Information and Exchanging Views

Information sharing is directed to establishing, in however rough or incomplete a form, a common data base. The administration needs to decide which materials or information need to be made available to faculty in order to conduct a sensible discussion. It is important that the faculty, the president, and perhaps even the trustees are talking about the same issues. Expressed another way, all sides should be aware of the same facts. Although this is a useful starting point, it may not always be feasible. For example, the issue of a university's investment in a real estate enterprise is entirely different in both the nature and the extent of the financial commitment from the issue of a university's owning stock in a corporation doing business in South Africa. In the stock-holding situation, there appears to be no impediment to sharing the full details. The issue is not whether owning the stock is a wise financial move but whether it is morally justified. Whether faculty should be privy to the details of a real estate transaction depends on such factors as the general financial state of the university at the time the investment is proposed and the need for privacy in transacting business. To take another example, when a former or current faculty member is engaged in litigation with the university, many faculty may believe the suit should be settled out of court. Because any settlement could have broad and often serious implications, it is doubtful whether the administration should do other than what legal counsel advises. Thus, the administration may have to establish with the faculty that for some issues information simply cannot be shared.

Within sensible limits, the importance of having both sides aware of the pertinent facts cannot be overstated. Even in an academic atmosphere, where professionals pride themselves on dealing with the problems raised in their disciplines on the basis of all the available facts, faculty are frequently exercised about issues about which they have only partial or fragmentary information. Frequently, the sharing of complete and accurate data will end an existing or incipient dispute. Even veteran decision makers are often amazed at how the relevant facts speak for themselves.

Once the decision is made to share information, administrators need to furnish the faculty with sufficient data in a timely fashion to avoid giving the impression that the information was given perfunctorily after the decision had been made without faculty advice. For this sharing to be effective, faculty must accept the credibility of the information presented. If they do not, demands for additional documentation will prolong the controversy, and in extreme circumstances these continuing demands will represent a thinly disguised vote of no confidence in the administration.

The administration also needs to decide whether it is desirable or politically appropriate for the information supplied to be widely disseminated. This is particularly difficult to determine when the number of faculty involved is small, but their reputation for persistence and effectiveness is impressive. Under these circumstances, it may be best to determine that only those faculty directly involved need be addressed. At the other extreme, if it is determined that the demands from vocal representatives represent a more significant segment of the professional staff it may be appropriate, before a response is formulated, to request that they form a committee and appoint a spokesperson. The facts would then need to be shared only with this committee. In the event that the demands come from all segments or a large number of faculty, the fact sharing could be effected through a memorandum to all faculty. Inevitably, in some situations, it will be best to limit the information sharing within the university precincts.

If fact sharing does not resolve the problem, the next step is an exchange of opinions, either written or oral. In general, the determination of whether the exchange is written or oral depends on the relationship of the parties. However, in some instances, the extent of the dispute is the most important variable. If the issue is one that has received campus-wide attention, reliance on oral presentation and responses may be dangerous. Even with the best intentions, transmittal of the details of an oral exchange to the community at large can give a severely distorted impression of what in fact transpired. This distorted perception may lead to heightened conflict. One of the virtues of a written exchange is that it limits distortion, although there is always the danger of misinterpretation. Written statements tend to be more precise and fully developed than oral presentations. Therefore, the positions generally tend to be more clearly defined. Written positions may highlight the differences, but they also allow the parties to avoid face-to-face confrontation; they can make clear to the campus community the areas of common interests and can create an atmosphere in which mutually acceptable positions can be developed. One of the most common means of written exchange is position papers. In most instances, it is appropriate for the faculty to present their position first, with the assurance that there will be a written administrative response.

The president and trustees should establish that their willingness to share information and exchange opinions with faculty does not necessarily represent a form of accommodation but rather, a willingness to seriously consider contrary arguments before making a final decision. These arguments may not necessarily persuade, but they will be entertained.

Mediation

If sharing information and exchanging opinions do not end the dispute, other techniques should be explored. Because these disputes are unpredictable, formal internal processes, such as grievance procedures, cannot be used. Thus the search is for informal approaches and forums. Fact finding inevitably involves hearings and recommendations, which tend to force the

parties into hard and frequently frozen positions; this adversarial atmosphere is unsuited for these problems. In the disputes discussed in Parts One and Two, the initial decision mak-
er's determination is subject to review on the basis of whether
it was based on relevant factors that were reasonably evaluated.
Here we are dealing with totally discretionary decisions, in
which as mentioned, the administration may allow the faculty a
limited degree of influence; these policy issues need not necessarily be discussed with faculty at all. Transforming this unilateral and voluntary approach into a formal hearing distorts the
nature and intent of the process. Furthermore, once there is an
agreement to take such a formal step, the door is open to make
it a permanent part of the decision-making process. One has
only to examine the history of regulatory agencies to appreciate that notice leads to hearings and hearings inevitably to
sanctions. This natural progression seems particularly inappropriate here.

Although fact finding seems inappropriately formal in
these circumstances, mediation, with its emphasis on privacy
and informality, seems a particularly suitable approach because
it encourages a full exchange of views without necessarily falling
into an adversarial mode. By encouraging discussion of alternative solutions, the mediation process may disclose new aspects
or implications of a policy and lead to appropriate decisions.

The use of mediation in policy disputes is similar to the
use of mediation described in Chapter Five, the exceptions
being that no detailed procedures are prescribed and that the
objective is for faculty to influence decision making rather than
to mutually settle a dispute with the administration. Many of
the same conditions apply: The parties must agree to discuss the
issues with those whose positions differ from their own and
must be willing to permit the designated mediator to work with
them in an attempt to reach an acceptable solution. The mediation process thus provides an opportunity for some faculty influence, and when it is fully accepted, it can address the substance of the problem.

Mediation is a particularly attractive approach for resolving disputes that involve a number of constituencies with sepa-

rate agendas and views of the institution. For instance, it has proved effective in disputes over the reorganization of a college. The president may propose a plan to merge departments, restrict the number of divisions, and otherwise streamline the structure to save money as well as to increase line authority. Not infrequently, faculty see these moves as a way to reduce their autonomy and increase their accountability. These actions or proposed plans are bound to create distrust and lead to faculty assertions that the president's autocratic leadership fails to take into account the dedication of the faculty and its sense of shared, if not primary, responsibility for the educational enterprise. Students may also feel the effects of the proposed reorganization either directly, as when an increase in class size is being proposed, or indirectly through their allegiance to disaffected faculty members. Then, too, members of the board of trustees, as the ultimate decision makers, cannot help but be affected by demands on the one hand that they remain steadfastly loyal to the president and on the other that they recognize the president is proposing irreparable damage. In these multiparty, highly volatile situations, where no clear-cut answers emerge, a mediator who is trusted by the parties can sometimes help them work toward an acceptable solution.

As another example, mediation may be useful when a financially vulnerable college seeks affiliation with a stronger institution that seeks merger as a way to develop or strengthen academic programs. A mediator can encourage full discussion of the options and can assist the parties to reach decisions that have the broadest possible support. In many instances, when parties of unequal negotiating skill and experience hold merger discussions, the stronger institution may come close to dictating merger terms. These uneven negotiations can be a disservice to students, faculty, and staff at the weaker institution and provide less than an optimum result for higher education in the region. Through the mediation process, the interests of the ailing institution can be fully represented.

One of the first tasks of a mediator is to defuse a highly emotional and adversarial atmosphere by providing an opportunity for dispassionate analysis and by allowing reasoned com-

munications to take place outside the glare of publicity. The
mediator may suggest and obtain agreement on the data needed
for such an analysis and on a timetable for meetings at which
this information will be exchanged. The mediator seeks to substitute meaningful discourse for inflammatory rhetoric, to encourage discussion and consideration of a range of options. In short,
the mediator tries to put the focus on constructive problem
solving that is based on a full understanding of institutional and
group objectives.

The mediator can use a number of approaches to stimulate progress toward a solution. A time limit is usually advisable
so that everyone understands that closure will be reached and so
that those with final authority recognize that the process will
not be prolonged unnecessarily. To keep within time limits, the
mediator, characterized as the "agent of reality" by many prac-
titioners, may continually remind each of the interest groups
that they have much to lose if they fail to reach a solution. The
mediator may point out that continued disruptions will distract
from the education of students and from the research activities
of faculty. The mediator may also observe that the president's
position of respect and authority may be at least temporarily
eroded by a continuation of rancor and hostility. Time-consum-
ing discussion can also divert trustees from their other responsibilities. In addition, a board that continues to be divided cannot
appropriately oversee the institution. Continuing arguments
may spark personal animosities and damage long-standing respectful and productive relationships among board members.
Running through the entire dispute, if it is being conducted in
the open, is the possibility that adverse publicity will affect enrollment. By continuing to direct attention to the need of all
parties for settlement, the mediator exerts pressure on each of
the groups to present workable alternatives.

The mediator also needs to control communication about
the mediation process and its results. If continued exposure in
the press and local community may damage the institution, it
may be critical to obtain an explicit understanding that only the
mediator will issue a statement while the negotiations are being
conducted. When agreement is achieved, the mediator may

assist the parties in preparing a memorandum that describes the agreed-on solution.

An acceptable mediator will probably be drawn from the campus community and in all probability will be a faculty member because there is a general sense within higher education that its norms and methods of governance are different from those in other fields. By using an insider, the parties can have confidence that the mediator shares their understanding of the institution's mission and place within the educational environment and can be assured that private and potentially embarrassing matters will not be exposed to public view. A faculty member is more likely to be perceived as neutral than a comparable fair-minded, well-respected administrator because the faculty member is less likely than the administrator to be seen as a mouthpiece for the administration. Furthermore, faculty, in contrast with administrators, are not required on a regular and daily basis to make management decisions that, at least in some instances, have the potential for antagonizing individual faculty and faculty groups.

If the president and the board of trustees do not permit mediation to take place or if faculty have not been given an opportunity in other ways to influence the decision-making process, faculty have other options at their disposal.

Faculty Alliances with Other Groups

If the president is stonewalling, there may be strategies for faculty to at least gain an opportunity to air their views; the faculty goal here is to be consulted. As previously indicated, if the president's or the board's position is either to appear conciliatory or in fact to be conciliatory, then real opportunities may exist for influencing the outcome. Managing a stonewalling president is both easier and more complex. Easier because the tactics are more straightforward; riskier because, if unsuccessful, faculty can lose any influence they may have attained in other disputes with the college leadership. Faculty have two principal mechanisms for gaining the attention of recalcitrant presidents or trustees. Both are variations of the same tactic. First, and probably the preferred, is to mobilize student opinion in favor of the faculty position. The second is to gain alumni support for a faculty cause. Both avenues can be pursued simultaneously.

Students taught faculty the tactic of forging alliances with other groups. In the late 1960s and early 1970s, many faculty desperately scurried to catch up with student activists. Here the process is reversed, although if it becomes apparent that faculty are using the students as surrogates, the tactic will not be entirely effective. The objective is for the students' own expressions of concern to coincide in large measure with the position of faculty seeking a similar outcome.

This could be the case, for example, in a dispute over the merits of specialized accreditation. Members of the faculty may object to filing for accreditation, and the trustees and president may lean heavily in favor of doing so. This situation is typical in schools of business, where there is a claimed need to offer a distinctive and superior product to capitalize on growing student interest and enrollment. Faculty may highlight to students a number of disadvantages of accreditation in an attempt to show that a decision to seek accreditation may not be in the students' best interest. For illustrative purposes, it may be instructive to consider these arguments. The following points might be used:

- Accrediting agencies stipulate the ratio of Ph.D.s to students. As more business schools seek accreditation, the number of Ph.D.s cannot keep pace with demand. The quality of education declines because professors lack commitment to any institution; they are constantly lured elsewhere by higher salaries.
- Given the small pool of first-class scholars and teachers, many institutions must hire less qualified Ph.D.s. Despite their credentials, these Ph.D.s may be less experienced and effective teachers than professors who do not possess the Ph.D.
- Small classes may be a victim of accreditation as schools increase the size of classes in order to meet the stipulated ratio of Ph.D.s to students.
- The accreditation agency's emphasis on research and publica-

tions may lead to decreased attention to improving teaching skills. Fine institutions with outstanding local or regional reputations nurtured over decades may find their reputations rapidly deteriorating when students complain to guidance counselors and graduates complain to employers about the decline in teaching effectiveness.

- Complying with agency criteria means that discretion with respect to hiring, selection of texts, and curriculum is surrendered.
- Periodic examination is part of the accreditation process. Although the gaining of accreditation does not necessarily carry with it expanded prestige, the loss of accreditation is a story guaranteed to achieve wide media exposure.
- Institutions that remake themselves at great financial cost and with a serious impact on students may find that in a few years the standards of the accrediting agency are changed and its methods of measuring quality are drastically altered.

Armed with these arguments, students would be effective advocates against accreditation. Even an autocratic leadership would find it difficult to resist informed student demand expressed through petitions, meetings, and in-school publicity. If these forms of persuasion are ineffective with the administration, students can direct their efforts to educating the trustees, who may not be in full command of the details and arguments. Quiet and reasoned appeals to trustees who may be favorable can sometimes produce the desired result. Ultimately, students may decide to bring their concerns to the local press, who are usually quite eager to deal with potentially sensitive material. Faculty do not necessarily have to steer students in that direction; students, once aroused and armed with compelling arguments, are not shy about proclaiming their demands outside the university.

Here, as in other areas where the decision-making authority clearly rests outside the protesting group, key factors increase the odds for achieving an impact; thorough preparation, significant numbers, and dogged persistence are among the most important. The ever-present threat of outside publicity often provides an incentive for decision makers to examine a range of alternatives. A constraint on the effectiveness of student action, however, is their relatively short connection with the institution. Nonetheless, administrators usually watch student efforts to effect change carefully because of the potential for surprise and embarrassment and as a bellwether of emerging issues.

A range of student responses has been suggested. The approach is equally applicable in attempts to mobilize alumni support. Once again, faculty can disseminate the facts or their interpretation of them. Alumni usually have their own formal and informal structures for influencing university policy. Whether presentations to established councils or a telephone campaign works best, the key here, as with student involvement, lies in numbers. Naturally, alumni who provide substantial resources to the institution are the most likely to be effective. A constraining factor, however, is that faculty usually do not have easy access to such alumni.

Faculty should note that students and alumni tend to differ about the importance of certain issues. Alumni, by virtue of age, experience, and success are often moved only by issues that they view as fundamental to the well-being of the institution—perhaps a new football facility or a new laboratory, depending on the nature of the institution. Active alumni who are themselves executives naturally view student or faculty complaints with a somewhat skeptical eye, reasoning from their business experience that few complaints deal with basic issues. They also are less volatile than students and therefore less likely to take extreme actions. For many alumni, the supreme effort in support of a faculty position is a telephone call to an administrator who was a classmate. And the chances are the telephone call will be a query rather than a definite statement of position.

Some realistic constraints exist on the ability of faculty to activate other groups. Most individuals connected with the institution, be they fellow faculty, students, or alumni, are not active in the service of any cause. Even the most sophisticated generally believe that the president, the trustees, and the top administrators are in possession of all the facts. They believe that these people make decisions after comprehensive consideration of a multitude of details provided by their staffs and advisers.

This is usually not the case. Important decisions are often based on fragmentary information. If this is true for the college president, it is even more true for trustees, who are remote from the day-to-day activities of the college and distant from the sources of information. Furthermore, the information they receive is filtered through trustee committees and administrative staff and probably reflects a point of view.

Therefore, the faculty's ability to influence decisions depends on providing both administrators and trustees with as much pertinent information as possible. The leadership then must either arbitrarily dismiss the evidence with the attendant adverse consequences, or present a reasoned basis for rejecting the conclusion that the evidence suggests. Put in the simplest terms, the crucial factor is the faculty's ability to embarrass the administration. Even autocrats on occasion will make heroic efforts to avoid such a result.

This discussion of strategies faculty can pursue when their advice is not requested recognizes that faculty who believe their views are not given appropriate weight will in many cases take steps to receive their due. Recognition on the part of management that faculty can and do act to express their displeasure may help create a collegial and interactive environment. Our aim is to encourage management strategies that deal constructively with faculty disputes. We have presented faculty options in the absence of consultation not to engender conflict but to emphasize the fact that faculty have options in the absence of an administrative response to their demands.

Strategies Available to the President

In the broadest sense, a president's effectiveness rests on support from all constituencies: trustees, faculty, administrators, students, alumni; in some cases, the community; and, at public institutions, local or state legislators. In the short run, the key constituency for the president is the board of trustees. When the trustees tire of a president, he or she will be replaced. Although faculty in all types of institutions censure their presidents from time to time for one action or other, these votes are not legally binding, and their impact on trustees varies with each institution. The trustees may ignore a vote of no confidence by the faculty, or they may consider it as evidence that hard choices are being made. But when the trustees are determined to replace the president, a faculty vote of no confidence can be a welcome pretext.

Over the long term, the president needs support not just from the trustees. Students, as the most transient group, are probably the least useful. It may be argued that transient students ultimately become active alumni, but that takes a good deal of time, and in many institutions the alumni are not a significant factor. The president usually already has the support of administrators because they are beholden to the president for their advancement; but administrators by nature are reluctant to be combative and therefore may not be useful allies when the president needs strong support. The political implications of heading a public institution are a separate study in themselves.

What remains, then, is the relationship of the president to the faculty. It has been suggested that the need to cultivate faculty is greater at prestigious than at nonprestigious institutions because faculty with wide reputations in their fields may exert substantial influence on the trustees. A more important reason, however, is that, in many institutions, needless conflicts arise because of the substantial distance between the president and the faculty. This situation occurs when the provost, deans, and department chairs either are merely vehicles for carrying out administration policy or are relatively impotent functionaries. These administrators should serve as intermediaries between their superiors and the faculty; for example, department chairs should be advocates for their department members with the dean and provost and should at the time present school policies to the faculty in a positive manner.

Much has been made of the difficulties of realizing this ideal. Given collective bargaining and the presence of many autocratic administrators, the attainment of the ideal must start at the provost's level. In most institutions, the provost has power to make both academic and administrative decisions. Although provosts historically have been deans of the faculty, the administrative duties of the position usually far outweigh the academic responsibilities. Perhaps it was natural for administrative responsibilities to overshadow the provost's traditional role of representing faculty to the president and trustees. After all, the number of faculty have declined, and their share of the overall budget reflects this trend. In addition, collective bargaining tends to place the provost in a position somewhat akin to that of school superintendents with unionized teachers. Also, the provost spends much time dealing with the business aspects of large acquisitions such as computers. Despite these administrative preoccupations, in many cases provosts still retain their historical role of representing faculty, as do deans and department chairs to a lesser extent. Thus, presidents who desire to establish credible networks for early identification of significant areas of faculty discontent should pay attention to precisely describing the role of provosts, deans, and chairs.

In some instances, a president who has particularly close and cordial relationships with individual faculty members mistakenly believes these relationships assure that problems will be identified as they arise. However, friends are often reluctant to be bearers of bad news. Also, faculty members who have the president's ear may not be truly representative of the faculty. And, of course, faculty whose primary concern is their own access to the president can cause great damage. Although a false sense of security in these matters is endemic in executives of all large organizations, the element of collegiality makes college administrators all the more susceptible. This observation is not made to downgrade the importance of collegiality but as a caution that the collegial atmosphere alone may not sufficiently alert the president and members of the administrative team to the presence of developing problems.

Although presidents need to obtain useful signals from faculty, it does not follow that presidential accessibility will necessarily minimize problems, particularly in a period of imposed fiscal constraints. It may, for example, be necessary to strengthen certain academic areas that provide current and future growth while at the same time sacrificing departments and instructional personnel in disciplines where enrollment is declining. Regrettably, collegiality recedes in the face of difficult choices and the accompanying disappointment. The best that faculty can hope for, legal considerations aside, is an equitable solution.

In actuality, the relative importance of the various groups for a president is unique to each institution. A sensible position for an independent president is to avoid catering to or relying on any single one. This is not to say that in extreme situations heavy reliance on faculty should be eschewed. If the trustees embark on a course that both the president and faculty believe to be detrimental to the future of the university, the president has the choice of resigning or resisting. If the president chooses to resist, faculty support is crucial. In most circumstances, however, the best course of action is to be open to comments and suggestions from all constituencies without being the captive of any.

CHAPTER 9

Faculty Participation
in Resolving Financial Problems:
A Case Study

Among the most threatening issues facing faculty, administrators, presidents, and trustees are those concerning the financial health of their institutions. Declining enrollments, inflation-eroded budgets, sharp increases in the costs of basic services, and reduced levels of support from state and federal sources exert unprecedented financial pressure on most academic institutions. Institutions have adjusted to budgetary constraints by deferring building and grounds maintenance and cutting other nonpersonnel budget items. As the budgetary pressures mount and discretionary budget items are pared or eliminated, cuts become increasingly difficult to accomplish. In addressing these unpleasant financial realities, trustees look to faculty to absorb a share of burden, either through salary reductions or provisions for increases far below the level of inflation.

The purpose of this chapter is to demonstrate that faculty can play a helpful role in analyzing financial problems and presenting suggestions for their resolution. The recommenda-

167

tions at the end of the chapter highlight elements to be considered if faculty participation is to be realistic. The way Hofstra University (New York) faculty participated when there was a financial crisis illustrates the rich possibilities that exist for faculty in many institutions. The Hofstra experience is particularly relevant because its size and program offerings are characteristic of those of many independent liberal arts colleges and universities. The way faculty involved themselves in examining the financial affairs of the university may be instructive to faculty and the leadership of other institutions that face problems similar to those that confronted Hofstra. In examining Hofstra's approach to its financial difficulties in the mid-1970s, we have the benefit of sufficient distance from which to evaluate the full impact of this experience.

Hofstra University and Its Financial Problems

Hofstra College opened its doors in 1935 as a small, local, primarily liberal arts college associated with New York University. The college was named for the principal property on which it is situated, the William S. Hofstra Estate on Long Island. Hofstra, a successful lumber merchant, built his large home on fifteen acres and landscaped the property with a great variety of trees. His widow remained on the estate until she died, when the property was turned over to a charitable institution designated in the will. However, the Masonic lodge named as beneficiary declined the property because there was no accompanying endowment to cover maintenance expenses. A trustee of the estate suggested the property be used for a college. At the time, New York University was holding classes for teachers in the local high school. The university agreed to sponsor Hofstra as a branch campus and thus Nassau College–Hofstra Memorial began with 159 day students and 621 evening students and a curriculum featuring liberal arts, teacher training, and business for part-time day students and evening students. This continued to be the main curriculum until the early 1970s. The association with New York University was concluded in 1940, when Hofstra received its own state charter.

The first classes were held in the former family mansion, renamed Hofstra Hall, and in quonset huts and other temporary buildings. Eventually, an architectural theme emerged with the construction of permanent classrooms and offices. This was a period of slow, steady expansion. Hofstra operated in the black, and physical-plant improvement was financed primarily out of operating revenues.

This fiscal success brought Hofstra to the attention of the Ford Foundation at a time when state legislatures were making substantial funds available to their institutions and private sources were supporting physical expansion at independent institutions to accommodate vastly increased enrollments. In the 1960s, Hofstra was selected, along with twenty other institutions, for a Ford Foundation matching grant program; it provided Hofstra with $1 million after a successful two-year campaign to raise an equal amount from other sources. This fundraising success reinforced interest in outside financing to expand plant and facilities. At the same time, the military vacated Mitchell Field, a nearby naval air base. Hofstra, along with other local community organizations, obtained a portion of this acreage, which was directly across the road from the original campus. The acquisition of this property, together with the desire to obtain outside financing, led to an arrangement with the New York State Dormitory Authority to provide $11.45 million for expansion, including permanent dormitories, a physical education center, a large student center and cafeteria for the new campus, and an impressive nine-story library. Up to this point, Hofstra had been almost exclusively a commuter college catering to middle-class students on Long Island. The few resident students lived in boarding houses in the surrounding villages.

While this physical expansion was occurring, Hofstra also participated in the national trend to grant advanced degrees. Hofstra College became Hofstra University, providing advanced degrees in business, psychology, education, and, eventually, law. With the expansion in both degrees granted and physical plant, the student body grew to 12,000, or approximately 8,400 full-time equivalents.

Just as the dormitories and library opened in the early

1970s, Hofstra began to feel the adverse effects of the nation-wide higher education building boom that dramatically increased the number of colleges. Fixed costs, which continued to grow, were not offset by increased income. The new dormitory space was fully utilized for only a short time; thereafter, enrollment declines left vacancies. The opening of two state institutions in the area (at Stony Brook and Old Westbury) and the rapid expansion of the community college system in Nassau and Suffolk counties came just as Hofstra's new physical plant was completed. From 1972 to 1975, Hofstra's enrollment loss of approximately 1,200 full-time equivalents was almost exactly balanced by the combined enrollment gains at Adelphi University and the C. W. Post Center of Long Island University, two of the independent colleges in the region. In the same period Suffolk Community College and the nearby Stony Brook campus of the State University of New York gained more than 9,000 students. Hofstra was particularly hard hit because its financial resources were also being strained by auxiliary enterprises and the dormitory bonds which gave the university a substantial debt service. The university endowment was of little help, for its value in the then-depressed stock market was only slightly more than the annual short-term line of credit the university was required to cover each year.

The administration plan for improving Hofstra's financial position relied heavily on bolstering enrollment by enhancing the quality of education. The premise was that higher admission requirements would attract additional students and financial support. Although laudable as a long-term objective, the enhanced quality of education would not increase enrollment in the immediate future, and the absence of significant financial reserves precluded any deliberately paced transition. The growth of the administrative staff, reflecting the increasingly complex operation of the university, further exacerbated the situation.

As serious financial problems became apparent, suggestions were offered from many quarters to correct the imbalance. Faculty, among others, were not shy about making proposals. Financial pressures necessitated extensive layoffs of secretarial and support staff; close to 100 employees were laid off in November 1975. Shortly thereafter, the financial crisis came to a head when the president suggested that faculty take a 6 percent cut in salary, a particularly disturbing suggestion because the faculty were traditionally conservative in seeking salary increases.

Faculty Response

The faculty senate reacted to the president's suggestion that faculty salaries be cut by creating a special faculty committee to examine the financial status of the university. Although the faculty senate had a budget and planning committee, the creation of a new committee was apparently an admission that a fresh start was needed. The committee was requested to prepare a report for the faculty senate before action was taken on sacrificing 6 percent of faculty salaries. The initial committee, appointed by the speaker of the faculty, included an accounting professor, a business law professor, the chair of the sociology department, and a professor of German.

The committee determined the first order of business to be an examination of the books and records of the university. Given the approximately $35 million budget, such an inquiry was a massive undertaking. Recognizing the enormity of the task at hand, the committee received approval to expand its membership. The final report was signed by seven members with the additional signatories representing important faculty constituencies. The original four members, however, remained the principal initiators, coordinators, and spokespeople for the project.

Initially, the administration and trustees were reluctant to permit faculty access to the detailed financial records of the university; however, they subsequently complied with committee requests for the fiscal data, including line-item budgets. The precedent for permitting faculty to review such records occurred about one and a half years earlier when the planning and budget committee of the faculty senate, chaired by William Leonard, requested and received university financial statements. Leonard, a well-known economist, conducted a careful analysis of the university budget, with particular attention to the growing impact of auxiliary enterprises (the university-run bookstore, the university club, and other properties) on Hofstra's financial health.

Although the Leonard Report produced no administrative action, the three most important findings in the Leonard Report proved relevant in the unfolding financial difficulties: the decline in direct costs of faculty as a percentage of the total budget, the manner in which capital improvements were handled in the financial statements, and the growing burden of auxiliary enterprises. The Leonard Report also established that individual faculty members were fully competent to deal with the business side of the university. For example, one member of the Leonard committee had substantial experience in accounting and in advising bookstore management.

The trustees, in authorizing committee access to the data, including the line-item budget, made it clear they wanted a timely response, preferably within two weeks. The committee, stating its intention to work through the five-week mid-year break on the intensive examination of the financial data, requested and received from the trustees an agreement that the report would be completed by the time school resumed for the spring semester.

During intersession, the committee analyzed the history of the crisis, including the nature and sources of the debt and the evolution of administrative policies to pay it; compared the enrollment and budget of a somewhat similar institution located close by; compared the relationship of endowment and debt service at other colleges in the general area; and examined the rapid growth of administrative costs at a time when a declining percentage of the budget was allocated for faculty. The report also analyzed the financial contribution of the Law School (a somewhat autonomous structure) and evaluated the revenues and expenses of auxiliary enterprises. In addition to these large issues, the report considered such relevant areas as the efficiency of the heating and air-conditioning systems and expenses for telephones and postage.

The report was carefully crafted. Clearly a broad, unfocused critique of trustee and administration policies would be counterproductive. The seriousness of the financial situation demanded solutions not confrontation. At the same time, a hard, objective examination of the policies and practices that culminated in the proposal to reduce faculty salaries was required if the committee's report was to be useful.

Two audiences had to be considered. First, the faculty had to be apprised of the current fiscal status of the university. The major investment of 6 percent of the salaries of hundreds of faculty dictated that the "investors" understand both the structures and managerial approaches of the beleaguered enterprise and be persuaded that policies and practices that caused or aggravated the problem would not persist. Second, the trustees had to be persuaded to overcome their impression of the faculty as chronic complainers adept at pointing out problems but shying away from the hard solutions. The committee therefore made the survival of the institution its ultimate objective. This focus required the utmost objectivity in presenting practical solutions.

The committee concluded that the actual financial crisis was more severe than the administration had made it out to be. Further, in evaluating the administration's claim that the Law School was generating substantial income, the committee used three different accounting approaches, selecting the one that maximized the Law School's contribution to the university, and concluded that the contribution was modest. The report criticized the rapid growth of administrative expenditures and the slow growth of the endowment and development funds but also proposed a cap on faculty salaries and included a preliminary scheme whereby the faculty could make loans to the university to tide it over the crisis. The unifying theme of the report was mutual sacrifice. The trustees should build the endowment, the administration should become smaller and more efficient, and the faculty would make financial sacrifices to save the institution.

When the Law School was created, the trustees committed the university and, implicitly, the faculty in liberal arts, education, and business to finance start-up costs. Ironically, at the same time, the faculty agreed to give the Law School autonomy in its operations. Consistent with NLRB policy, the Law School was not part of the collective bargaining unit that only recently had begun to represent faculty and library staff in the rest of the university. Thus, compensation of law professors was determined by a different set of negotiations.

Many on campus felt that the Law School, having subsisted for a number of years on general university funds without becoming self-sustaining, should give careful consideration to tapping the market for a night law school on Long Island. Proponents sensed that a night program would be attractive in the suburbs and could provide additional sorely needed income. The Law School, however, decided to remain a day school on the basis that its educational function was separate and distinct from that of other parts of the institution and that a school's stature is measured in part by whether the program is a full-time day program or a mix of a full-time day and a part-time night program.

Fairness requires the observation that the Law School's position would probably have been taken by other professional schools on other campuses. Parts of the university subject to professional accreditation are always under extreme pressure to protect their standing. For example, in later years, Hofstra devoted additional resources to the School of Business to enable it to pay competitive salaries to Ph.D.s and to permit about one-third of the faculty to enjoy a 25 percent decrease in teaching load. These changes were made to meet accreditation requirements.

In addition to the Law School, a particularly upsetting problem to the faculty was administrative preoccupation with public relations and enhancing educational quality in order to attract students without the necessary reserves to finance these improvements. Administrative costs were growing; in the two-year period before the crisis (1973-1975), they increased dramatically, adding substantially to the budget. Although instructional costs increased, they were relatively minor.

The committee submitted two reports to the faculty senate. An interim report on the financial situation emphasized that the problems were real and more extensive than had been recognized. This report was terse and acerbic, noting that "our debt and debt service put us in the same league with Columbia, but for the insignificant fact that Columbia's endowment is fifty times ours." The interim report was more openly critical than the comprehensive and thoroughly documented forty-page report that was directed to the faculty with copies to the president and chair of the board.

The progress report did strike a conciliatory note, observing that "the present administration has done an excellent job in reestablishing the priorities of the university from bricks and mortar to quality education." The committee requested, however, that improvements in educational environment be carefully planned and adequately funded.

The final report, submitted at the end of January 1976, attracted the attention of the trustees. The report's summary dramatically highlighted the problems of the deficit, enrollment, the financial drain from auxiliary enterprises unrelated to educational purposes, and the rapid increase in administrative costs. Six specific budget areas were targeted for savings amounting to $500 thousand in yearly operating expenses. The committee suggested the bulk of the savings ($300 thousand) be achieved through fixing outlays for part-time teaching, special programs, and stipends at present levels. In all, twenty-one recommendations affected all phases of the university, including administrative structure and staffing, faculty salaries, auxiliary enterprises, and enrollment policy. One of the most startling recommendations, which was not implemented, was a voluntary loan program under which faculty and staff would provide short-term financing for the university.

The major recommendations were supported by extensive exhibits that unmistakably demonstrated the committee's grasp of the financial problems. The exhibits detailed the genesis of the difficulty and documented specific areas, such as heating, telephone, and postage, where cuts could be made. The report also presented comparisons of debt, debt service, and endowment at similar institutions in the region, at major universities, and at other selected quality institutions. In making the case for administrative belt tightening, the report compared administrative costs at Hofstra with similar costs at a nearby private institution. Over the three-year period through the 1975–76 academic year, that institution recorded a striking rise in tuition income, while the costs of central administration increased by only 10 percent of that amount. In the same period, Hofstra's tuition income rose by only one half of the other school's increase, while central administrative costs rose by about 25 percent of the addition to revenue.

Trustees' Strategy

With the submission of the report to the faculty senate and copies to the chair of the board of trustees, the committee had completed its work. Because the committee had been so careful and detailed in its analysis of the financial data and so reasonable in its approaches for resolving the financial crisis, the faculty accepted the report as a useful, informative, and effective document. Its impact on the trustees was subtle. Members of the committee were invited to a board meeting at which the president was also present; and committee members were permitted to participate to a limited extent in a discussion of the report. No direct action came from this meeting. But the highest praise for the report can be gleaned from the fact that significant changes were made by the trustees, albeit spread out over a substantial period of time. The administrative structure was simplified, concern with cost cutting became paramount, and a realistic debt-retirement program was implemented.

It would be improper to attribute these measures solely and directly to the work of the faculty committee, inasmuch as the policies moving the university toward fiscal recovery were ultimately those designed and implemented by the trustees. Nevertheless, the report was successful in that the major policy concerns of the committee were ultimately shared by the trustees as well. Trustees were deeply concerned with the drift of the institution toward insolvency. The report sent unmistakable signals to the trustees that there was a solid constituency among the faculty in favor of basic reform in the way the institution was conducting its business.

Ironically, the report was too successful in some regards. The central thrust of the report was that the university, in an era of rapid expansion followed immediately by enrollment declines, had not been sufficiently cost conscious. The faculty report's fervent plea for strict budgetary controls was no doubt responsible in part for a series of cost-cutting actions and the stabilizing of expenditures. Having endorsed such controls, the faculty was essentially precluded from protesting in the ensuing, increasingly prosperous, years that the university had become overly cost conscious.

In the end the faculty did not take a pay cut. Instead, the trustees developed and implemented a three-stage recovery plan spread over the following six years. First, a debt-management strategy was implemented to rapidly retire a substantial portion of the debt. Second, improvement of deteriorating plant and equipment was undertaken, including a campus beautification program. Third, the university focused on meeting the enrollment challenges of the late 1980s. A new and rigorous marketing program was planned and implemented to recruit students from a wide geographical area.

Because belt tightening meant restraints on faculty salaries, in a subsequently negotiated faculty collective bargaining agreement, faculty took less of an increase than they might have if the institution were financially sound, with the understanding that they would share in any financial improvement according to an agreed-on formula. The improved financial situation permitted faculty to receive additional compensation, based on the formula, in each of the following three years.

The trustees also took action on issues concerning the economic future of departments and programs: the number of classes offered, the allocation of faculty lines, and the granting of tenure. They shifted some resources from departments with declining majors to those experiencing or showing promise of expansion. Inevitably, there were cuts in course offerings and in areas of concentration; in some departments, emphasis was redirected to servicing other departments. For example, cutbacks were made in the number of faculty in education and in course offerings in the philosophy department. In some departments retiring faculty were not replaced, and in the School of Education several small departments were consolidated. Over several years, resources shifted toward the School of Business, which currently enrolls at least one half the undergraduate student body; the business faculty increased from thirty-five in the mid-1970s to close to eighty today.

The one major committee recommendation that failed to gain acceptance was for faculty participation in the decision-making process, although there are faculty observers at board of trustee meetings exclusive of executive sessions. A recurring theme in the committee report was the desire for faculty involvement through consultation and participation on trustee committees. In fact, the first recommendation in the report called for "a special commission of faculty and administration . . . to serve as a permanent monitoring/supervisory board and to be jointly responsible with the board of trustees in all fiscal matters." Not surprisingly, the board failed to respond to this suggestion. To have agreed would have gone a long way toward sharing authority, a rare occurrence in higher education. The Board of Trustees continues to make all the basic decisions about the direction of the university without effective or sustained input from the faculty. But the success of the committee should not be measured by whether it was a vehicle for permanently increasing faculty involvement in trustees' decisions. Rather, the true measure of its success was that it assisted all segments of the institution in dealing with pressing financial problems.

Recommendations for Faculty Involvement

The Hofstra experience suggests that faculty can provide valuable practical assistance to their institutions in times of financial stress. Perhaps the most important reason for involving faculty in the examination of options for institutional survival and improvement is that the faculty determine the quality of the students' educational experience. If faculty feel isolated or shut out of the process by which financial problems are resolved, their sense of commitment to institutional goals may be damaged and, in turn, the teacher/student relationship. Particularly during periods of financial difficulty, it is important to enhance the spirit of community that is essential for the survival of imperiled institutions. One way in which the collegial environment can be strengthened is to draw on faculty to assist in fashioning solutions to problems. The timing of their involvement, the way this assistance is structured, and the objectives and expectations of the faculty are all factors that determine the impact they have in helping the institution to overcome financial problems. A number of recommendations based on the process used at Hofstra may be helpful to faculty and administrators who confront similar situations.

1. Activate or enhance existing institutional structures to deal with financial problems.

An existing faculty committee is probably the best vehicle for tackling financial issues. Although in a critical situation a special committee might be preferable, this is the exception rather than the rule. Because there may be a need for special skills that present members of the committee do not have, a mechanism should exist for enlarging the committee to take advantage of faculty specialists. However, it is not necessary to include on the committee representatives of every segment of the university. Professional schools may not have the same interests as schools of liberal arts, and the expertise of some faculty is more relevant than that of others. What is needed is significant representation of the undergraduate programs, which in most institutions are the major share of the educational offering. Although the faculty senate at Hofstra chose to select a new committee, perhaps as a way of giving attention and importance to this venture, the tasks of the committee could have been completed by an existing committee if provision had been made for expanding the number of members to permit participation by faculty with relevant and specialized qualifications.

2. Tap specific expertise of faculty.

Use can be made of the skills of people within the institution, such as professors of accounting and finance who have had business experience or practice their professions outside the university. For example, faculty from the engineering school may be able to offer valuable insights into cost savings in heating, maintenance, communications systems, and computer operations. Trustees and administrators, however, may be reluctant to use the expertise of faculty because they fear being locked into a result. For example, the support staff, deeply concerned about salary inequities, may propose a comprehensive, once-and-for-all job survey. The business school dean, aware that the university is in financial difficulty, may seek to minimize expenses by offering faculty acquainted with job classifications to do the proposed survey. The dean may find, however, that the offer is stillborn, probably because the administration would be hard pressed to publicly reject recommendations from its own faculty. Resort to outside management consultants offers both ease of rejection and the opportunity to shape the results. This problem can be finessed if all parties understand at the outset that the faculty is an additional analytical resource available to be tapped at the discretion of the president and trustees.

3. Base participation of faculty on the principle of full disclosure by the trustees.

Without full disclosure of pertinent data, the faculty will be engaged in an empty exercise at best, and feel used and patronized at worst. Faculty in some instances may be surprised to find trustees willing to authorize full and complete disclosure. In most institutions, such disclosure would represent a desire to make the inquiry effective. In some, however, it may represent an expectation on the part of administrators and trustees that faculty, although quite energetic in voicing complaints, will not want to do the detailed work necessary to analyze all the data and will default by returning the problem to the trustees for a solution.

To gain full disclosure, the committee representing the faculty must achieve credibility with the trustees. It can do so only by demonstrating that it has done its homework with respect to the already available financial data, is willing to make use of technical experts available on campus, is willing to put in the time necessary to do a decent job, and above all is armed with suggestions for improvement.

4. In presenting proposed solutions, consider the good of the entire university.

If the committee had viewed Hofstra's financial problems solely from the perspective of faculty members, with the principal objective being the protection of faculty positions, the trustees would not have viewed the report as a responsible attempt to contribute to the improvement of the institution as a whole. A corollary to the principle that faculty should take an overall view of the institution is that all parts of the university must be part of the solution. For instance, program cuts and eliminations should be accompanied by reductions in administrative overhead whenever possible so that everyone recognizes that sacrifices are being made throughout the community.

Without outside support, resources will be shifting from program to program as the interests and expectations of students change. It makes sense for faculty to be prepared to accept the inevitable and whenever possible to participate in shaping change. It should be clear, however, that hard choices will be the faculty's burden. For example, faculty representatives from a school that is prospering should not focus solely on retaining their favored position but should consider the total university in fashioning proposals. Faculty may have to accept that shifting tastes in majors may distort an already disparate salary picture. Difficult as it may be, timely consideration of the health of the entire institution is the only way faculty can gain the credibility necessary to be a positive force for improvement.

5. Accept the possibility that the solution may require a decrease in teaching lines.

Economics now assumes overwhelming weight in tenure considerations. Faculty must be aware of shifts in student interest as reflected in departmental and school enrollment levels. For example, schools of education, formerly important locomotives in pulling institutions toward fiscal health, now find that programs, and in some instances departments, are no longer necessary. Here, cost savings are obviously necessary. Even if a professor possesses all the credentials that would have assured tenure in the past, his or her salary now can be saved by an adverse tenure decision, and less expensive and more flexible replacements can be made if the line is to continue. Likewise, interest in early-retirement packages should be encouraged in departments that are, according to the administration, over-tenured.

6. *Consider retrenchment alternatives as early as possible.*

If a reduction in faculty is inevitable, the process should be planned as early as possible. The reason is obvious: If the institution is already on the brink of bankruptcy when the faculty becomes involved, there may be no room for adjustment and accommodation. If, for example, declining enrollments and decreasing funds are anticipated in a certain department, a nontenured professor whom that department wants to keep can be given an interdisciplinary or interdepartmental teaching assignment early to ensure that when that person comes up for tenure, he or she is not locked into a department that cannot grant tenure for economic reasons.

Naturally, if the policy of the trustees is simply to eliminate tenure tracks, any such suggestions will be rejected. It may be difficult to sell this approach to some administrators who believe, as do some sports-club owners, that two or three new low-salaried, short-term-contract players are worth the price of one star. However, all efforts should be made to impress on administrators the fact that in the 1990s, when enrollments again increase, the quality of surviving institutions may be measured for the most part by their reputation for excellence in teaching. If there are excellent teachers now on campus, it may be foolish to let them go and then have to pay a much higher price later for the chance to bring equivalent skills back into the classroom.

7. *Recognize the importance of physical-plant maintenance.*

Contrary to the opinion of many academics, the state of the physical plant and the need to provide for its proper upkeep and maintenance are ultimately as important to the teaching process as the choice of texts and class size. The state of the plant is often as much a factor in competing for and retaining students as location and faculty reputation. Thus, certain physical improvements can demand priority over other claims on the revenue of the institution. In short, realism about the needs of the physical plant is essential.

8. Be aware of marketing considerations.

With the exception of a few institutions to which outstanding students will continue to apply in great numbers, a college or university must be keenly interested in marketing its product. Faculty must realistically address the difficult question of which markets to tap and be prepared to make suggestions for improving the marketing process.

9. Make the trustees responsible for final decisions and implementation.

Once the faculty report is submitted to the board, faculty probably will not be invited to participate in its implementation. In many institutions, the trustees, and specifically the executive committee, have the power to determine and implement recovery plans. In others, an aggressive president is the ultimate source of authority. But the objective of faculty involvement is not self-aggrandizement and ego enhancement. It is to furnish a creative series of recommendations to assist the leadership to reverse the adverse fiscal tide.

Although the faculty will probably not be asked to participate in further discussion of the recommendations, let alone their implementation, such a result does not mean their efforts have been to no avail. If trustees and administrators consider the report temperate and sophisticated, it will have an impact. The chances are that some of the recommendations will be implemented, albeit at a pace that seems politically and economically sensible to the trustees. The planting of seeds, assuming some fertile ground, may be as significant in one situation as a sudden and dramatic adoption of faculty proposals may be in another.

10. Make faculty contacts with trustees constructive.

In some institutions, faculty have an opportunity for informal contacts with the trustees. They should not use these opportunities to gripe about parochial or inconsequential issues, but to discuss problems with university-wide impact. Trustees, regardless of their background, tend to consider their responsibility to be the large policy questions. Nothing erodes faculty credibility as quickly as petty complaints for which other offices in the university are the appropriate recourse. Once the work of the committee is completed and the report is available, the committee or other faculty representatives should make a strong effort to meet with the trustees to discuss its content. Whether this occurs before or after the report is formally published can be determined only on a case-by-case basis.

11. Once the crisis is over, expect the administration to reassume its aloof position and the faculty to fall back to their parochial ways.

These recommendations are full of admonitions and exhortations for the faculty, but do not press management to any great extent. The disparity is necessary because we are dealing with some degree of informal power sharing. Traditionally, trustees and top administrators have regarded direct faculty efforts to achieve significant involvement as an adversary thrust. Therefore, the burden of persuading the window of power to be opened but a crack rests with the faculty. It matters not that those in charge were the authors of prior disasters or that the people "who brought us Pearl Harbor" appear to be at it again. In the absence of any legal obligation of the trustees to listen (aside from the drastic and impractical remedy of faculty appeals to the state higher education authorities to review the activities of the trustees), faculty must persuade those in charge of the institution to listen. Once they have, however, the relationship between faculty and administration may return to the status quo ante.

The faculty successful in presenting a proposal for economic discipline must anticipate an ironic result. An administration that is too little concerned with costs can be succeeded by an administration whose only concern appears to be costs. As the primary efforts of the administration are directed to cost control, reduction of the debt, and improvement of the physical plant, administrators have little time left for involvement in the educational process. Thus, as the financial situation strengthens, the administration becomes increasingly removed from the faculty and its educational concerns. Perhaps the solution lies in anticipating such a result and in imposing some vehicle for consultation until the desired balance between cost and performance is achieved.

12. Recognize that faculty involvement and problems of institutional management are cyclical.

The submission of the faculty report to the trustees and action by the trustees to remedy financial problems conclude a cycle that is bound to recur. With the immediate crisis past, faculty and administration tend to fall back into old patterns unless some new permanent relationship has been developed; the gulf between them begins to grow again until faculty become deeply concerned with new problems of institutional management. This cyclical phenomenon occurred at Hofstra approximately four years after the committee submitted its report to the trustees. Concerned about the ever-increasing distance between the faculty and administration once the crisis had abated, the faculty senate passed a resolution empowering the speaker to form a council to explore ways to remedy the distance between the managers and teaching faculty. The speaker's council included faculty from all parts of the university except the Law School. One phase of its work culminated in a meeting with a committee of trustees to exchange views on university problems. To some extent, the council and the trustees were working at cross purposes: the council concerned with the widespread feeling that faculty had become the least important element in the university family, the trustees concerned, as the president put it, with repositioning the university to meet the financial and enrollment challenges of the 1980s.

It would be difficult to ascribe any particular result to this relatively brief meeting, but shortly thereafter the president announced that the role of the provost's office would be reexamined as to both need and scope. The incumbent provost resigned to spend time on research, and there appeared to be no intention to replace him. As a result, the faculty senate overwhelmingly passed a resolution that a provost be appointed lest there be a missing link in the traditional structure of the university. In response, the president appointed an interim provost, while still explicitly retaining the right to determine the need for such an office in the administration. Ultimately, the interim provost became the permanent provost. It can be inferred that in a scaled-down manner, the speaker's council and the senate played a role similar to that of the early committee.

Faculty concern over resource allocations at Hofstra has also reappeared. The decision of the trustees to build additional dormitories and facilities and the extensive beautification program stimulate memories of past financial problems even as faculty appreciate that the character of the university has been changing markedly because of the shift from a commuter to a residential student body.

Generally speaking, faculty should not be discouraged or feel their continuing efforts to make useful and significant suggestions are a waste of time. Continuous concern with their employers' economic conditions must enhance their ability to deal effectively with problems as they arise.

Conclusion:
Managing Faculty Disputes

Changing economic, political, demographic, and social conditions suggest that disputes involving faculty will continue to demand the attention of college and university administrations. Cuts in state and federal funding for higher education, coupled with the dramatic and continuing decline in the population that is eighteen to twenty-four years old, will require readjustments in the relationships between faculty and their institutions. The presence of disgruntled faculty members who have been passed over for promotion or tenure is not a new phenomenon. A new element, however, is the sheer number of these disputes and the growing complexity of the issues involved. In the days of expanding enrollments and abundant financial resources, faculty members could move to other institutions with relative ease when they considered the teaching or research environment unsatisfactory. Now they are likely to remain and register their discontent. In addition, institutions facing difficult decisions concerning layoffs of tenured faculty must balance their commitments to affirmative action in the hiring and retention of women and minority faculty with the seniority rights of the faculty at large.

Societal factors that point to a growing number of disputes include the increasing awareness of individual rights and antidiscrimination laws, as well as a perception of the enhanced role of the individual within the organization. Then, too, the emergence of collective bargaining in higher education, although it covers only a small number of faculty, heightens the sensitivity of academics to avenues for challenging administrative decisions and to the need on occasion to confront the administration.

Colleges and universities that in the past insisted they could manage themselves now must consider that courts and legislative bodies have broad oversight. This intrusion affects employment practices, due process rights, and even to some degree organizational changes. Nowhere is this political factor more evident than in state and federal statutes on civil rights. Governmental initiatives and controls have a significant impact on the administrative structure of academic institutions. Institutions that formerly relied on informal advice from a trustee who was an attorney to handle occasional real estate transactions now have fully staffed legal offices to handle the varied aspects of the institution's day-to-day affairs. Furthermore, many academic institutions retain outside counsel to assist in litigation and advise on unusual situations.

The increasingly adversarial relationship between faculty and their institutions, as evidenced by the increase in faculty-initiated litigation, suggests that many faculty consider internal processes, unilaterally imposed by the administration, to be unfairly weighted against them. By implementing complaint procedures that are widely viewed by faculty to be fair and impartial, the institution is in a position to protect itself against unnecessary litigation because a positive experience will encourage faculty to resolve differences within their own systems. Furthermore, courts look favorably on the exhaustion of internal remedies that are considered to be equitable.

Confrontations over individual faculty-status decisions, however, constitute only a narrow segment of the dispute spectrum. Less dramatic disputes over policy occur with regularity and involve both individual faculty members and the faculty as a group. Although these seemingly minor disputes are sometimes characterized by jaded academics as obvious or trivial, the issues often have a larger significance than is immediately suggested by the problems themselves. Disputes over course schedules and assignments, however minor, have the potential for creating antagonism. If allowed to fester, they may disrupt or critically impair the teaching process. Thus, it is important that these disputes be resolved in a way that does not undermine the collegial relationships that are essential for academic teaching and research. These relationships are particularly vulnerable because of the faculty's role in assessing the credentials and performance of their peers.

Academic disputes of either kind, however, are more complex and varied than those that occur in industrial and commercial enterprises. Because diversity is a hallmark of the academic community, the substance of these disputes and the approach to their resolution differ markedly from institution to institution. A college or university that is devising a mechanism for the resolution of disputes needs to take into account its own educational mission, governance structure, student population, and sources of financial support.

Approaches to Dispute Management

Disputes and adversarial relationships cannot always be avoided. The number of issues that lead to entrenched positions can be minimized, however, through an understanding of the way individuals and groups customarily react in sensitive situations and through an appreciation that there are generally more options and alternative courses of action than may be apparent at first glance. As is the case in all successfully managed enterprises, academic administrators need to anticipate, to the extent possible, the issues that may erupt into disputes and to consider in advance the methods available for coping with them.

In examining the range of approaches for managing faculty disputes, we can distinguish between two separate categories of disputes on the basis of the frequency of their occurrence and the nature of the issues involved: disputes involving individual faculty members over issues such as promotion and tenure that arise with some regularity and disputes that occur infrequently and involve groups of faculty (sometimes aligned with other groups). Within this conceptual framework we can analyze the range of appropriate responses for handling disputes.

This distinction is also dictated by fundamental differences in the way these disputes are viewed by faculty and administrators and by differences in the role faculty play in their resolution. In the interest of fairness and as a protection against arbitrary action, disputes concerning individual faculty members require regularized, standing procedures. The procedural approach must be balanced to meet the needs of both faculty and administration. Faculty need assurance of due process and impartiality. The administration requires an orderly approach for faculty complaints and finality in their resolution. Both require a timely decision. These objectives can be achieved within a procedural framework that is custom tailored to fit unique institutional circumstances.

In contrast, the administration can use various alternative ways to resolve broad policy disputes. These disputes, which can be anticipated as to subject matter if not to timing and intensity, require special actions initiated by the administration because they have the potential of involving students, alumni, and off-campus groups. A failure to respond appropriately can generate adverse publicity for the institution and affect the institution's relationship with the community at large. Faculty can play an important role in resolving policy disputes, although this role is usually limited to giving advice inasmuch as the ultimate authority for resolution lies solely with the president and trustees. Provision for a consultative role for faculty is based on the conviction that this collaborative process may yield a better solution than a unilateral determination.

The differing requirements for handling these two kinds of disputes necessitate different designs for their resolution. Systems for managing individual faculty disputes are generally a permanent element of institutional policy. Resolving these disputes involves the direct application of this policy to an individual faculty member's situation with procedural regularity. The need for an additional review after a supposed final outcome because procedural details were not honored represents a failure of management. Rigorous adherence to procedure not merely avoids suspicion that the process is illusory but has the practical effect of minimizing litigation.

The design of procedures for individual faculty disputes should reflect the influence of faculty. At institutions where faculty wield substantial power in peer review and other aspects of governance, this power should be expressed in an active role for them in formulating and implementing the procedures. Fairness also requires that the grievance process include at some point the participation of those not directly involved with the department or school. In other words, the review should include consideration by those outside the original decision-making process. The Resources at the end of the book are useful to those designing grievance procedures.

Systems can also be designed to handle new and special situations and relationships. New arrangements within the university may require adaptation of the grievance procedures used for handling faculty problems. For instance, collaborative industry/university research may involve a contractual agreement with regard to publication and other exchanges of information. The process for resolving disputes must take into account these new obligations of faculty members in independent or at least semiautonomous centers. University-based procedures may also need to be adapted for deciding disagreements regarding faculty status in these research centers. Thus, the collaborative research center's procedures, if any, and the university procedures should both mesh and clearly indicate the jurisdiction for specific problems.

In these joint ventures also, university leadership should distinguish in advance between the faculty members' academic responsibilities and those that relate strictly to the research venture. Issues such as discipline for disclosure of industry secrets probably will require consideration by and perhaps sanctions from the sponsor, possibly including termination of the faculty member's participation in the center. Realistically, termination from the research activity may well affect the professor's status within the university. If, for example, the faculty member has had a half-time teaching load because of research obligations at the center, the professor may not fit comfortably within the department on a full-time basis. Most institutions and industry sponsors are aware of the fundamental differences between academic and proprietary values, but few consider how such differences are translated into grievances and institutional responses.

Disputes that do not lend themselves to systematic resolution frequently erupt without warning and may involve faculty who side with student activists or community leaders. Although not susceptible to resolution through a grievance mechanism, these recurring problems have enough similarities to assist the besieged college official in deciding how to handle them.

Probably the most common of these disputes arises over economic issues. Although it is conventional wisdom that in bad times people tend to lie low, a case can be made for the opposite result. As conditions become particularly difficult, faculty can be expected to openly demonstrate their frustrations. The challenge in this policy area is to develop executive flexibility. The temptation during times of financial hardship is for the administration to exercise ever-increasing control in an effort to save money. Although, in most instances, ultimate responsibility for changes brought about by economic conditions rests with the administration and trustees, the climate in which such changes occur, as well as the quality of the changes themselves, can benefit from some level of faculty involvement in the process.

There is usually sufficient talent within the institution's faculty to realistically address severe economic problems. Although the problems may not be recurring ones, it is possible to use existing governance structures, such as senate budget committees, for this purpose. The first objective is to establish sufficient faculty credibility with the trustees and administration to bring about full disclosure of the relevant financial data. The second objective is for the faculty to produce a viable series of recommendations. It should be anticipated that in the implementation of a recovery phase of the program the faculty may be excluded. Their exclusion does not, however, represent a failure but simply illustrates the existing divisions of power within the institution. The most important element is not who takes credit for saving the institution but that the institution survives.

The distinction between individual faculty-status disputes and policy disputes is not meant to suggest that there are no common approaches that can be used for their resolution. For both types of disputes, participants can use a variety of accepted dispute-settlement techniques. Traditional reliance on informal resolution through discussion continues to be the primary vehicle for resolving disputes of both types. When this approach fails, a hearing conducted either under established procedures or as an ad hoc review is the standard and best-recognized next step. An alternative or additional step that has effectively resolved disputes is mediation; here again, it may either be instituted within the provisions of a grievance mechanism or be designed especially for a particularly intractable problem. However, not all issues can be handled entirely internally. Questions involving legal precedent and statutory interpretation can be resolved only through litigation. For instance, the courts may be asked for a final determination regarding compliance with federal laws barring sex, race, or age discrimination.

As a part of the preventive management strategy, it is important to identify individuals within the institution who are respected for their wisdom, balanced judgment, and evenhandedness. In the professional world of dispute settlement, these individuals would be labeled mediators. Although in a university setting such a designation may be considered threatening, the functions these persons perform are essentially the same regardless of title. Acting as liaisons, as sounding boards, as initiators of ideas, and as conveners of individual and group meetings, they assist those directly involved in a conflict to act constructively in the best interests of the institution. Individuals of this type are present on every campus. Academic institutions are particularly fortunate because the educational process seems to develop more than its fair share of such facilitators. Faculty mediators or neutrals may gain this position through recognized research, through rapport with fellow faculty and with students, through experience on faculty committees, and in some cases through professional activities off-campus. Although the presence of individuals with strong conciliatory abilities will not prevent the development of a controversy that divides the campus, they can facilitate discussion and resolution of these problems with a minimum of recurrent bitterness and hostility.

A president who recognizes the importance of the early identification of potential disputes and who appreciates that there is substantial latitude in selecting a management style and implementing the settlement process is likely to foster an environment where faculty, students, and administrators believe their concerns are fairly taken into account in the institution's decision-making process. A responsive management style should permit the president to identify significant areas of faculty discontent before they ripen into serious confrontation. The provost, deans, and department chairs will feel free to express their sense of emerging problems. Inevitably, this approach will make the president aware of the important concerns of the academic community.

Often, it is less the substance of a president's decision than the way the decision was reached and promulgated that arouses the wrath of faculty. In the area again of financial constraints, for example, most faculty appreciate that even the best financially positioned schools are vulnerable. The sacrifice, primarily in the form of reduced salary and increased teaching load, may not be the source of pain as much as the sense that limitations on economic or professional growth are being imposed in an arbitrary fashion. Put another way, a frequent faculty complaint against presidents is that faculty advice is not requested and they suspect their sacrifice is greater than that being made by other groups in the university.

A final useful management strategy is to be alert to patterns of disputes. Patterns will be seen when a sequence of similar disputes arise under similar conditions. When it seems likely that certain issues will recur, the administrative leadership should examine institutional policy for possible changes or additions.

In some instances, the appointment by the president of a joint faculty/administration committee to recommend guidelines for managing these issues will avoid the emergence of disputes in the future.

Conflict as an Opportunity for Institutional Improvement

The way administrators handle conflict has a pronounced influence on how the institution is viewed, both within the college and in the larger community. If administrators believe that conflict is an unwarranted intrusion into the smooth running of the institution, they become annoyed and impatient with demands and tend to procrastinate in responding to grieving faculty members. This apparent insensitivity fosters an impression of institutional intransigence. If, however, administrators see conflict as a natural and even healthy aspect of their relationship with the faculty, they will be responsive to faculty concerns and demonstrate the institution's commitment to thoughtful and thorough consideration of issues within a rational problem-solving framework.

Throughout this book, the emphasis on viewing conflicts constructively and on cooperatively fashioning solutions may suggest an amorphous process—everyone pitches in to come up with an answer. It is vitally important, however, to understand that we do not believe that in most cases everyone happens to join together in some spontaneous way to work out a solution. Put another way, what is constructive and cooperative is the systematic, mutual fashioning and implementation of the procedures rather than some rare coming together to solve a particular problem.

It should also be clear that although we frequently expound the benefits of a reasoned and regular process, similar emphasis should be placed on the costs, to the institution and to the individual, of engaging in the process. For example, the institution may accept binding outcomes that are not, in its view, the optimum way of concluding the dispute. An individual grievant must be prepared to submit to time limits and to adhere rigidly to mechanics. Thus, in evaluating the efficacy of the types of procedures described, one should keep in mind that the proper yardstick is whether a procedure works on net balance over a sustained period of time.

A constructive view of conflict enhances open communication. It encourages the administration and faculty to establish channels through which to exchange information and suggestions for solving problems, to anticipate troublesome issues, and to obtain systematic feedback for timely, corrective action when necessary. An administration that appropriately addresses emerging issues may avoid a series of disputes all relating to the same problem area. If, for example, a dean is a frequent source of formal complaints from a department, the president may determine from the nature of the complaints that the dean and not the department is the source of friction. The president can then examine the dean's relationship with the department with a view to suggesting improvement.

We are not implying that the institution should give way on principle. The emphasis is on a readiness to evaluate the issues rather than to defend an initial position simply because a decision was reached. This emphasis on evaluating issues acknowledges that administrators can and do make incorrect or ill-considered decisions. The objective is not to protect past decisions regardless of their wisdom; it is, first and foremost, to solve problems. If the administration approaches conflict constructively, faculty will be confident that the issues they raise will receive thoughtful consideration. Gossip and rumor of unfair treatment will be minimized as faculty gain confidence in both the established procedures and in the leadership's willingness and ability to fit the process to the problem. With adequate procedures, grieving faculty members may be satisfied even when the outcome is unfavorable. The importance of having an opportunity to express positions and to be fully informed of the basis or rationale for an administrative decision cannot be overstated.

Preventive management strategies, such as an open-door policy, an expressed willingness to discuss problems, and other techniques based on expanding communications and the early identification of disputes, will not be successful in all situations. No amount of discussion concerning contingencies will prepare faculty and staff for the pain and disruption involved with activating retrenchment plans. Student groups, buttressed with support from faculty, may not be dissuaded from confrontation because a joint committee is appointed to discuss the issues. However, an understanding of dispute-resolution processes and how they apply to specific disputes will enable educators to distinguish between issues that should be treated formally and those that require special handling. In policy disputes, it is important to consider the full range of options and techniques available. The knowledge that effective responses for managing disputes exist will often offset the tendency to temporize in the hope that the dispute or incident will run its course without official intervention.

RESOURCES

A. Checklist for Assessing
Grievance Systems

B. Model Procedures
for Resolving Faculty Disputes

C. Components
of Faculty Grievance Procedures

D. Grievance Procedures:
Northeastern University

E. Grievance Procedures:
Pace University

F. Grievance Procedures:
Unity College

RESOURCE A

Checklist for Assessing Grievance Systems

This checklist includes questions that should be answered in reviewing institutional procedures for handling faculty complaints. The items in the checklist are not necessarily in the order they would appear within the procedures, and the weight or significance of each element is not necessarily reflected in the sequential listing or the prominence within the checklist. Both procedural and substantive elements are covered because both are components of effective complaint procedures. Faculty complaint procedures are closely tied to an institution's policies. These policies should be carefully reviewed to be sure that they are clearly enunciated and reflect the goals, governance structure, and management philosophy of the institution.

In order to assess existing complaint procedures, the volume and nature of complaints should be reviewed. Procedures may be used infrequently because faculty do not consider them fair, because faculty are not aware of their existence, or because faculty distrust the administrators handling complaints. However, infrequent filing of complaints may mean that the procedures are serving the purpose for which they were designed. If many complaints are filed, institutional policies may need to be more clearly stated than they currently are.

Procedures

Do the procedures encompass the range of complaints that are likely to arise?

Are the issues covered by the procedures clearly described?

Are the procedures described in clear, unambiguous language with a minimum of legalisms?

Are the steps and the appeals process simple?

Is information requested in the statement of the complaint uncomplicated so that preparation of the statement is not an obstacle to filing?

Is information widely available regarding the existence of the procedures?

Is a mechanism provided for receiving information that may serve as the basis for institutional improvement?

Time Periods

Are the time limits for preparing the complaint and deciding on appeals reasonable?

Is the complaint process completed within a reasonable time so that the faculty and the college can plan for the future?

Does the timing for the procedural steps correspond to the personnel decision-making timetable?

Hearing

Is the hearing conducted by an individual or committee perceived as neutral concerning the issues and the parties?

Is full opportunity provided for the parties to present testimony and information supporting their positions?

Is an opportunity provided for an external or independent review of the decision or recommendation?

Are the responsibilities of the hearing officer or committee carefully delineated?

Administration of Complaint Process

Is the method for transmitting decisions clearly delineated at each stage?

Are the titles and responsibilities of staff and faculty members who administer the procedures included?

Protection of Parties

Is confidentiality of information provided to protect the parties and others involved in the complaint?

Are the parties protected against invasions of privacy?

Are the parties and others involved protected against retaliation for filing a complaint?

Model Procedures
for Resolving Faculty Disputes

The model procedures presented here were prepared by the Center for Mediation in Higher Education and are discussed fully in *Resolving Faculty Disputes* (1981), by Jane McCarthy and Irving Ladimer. Faculty and administrators can use these procedures in designing grievance systems compatible with the unique characteristics of their institutions. The model incorporates the elements of due process, administrative simplicity, and responsiveness as outlined in Resource A. (Time periods suggested are illustrative; they may be acceptable at some institutions but too long or too short at others.)

Purpose

These procedures, when officially adopted, are intended to promote the voluntary resolution of differences between faculty members and the institution in a fair and equitable manner. The procedures may be used to resolve any dispute between a faculty member and the institution except for matters expressly covered under other procedures.

The procedures recognize and endorse the tradition of informal consideration and resolution of problems between faculty and other members of the institution. It is expected that most disputes will be resolved in this manner or through mediation, to which this institution is precommitted. When resolution cannot be achieved, faculty may proceed to the subsequent steps in these procedures.

The procedures emphasize mediation, a process by which the parties come to voluntary agreement with the assistance of a neutral, and provide for a formal hearing on issues not resolved through mediation. Arbitration is available to obtain an external review of complaints involving tenure, contract, promotion, dismissal, or other issues involving professional activity, discrimination, or academic freedom.

Definitions

A *complaint* is a written statement alleging a misinterpretation, incorrect application, or violation of a policy, procedure, or practice of the institution not pursued by the faculty member in some other forum.

The *faculty-relations administrator,* appointed by the president, has central management responsibility for administering these procedures, including acceptance and referral of complaints and requests.

The *hearing officer* is a member of the institution appointed by the president to conduct the formal hearing and to make a decision regarding the disposition of the complaint.

The *faculty review committee* is a standing committee of the faculty that reviews and mediates complaints and suggests revisions in these and other procedures and policies of the institution.

Professional activity includes all functions and responsibilities of the faculty member in pursuing his or her customary research, teaching, and institutional duties.

Complaint Procedure

Information About Procedures

The faculty-relations administrator is responsible for providing information regarding these procedures and their relation to other policies and procedures of the institution. This administrator shall explain the conditions for using the various steps in response to inquiries by faculty members.

Filing a Complaint

On request, the faculty-relations administrator will assist the faculty member in preparing the complaint.

A complaint must be filed with the faculty-relations administrator within a reasonable time after the faculty member learned of the act or omission that is the basis for the complaint. The statement of the complaint should include: (1) a brief description of the alleged act or omission giving rise to the complaint; (2) the basis for the complaint, such as a misinterpretation, incorrect application, or violation of a policy prohibiting discrimination, a policy guaranteeing academic freedom, or some other policy, procedure, or practice of the institution; (3) the remedy the faculty member seeks; (4) the address and telephone number where the faculty member wishes to be reached; (5) the name of the faculty member's representative, if any. (If the faculty member's representative files the complaint, it must be signed by the faculty member.)

Within three days of the receipt of the statement of a complaint, the faculty-relations administrator shall send a copy of the complaint to the chair of the faculty review committee.

Mediation

Request for Mediation. Filing of a complaint shall be deemed a request for mediation. If mediation is declined, the complaint shall be deemed a request for a formal hearing. If me-

diation is tried but does not result in full agreement, the faculty
member may request a formal hearing on the unresolved issues
within thirty days of the date the complaint is filed unless the
parties consent to an extension.

Mediation Process. After the acceptance of mediation by
the faculty member, the faculty-relations administrator shall request the president to designate an individual to represent the
institution and shall so inform the chair of the faculty review
committee.

The chair of the faculty review committee shall appoint
as mediator a member of the committee and an alternate who
will meet informally with the faculty member and other involved parties and attempt to mediate the complaint.

The mediator shall meet with the parties for the purpose
of reaching an agreement mutually acceptable to the parties and
in conformance with the policies of the institution.

Confidentiality. The mediator's authority does not extend to obtaining confidential information; however, by joint
agreement, the parties may authorize the mediator to review
confidential information.

Mediated Agreement. If a satisfactory settlement is
reached through mediation, it shall be signed by the parties and
submitted to the faculty-relations administrator and the chair of
the faculty review committee.

Termination and Extension of Mediation. If the complaint is not resolved through mediation within thirty days, the
mediation shall be deemed terminated. If at any time during the
thirty-day period, the mediator believes the parties cannot reach
agreement, the parties shall be so informed, and the mediation
effort shall cease, unless the parties agree to the contrary. By
mutual consent, the parties may extend the mediation period
for a reasonable time.

Formal Hearing

Jurisdiction. The formal hearing is the institution's method for adjudicating any issue that comes within the scope of the
complaint procedure that has not been previously resolved.

Selection of Hearing Officer. The hearing officer is the administrator appointed by the president to hear complaints or, on the request of the complainant or the hearing officer, an alternate acceptable to both the complainant and the institution. The appointment of an alternate hearing officer will be made following selection procedures designated by the institution, including use of persons in or outside the institution.

The alternate hearing officer may be one person or a three-person panel, the latter to be used principally in cases of academic judgment and composed of persons who may serve as a peer-review body.

Scheduling the Hearing. The hearing officer shall schedule a hearing of the complaint. The hearing shall be held within twenty days from the date the request for a hearing was received, unless the parties mutually consent to an extension of time.

The hearing officer shall send five days' written notice of the scheduled hearing to the parties and to the chair of the faculty review committee. Persons having a direct interest in the hearing are entitled to attend, including members of the faculty review committee. Other persons may attend at the discretion of the hearing officer.

Confidential Information. Confidential information shall be made available to the hearing officer upon the written request of the faculty member. Under no circumstances will the hearing officer reveal the contents or authors of confidential information.

Hearing Process. The hearing officer will take evidence and listen to the testimony of all persons concerned. The hearing will be conducted in accordance with the special rules for this purpose. The procedure will be responsive to the needs of the parties, who shall be given an opportunity to make a complete presentation, with due regard for privacy.

Decision. The hearing officer's decision shall include an appropriate remedy with respect to matters within the authority of the administration. If the remedy requires action by the board of trustees, as in cases of tenure, the hearing officer's decision shall include only findings and recommendations.

The decision of the hearing officer is conclusive unless the complaint involves issues of tenure, contract, promotion, dismissal, or other issues involving professional activity, discrimination, or academic freedom.

The hearing officer shall submit a written decision and opinion within thirty days after the hearing is completed. A copy of the decision and opinion will be sent to the parties and the chair of the faculty review committee.

Arbitration

Jurisdiction and Arbitrability. Arbitration is available to either party as an appeal from the decision of the hearing officer for issues involving tenure, contract, promotion, dismissal, or other issues involving professional activity, discrimination, or academic freedom.

Initiating Arbitration. Within ten days of the receipt of the decision of the hearing officer, arbitration may be initiated by filing a written request with the faculty-relations administrator. The faculty-relations administrator shall forward the request for arbitration to the American Arbitration Association and the chair of the faculty review committee.

Selection of Arbitrator. The faculty member and the administration will select the arbitrator in accordance with the *Special Rules for Post-Secondary Faculty Disputes* of the American Arbitration Association. The American Arbitration Association will submit names of arbitrators from a panel of arbitrators who have experience with arbitration in higher education.

Arbitration Proceeding. The arbitrator shall determine whether the complaint is arbitrable. The arbitrator may consider the opinion and decision of the hearing officer as well as the arguments of the parties on the issue.

The arbitrator shall conduct the arbitration in accordance with the *Special Rules for Post-Secondary Faculty Disputes* of the American Arbitration Association, which must be furnished to the parties.

Scope of Award. The award of the arbitrator shall determine the issues submitted, based on the evidence presented by the parties, within the terms and provisions of the agreement, policy, institutional charter, or statute governing the controversy. If the arbitrator's award requires action by the board of trustees, as in tenure cases, the award shall contain only findings and recommendations.

Form of Award. The award and a written reason for the decision shall be signed by the arbitrator. A copy of the award shall be sent to the faculty member, the hearing officer, and the chair of the faculty review committee in accordance with American Arbitration Association rules.

Enforcement. The award of the arbitrator, except as to issues requiring action by the board of trustees, shall be final and binding on the faculty member and the institution.

Board of Trustee Review. If the board rejects the findings and recommendations of the arbitrator, the reasons for such rejection shall be stated in writing and sent to the faculty member and the faculty-relations administrator within thirty days. Otherwise, the arbitrator's award shall stand.

Costs of Arbitration. The administrative fees of the American Arbitration Association and the arbitrator's fees shall be shared by the faculty member and the institution, with the institution providing payment for two thirds of these costs and the faculty member providing one third, up to a limit of $500. All other costs shall be paid for by the respective parties.

Reports and Annual Review

The chair of the faculty review committee will report at least once each year to the faculty stating the nature of complaints filed and their disposition (without identifying the complainants) and suggesting, if appropriate, improvements in this procedure or other policies or practices of the institution that result from experience with the complaint procedure.

Components
of Faculty Grievance Procedures

The procedures for handling faculty grievances should be appropriate to the institution within which they will be used. On a campus where faculty actively participate in the decision-making process, they should be involved in the grievance procedure. Likewise, the procedures should be compatible, in style and substance, with other policies and procedures of the college. The procedures should also reflect the degree of involvement of the governing board in the college's affairs.

General Components

The following items are general considerations that may assist designers of procedures to reach decisions concerning a suitable overall approach.

Jurisdiction

Definition of the grievance (comprehensive or special issue)

213

Steps in the procedure

Informal resolution/mediation
Hearing
External review

Authority of the faculty

Faculty grievance committee
Participation in the hearing
Decision-making role

Role of the administration

Staff responsibilities

Review of relevant institutional policies

Financial exigency
Reappointment, promotion, and tenure
Dismissal and termination
Selection of deans and department chairs
Retirement (age, privileges)
Work load
Outside employment, research activities
Discrimination, including affirmative action program

Specific Components

The following specific structural elements are included in the procedures used in many academic institutions. The design committee should determine, at least on a preliminary basis, which of these elements should be part of the procedure.

Informal Resolution

Attempts at informal resolution are generally made before a grievance is filed. A provision for informal resolution is included in the procedure to underscore the college's commitment and willingness to take steps to resolve complaints at an early stage.

In considering the inclusion of an informal-resolution stage, designers should discuss the following issues:

1. If the informal-resolution stage is to be conducted before the complaint is filed, how are the time limits for filing affected?
2. Should the grievant be required to attempt informal resolution by discussing the grievance with his or her immediate supervisor?
3. If so, will the grievant always be in a position to identify his or her immediate supervisor for purposes of the grievance? For example, a biology professor grieves the lack of air conditioning over the weekend, citing the potential damage to controlled experiments or the need to conduct research activities. Is the immediate supervisor the dean, the department chair, or an administrator dealing with building maintenance?
4. If informal resolution is a required step before filing a grievance, should the grievant be required to include on the statement of the grievance a description of these attempts and contacts?
5. Should the administrator or faculty member designated to accept grievants' statements be given the authority to contact an immediate supervisor or others in an attempt to resolve the issues? If so, should these contacts be made only with the approval of the grievant? Should the results of these attempts be recorded on the statement of the grievance?

Choosing the Type of Grievance Procedure

The type of grievance procedure chosen is the foundation for the design process. There are two options: a comprehensive procedure for all grievances brought by faculty members concerning the application of the college's policies and procedures; and single-issue procedures for particularly sensitive areas of dispute.

Comprehensive Procedure. A comprehensive procedure is an expression of the willingness of the college to consider seriously any and all issues that faculty members believe affect their professional environment. Effective implementation of a comprehensive procedure requires a close examination, and per-

haps revisions, of the college's policies and procedures to ensure
that they accurately and clearly reflect the college's intent.

   Single-Issue Procedure. Single-issue procedures usually relate to general or specific employment practices. At a unionized
institution, the grievance procedure commonly covers all issues
arising under the collective bargaining agreement. But separate,
single-issue procedures may be designed to cover tenure, promotion, termination, dismissal, academic freedom, discrimination, and financial exigency. Problems can arise with single-
issue procedures when a faculty member bases a grievance on
several policies, such as a violation of both the policy against
discrimination and the policy on terminations due to fiscal exigency.

Filing the Grievance

   The section that describes the manner in which grievances
are to be filed should state:

1.   The title and duties of the administrator or faculty mem-
     ber with whom grievances are to be filed
2.   Time limits, if any, for filing
3.   The nature of the action that will follow the filing (to
     whom the grievance statement will be forwarded)

   Requested information may include:

1.   The basis for the grievance, including a description of the
     event that prompted the grievance and the policy or pro-
     cedure alleged to have been violated
2.   The remedy requested

   The design committee should determine the responsibilities of the faculty committee or administrator designated to accept grievance statements. These duties could include the following:

1.   Assist grievants to prepare statements
2.   Attempt conciliation with the approval of the grievant

3. Track the progress of grievances through the procedure
4. Act as liaison with faculty or administrative counterpart
5. Prepare report on number and nature of grievances for faculty and administrative review

Mediation

Faculty disputes frequently arise in an emotionally charged atmosphere. In mediation, the focus is on the issues and possible solutions and away from the background and personal circumstances that may have triggered the dispute. The mediator helps the parties to identify the substantive issues and explore areas of agreement. Mediation is successful when the parties voluntarily agree to a specific course of action or solution.

A variety of circumstances can prompt faculty members to present grievances. When a faculty member receives a negative evaluation, the grievance could be based on the following:

1. *Differences of opinion.* During the faculty evaluation process, a faculty member believes his teaching is satisfactory, but the departmental evaluators judge it to be deficient.
2. *Inadequate communication.* In discussing the evaluation with the grievant, the evaluators do not clearly state that the grievant's performance is unsatisfactory; the faculty member believes the report to be positive when, in fact, it is a hedged disapproval.
3. *Insufficient or inaccurate information.* In the discussion of the evaluation, the faculty member explains the reasons the evaluation was inaccurate (for example, he was sick on the day evaluated). The evaluators conclude the explanation is inadequate but do not fully inform the faculty member that these special considerations were unpersuasive.
4. *Unrelated events.* Although the grievance was filed over the substance of the evaluation, the real dispute, as far as the faculty member is concerned, is over the assignment of office space; he is in an office with three faculty with whom he is incompatible.

In situations such as the one described, the mediator's

task is to identify the source of the grievance and work with the faculty member and other involved parties to improve communication, clear up misunderstandings, recognize differences in perception, and exchange needed and accurate information. With these roadblocks removed it may be possible to work out an agreement.

In general, a mediator works with the parties, in joint and separate meetings, to explain the mediation process; identify misunderstandings; facilitate communications; explore areas of agreement; suggest possible areas of accommodation; and contact administrators or faculty who are not directly involved, when necessary, to gain their approval for a proposed settlement. The exact nature of the mediator's involvement will depend on the issues and the relationships between the parties.

The mediator's most valued attribute is neutrality; his or her effectiveness relates directly to the ability to establish trust. Mediators should be selected for their fair-mindedness, knowledge of the college, integrity, and ability to communicate.

These matters need to be considered by those deciding to include a mediation step:

1. Selection of mediators (number, term of office, responsibilities, substitutions)
   a. Standing committee
   b. Ad hoc
   c. One or more permanently designated
2. Role of mediation in the procedure
   a. Attempted on the request of one or both parties
   b. Compulsory step
3. Time limits
4. Nature of the agreement
   a. In writing
   b. Withdrawal of the grievance

Hearing

The grievance committee, composed solely of faculty members, is the group customarily charged with the responsibility for conducting a hearing.

In examining the role of the grievance committee, designers of procedures should consider the following items:

1. Composition and representation
   a. Faculty, administration, or joint committee
   b. Number of members, term of office, selection of chair (elected or appointed)
2. Nature
   a. Standing
   b. Ad hoc
3. Authority and reporting function
   a. Limitations on authority
   b. Person or committee to whom grievance committee reports
   c. Availability of appeal from the committee's decision or recommendation

Designers of procedures should determine the appropriate degree of formality in the hearing process. It should be sufficiently informal to encourage full discussion of the relevant facts and issues and at the same time be sufficiently structured to withstand a legal challenge on due process grounds.

In structuring the hearing, designers should discuss the following provisions:

1. A prehearing conference to
   a. Frame the issue(s)
   b. Stipulate facts
   c. Simplify and expedite the hearing
2. Presiding officer (possible alternate in case of conflict of interest)
   a. Member of the faculty or member of the administration
   b. Possibility of challenging the appointment
3. Grievant's representative
   a. Right to representation
   b. Faculty member or an outsider such as an attorney
4. Public or private hearing
   a. Designated in procedures
   b. At the discretion of the hearing officer

5. Availability of rules and agenda before the hearing
6. Time limits
   a. Scheduling the hearing
   b. Length of hearing
   c. Conveying the decision
   d. Filing an appeal
7. Record of the proceedings
   a. Minutes, stenographic record, tape recorder
   b. Allocation of transcription costs
8. Methods for ensuring confidentiality and protection of privacy
9. Acceptance of depositions and written testimony when witnesses are not readily available

The procedures should describe the actions to be taken when the hearing is concluded.

1. To whom will the hearing officer or committee report its decision?
2. Will the report be considered a recommendation or a final decision?
3. Will there be time limits within which the report must be completed and transmitted?
4. If the report is submitted to the president, will it be conveyed before the grievant is contacted?
5. Will minority or dissenting decisions or recommendations be submitted?
6. How, if at all, will the report be transmitted to the faculty as a whole and to the board of trustees?
7. At what point, and from whom, will the grievant receive the report?
8. Will the procedures include a provision for an appeal from the decision or recommendation provided in the report? If so, to whom will the appeal be made (president, board of trustees, external review)?

External Review

A complete and comprehensive complaint procedure includes a step for final decision by an off-campus neutral when a satisfactory solution is not achieved through mediation, hearing, or other internal procedure. Resort to court is, of course, always available, but such external review is usually limited to an evaluation of the sufficiency of the internal procedures and the extent of their use prior to the suit. The customary alternative to litigation is some form of arbitration, generally binding, which provides a speedy, inexpensive review and serves as a complete substitute for litigation. Although a small proportion of cases reach arbitration, it is nonetheless desirable to have such an option.

Arbitration is generally available for those issues that meet the definition of a complaint or grievance and for which the arbitrator can provide a remedy either through a final decision or through a recommendation that will be accorded respect by the governing board or trustees, who alone may be entitled to decide certain issues. Accordingly, arbitration may be reserved for disputes over tenure, contract renewal, promotion, and dismissal. Disputes over class assignments, curriculum, faculty privileges, and perquisites that can reasonably be decided by mediation or hearing may not be referred to arbitration.

The arbitration process requires certain formalities to ensure that only arbitrable cases, as specified in the procedure, are considered and that due process is observed in the presentation and hearing of the arguments. The rules may be designed by the institution and faculty representatives, may be provided by an administrative agency, or may be a combination of the two.

Those designing an arbitration step need to consider these matters:

1. What steps should be completed prior to arbitration?
2. For what issues should arbitration be available?
3. What provisions should be made for situations in which only one of several issues presented by the grievant is subject to arbitration?
4. Is a provision needed to ensure participation by all parties who may be affected?

These questions need to be asked when selecting arbitrators:

1. What qualities or experience, professional training, and familiarity with the issues should be required?
2. Must an arbitrator come from the field of higher education?
3. How does one ensure neutrality or impartiality?
4. Should arbitration be conducted by a single arbitrator or by a panel?
    a. Are there advantages to party-selected arbitrators who, in turn, select a neutral to serve as chair?
    b. Should the procedure permit the parties to have the option of selecting a single arbitrator or a panel?
5. Should arbitrators be selected from a neighboring institution or similar source, or should the choice be left to a professional agency?
6. How should a pool of arbitrators be established and maintained?
7. How shall costs of arbitration be determined and allocated?
    a. Should arbitrators be paid fees and expenses?
    b. What other costs should be permitted or provided?
    c. What proportion should be borne by the college?
    d. Should the allocation of costs depend on the outcome?

Arbitration is usually understood as a voluntary, binding process—that is, the parties agree in advance or at the time of claim to submit the grievance to arbitration and to accept the arbitral award. Under some circumstances, the arbitrator's award is advisory.

Those deciding on the form of arbitration need to ask these questions:

1. What is the appropriate balance between maintaining the authority of the president or board of trustees to make a final decision and gaining the advantages of final disposition by a qualified, impartial body?
2. If arbitration is limited to recommendations, should there be further opportunity for argument or hearing before the board of trustees?
3. Under advisory arbitration, what limits might be placed on the board's decision?

4. Should the arbitrator be permitted to make an independent judgment regarding the professional qualifications of the faculty member or be restricted to considering the method of review by the relevant academic committee?

Governing Board

At virtually all independent colleges, final authority in the grievance process is vested in the governing board. However, the process through which the board receives information on grievances and the availability of an appeal to the board vary widely. The level of board involvement generally depends on the policy implications of the issues presented.

Those deciding the degree of board involvement need to answer these questions:

1. What issues should be appealable to the board?
    a. All issues
    b. Employment issues (promotion, tenure, discipline, and dismissal)
    c. Employment-related issues (sabbaticals, professional activities, curriculum, class assignments, allocation of research facilities)
2. If an opportunity for appeal is provided, under what conditions should it take place?
    a. Should it be a review of the grievance or a new hearing, or should the form be determined on a case-by-case basis?
    b. What formats and procedures would be appropriate regarding such issues as time limits, grievant's representation and participation, and formality of the appeal?
3. To whom will the board report its decision?
4. Under what circumstances could a final board decision be subject to judicial review?

Administering the Procedures

Staffing. Designate an administrator or faculty member, by title, to receive grievances, move them through the process, track the stage to which grievances have progressed, maintain records on closed grievances, and close grievance files when the process is completed. This person's responsibilities could also include acting as liaison between the parties and arranging acceptable dates and locations for meetings and hearings.

Record Keeping. Determine the nature of information to be retained after the grievance process is completed and the location of the documents to be retained. Determine the length of time these records should be retained.

Reporting. Determine the information to be included in the report on grievances, the distribution of the report, the frequency of reporting, and the method by which recommended revisions are to be made in the college's policies and procedures.

Implementing the Procedures

Members of the design committee should agree on the steps necessary for implementing the new procedures.

1. Formal approval and acceptance by faculty senate, president, governing board
2. Possible revision of draft procedures based on informal discussion

Grievance Procedures:
Northeastern University

A. Step One: Department Chairman
    1. Before a faculty member brings a formal grievance, he/she must attempt to resolve the matter informally.
    2. If the faculty member has been unable to resolve the matter informally he/she may, within six weeks after he/she became aware of the grievable event(s), enter a formal grievance with his/her Chairman or immediate supervisor.
B. Step Two: Dean of College
    1. If the grievant is not satisfied with the disposition of his/her grievance at step one, or if no decision has been rendered within five school days after presentation of the grievance, he/she may file the grievance in writing with the Dean of his College, with a copy to the Chairman of the Senate Agenda Committee. The grievant will state the exact nature of the grievance and the remedy sought. At this point, he/she may request resolution through the Accelerated Grievance Procedure.

2. As soon as possible after the Senate Agenda Committee has received notice of a grievance, or notice that the Accelerated Grievance Procedure has not resolved the grievance, the Agenda Committee shall appoint an *ad hoc* Mediation Committee composed of three faculty members. In appointing this Committee, the Agenda Committee will normally appoint faculty members not involved with the grievant or his department. The *ad hoc* Mediation Committee shall conduct the meetings in steps two and three and shall attempt to mediate the dispute. However, the inability of one member of this Committee to attend such meetings shall in no way change the prescribed time limits.

3. Within five days of the establishment of the *ad hoc* Mediation Committee, its Chairman shall arrange for a meeting in an effort to resolve the grievance. The *ad hoc* Mediation Committee shall be invited to attend to assist in resolving the grievance. If the *ad hoc* Mediation Committee considers it advisable, it may request the attendance of the party whose action occasioned the grievance. The grievant may bring a Northeastern faculty member to this meeting.

C. Step Three: Provost

1. If the grievant is not satisfied with the disposition of his grievance at step two, or if no decision has been rendered within five school days after the *ad hoc* Mediation Committee meeting with the Dean of his/her College, he/she may demand that the Chairman of the *ad hoc* Mediation Committee arrange a meeting with the Provost (or his/her designee), the grievant, and the *ad hoc* Mediation Committee for the purpose of resolving the grievance. If the *ad hoc* Mediation Committee considers it advisable, it may request the attendance of the party whose action occasioned the grievance. The grievant may bring a Northeastern faculty member to this meeting.

2. After this meeting the *ad hoc* Mediation Committee may submit to the parties a proposed resolution to the grievance.

D. Step Four: Request for Arbitration

1. If the grievant is not satisfied with the disposition of the grievance at step three, or if no decision has been ren-

dered within five school days after the first meeting called for in step three, or within five days of receipt of the *ad hoc* Mediation Committee's recommendation, he/she may request, in writing, to the Chairman of the *ad hoc* Mediation Committee that the grievance be submitted to arbitration.

2. If the grievance involves 1) renewal of contract, 2) promotion, or 3) dismissal, the *ad hoc* Mediation Committee will institute arbitration proceedings immediately.

3. If the grievance involves other issues, the *ad hoc* Mediation Committee will, within five school days after receipt of the request for arbitration, decide by a majority vote if the grievance shall be arbitrated. In doing so, the Committee will not determine whether or not the grievance should be upheld, but only whether the grievance shall be arbitrated. The Committee shall decide in favor of arbitration if 1) the grievance falls within the definition of a grievance, and 2) the remedy sought is within the power of the arbitrator.

4. If the *ad hoc* Committee decides that the grievance does not meet the criteria for arbitration, the grievance is closed.

5. If the Committee believes that the grievance has disclosed needed improvements in policies, practices, or procedures in the University, it shall recommend such changes to the Senate by forwarding such recommendations to the Senate Agenda Committee.

6. If the *ad hoc* Mediation Committee decides that the grievance shall be arbitrated, the Committee will institute arbitration proceedings immediately.

E.   Step Five: Arbitration

1. If the grievance is to be arbitrated, the *ad hoc* Mediation Committee will so notify the Provost and the grievant.

2. Within fifteen calendar days after the notification of the Provost, the *ad hoc* Mediation Committee's Chairman and the Provost (or his/her designee) shall meet with the grievant for the purpose of explaining the process of filing a demand for arbitration with the American Arbitration Association. Such demand must be filed within 15 calendar days after this meeting.

3. The conduct of the arbitration proceedings shall be governed by the rules of the American Arbitration Association.

4. The decision of the arbitrator, within the scope of his jurisdiction, shall be final and binding on the parties to the dispute and the University. However, the arbitrator shall be without power to 1) make a decision which requires the commission of an act prohibited by law, 2) substitute his judgment on the professional qualifications of a faculty member for the judgment of the relevant academic committee, or 3) add to, subtract from, or modify provisions of the *Faculty Handbook* where provisions exist which cover the case in hand.

5. The costs of the services of the American Arbitration Association and the arbitrator shall be borne as follows:

a) If the arbitrator upholds the grievance (whether or not he grants the remedy sought by the grievant), the cost will be borne by the University in an amount not to exceed $1,000.

b) If the arbitrator denies the grievance, the grievant will pay 1/3 of the costs of the American Arbitration Association and the arbitrator up to a maximum of $200, and the University shall bear the remainder of such costs, but in no event shall the charge to the University exceed $800.

c) Each party will pay for its own expenses, services, and fees other than the costs of the American Arbitration Association and the arbitrator.

F.   Miscellaneous

1. A "grievance" is defined as a complaint by a faculty member that he 1) has been discriminated against on the basis of age, sex, race, religion, national origin, marital status or being a handicapped individual; 2) has been denied academic freedom; 3) has been dismissed without just cause; 4) has been denied due process in consideration for tenure, renewal of contract, or promotion; 5) has been subject to a violation, misinterpretation or inequitable application of provisions of the *Faculty Handbook*; or 6) has

otherwise been treated unfairly or inequitably. Grievances relating to tenure shall be governed by the provisions of E. Section VII, part D of the *Handbook*. The provisions of Section IX shall apply only to the extent they are expressly made applicable by Section VII.

2. It is important that grievances be processed as rapidly as possible. The number of days indicated at each step shall be considered a maximum, and every effort will be made to expedite the process. The time limits specified may, however, be extended by mutual agreement.

3. A grievant shall have two weeks to respond after each step. If he fails to respond by the end of two weeks, the grievance will be considered as waived. An involuntary delay such as illness or failure of the mails to deliver shall not be construed as waiving the grievance.

4. If, in the course of processing a grievance, there is a dispute over whether or not a grievance has been waived, the parties will continue to follow the procedure and the arbitrator will decide whether or not the grievance has been waived.

5. Copies of the arbitration decision shall be sent to the grievant, the Provost and the Chairman of the Senate Agenda Committee.

6. The University shall make available to the grievant relevant materials pertaining to his case.*

7. The Agenda Committee of the Senate will, upon request, provide the grievant and/or the person whose action occasioned the grievance with the names of faculty members or others who may be of assistance in preparation and presentation of his case in the grievance procedure.

---

*In an arbitration decision dated November 11, 1974, the following guideline relating to confidentiality was established: "Documents developed in the tenure procedure involving . . . the understanding and expectation that they were confidential do not have to be made available to [the grievant] by the University. Included in such documents are letters of recommendation, evaluation forms, and the minutes of the Promotion and Tenure Committee."

APPENDIX: Accelerated Grievance Procedure for Use in Case of Alleged Procedural Violations

1. Before a faculty member brings a formal grievance, he/she must attempt to resolve the matter informally.

2. If, within six weeks of perceived procedural violation a faculty member has not been able to resolve his/her complaint informally, he/she may file for grievance with the Senate Agenda Committee, requesting the accelerated grievance procedure. The grievance form should state the specific details involved in the alleged procedural violation and the desired remedy. The "clock" in this procedure stops at the date or receipt of this grievance and does not restart until the grievant receives written notice of the results of the accelerated procedure.

3. The grievant and a representative of the Senate Agenda Committee will confer with the Director of Faculty Relations within five workdays. If the Director of Faculty Relations recognizes merit in the grievance, he shall so notify the Provost. Otherwise, he shall inform the grievant, in writing, that the grievance is denied.

4. If the Provost recognizes merit in the grievance, he shall delegate the Director of Faculty Relations to work with the appropriate Dean or chairperson toward correcting the defective procedures. This process, which may involve any steps up to and including a full reconsideration of the grievant's original consideration with corrected procedures, should be completed within two weeks. At that time, the grievant will be informed of his/her status by the Dean or chairperson.

5. Whatever the outcome of this accelerated procedure, the grievant shall still have access to the standard faculty grievance procedure.

Northeastern University
Guidelines for the Conduct of Ad Hoc
Mediation Grievance Committees

This set of guidelines is meant to amplify the general statement in the grievance procedures with respect to the role of the *Ad Hoc* Mediation Grievance Committee appointed by the Senate Agenda Committee for each case. All the proceedings and statements made before the committee, excluding formal agreements and relevant factual disclosures, are to be regarded as in the strictest confidence, including all offers of compromise. It is hoped that these guidelines will be used to facilitate just and swift resolutions to grievances and to ensure due process for all concerned. This does not mean that all grievance committees must perform all of these duties, but merely that they should be open to the needs of both sides in the grievance and aware that they can play an active role whenever they deem it appropriate.

According to this activist interpretation of the permissive wording of the Grievance Procedure (Step 2-02), the possible roles of the *Ad Hoc* Mediation Grievance Committee are as follows:

1. *Overseeing the Processing of a Grievance*

It is the responsibility of the committee to oversee the progress of the grievance by convening the meetings at each step of the procedure in which it participates (Steps 2-02, 3-02). The chairperson of the committee should preside at each of the meetings and make sure that all parties understand the options open to them and the time constraints involved. It is up to the committee to ensure that all timeliness rules that are not explicitly waived are enforced, including the number of advocates who can attend hearings. (The regulation specifies a single advocate; however, if desired, and agreed to by both parties, one alternate may also attend.) The committee should ensure that lines of communication remain open at all times. Since university counsel plays no direct role in the mediation process, the grievant's attorney is not permitted to attend any meetings prior to Step 5.

It is important to realize that resolving some grievances takes a long time, sometimes over a year, along a path that occasionally twists back on itself. A solution is often worked out without arbitration and sometimes a grievance is suspended by mutual agreement while it is being worked out. During such a suspension both parties must continue to feel that they have ac-

cess to the offices of the Mediation Committee in case the grievance avenue needs to be reactivated or renegotiation is necessary. If a grievance is suspended the Mediation Committee
should continue to monitor the situation and be sure that the
Dean of Academic Affairs' Office has been so notified. The Mediation Committee should also press for a solution that is both
timely and just.

Under the current procedure, the *Ad Hoc* Mediation
Committee plays a major determining role in sending certain
grievances to arbitration (Sections D and E, Steps 4-01 through
5-02). Up to now, these provisions have been interpreted to
give the grievant maximum access to arbitration. Though the
committee's role is reduced in the proposed revisions now before the Trustees (Sections 4 and 5, Steps 4-01 through 5-01)
the committee should continue at this stage to be a resource to
all parties, and it remains responsible for a final report to the
Senate Agenda Committee (see Section 8, below). Thus, in a
limited sense, the Mediation Committee oversees the movement
of the grievance from the time of the committee's appointment
(in Step 2) up to arbitration.

2. *Advice and Counsel*

The Mediation Committee should make itself available to
all parties as a source of advice on the grievance procedures
themselves, on precedents, and in so far as its role as mediator
is not compromised, on the grievance itself. For instance, it may
offer advice on what is or is not within the province of the arbitrator to grant by way of redress. The committee should call
upon the records and expertise of the Senate Agenda Committee or on individuals or groups within the faculty who have
knowledge and/or experience in these matters (Section F-7 of
the existing procedures).

3. *Time Limits*

The Mediation Committee should be aware of the issue
of timeliness. It should feel free to apply informal pressure and
to warn both parties of violations of time limits. When suspen-

sions are agreed upon the committee should suggest time limits for them and attempt to have such time limits written into the agreement.

4. *Ensuring the Usefulness of Meetings*

In order to ensure the maximum possible gain from each meeting, it is important that the committee apprise all parties of the proposed function of the meeting. Mediation meetings serve little purpose if one side comes to them "prepared only to listen."

5. *Defining the Positions of the Parties to the Grievance*

The committee should encourage the parties in the grievance to make their complaints and proposals for redress as explicit and as sharply delineated as possible. In this way areas of agreement and disagreement can be quickly defined.

The Mediation Committee should meet separately with each party both prior to bringing them together and whenever during the procedure the committee deems it advantageous to do so.

As the grievance itself becomes better defined and as proposals for solutions are proffered, each side should be encouraged to commit these proposals to writing. The Mediation Committee should carefully note any procedures or solutions offered or accepted during the course of the mediations, and work to clarify them. If inconsistencies appear between oral agreements and their final written formulation, the Mediation Committee should work to clarify them also.

6. *Procedural Violations*

It occasionally happens that during the course of the procedure one of the parties may commit some violation of due process, or complain that the other party has committed such a violation. The most common source of such complaints is Section F-6 of the current procedure, which states that "The University shall make available to the grievant relevant materials pertaining to his case." The proposed procedure states that "Disputes over what are relevant materials may be brought to arbitration in accordance with the grievance procedure" (605) while the current procedure stands mute on redress. But even in the event that the new wording is adopted, the juggling of simultaneous grievances may be too much for anyone to handle. The Mediation Committee can serve a valuable function, when it is convinced that such violations have occurred or such complaints have some basis, in applying informal pressure to obtain compliance with the procedure. There is of course no injunctive authority on which the Committee can call, but it could possibly use the moral weight of its neutral position to press for a satisfactory resolution (particularly if failure to achieve one might result in a bad press or in negative evidence at later stages), and it can call upon the Senate Agenda Committee for advice and assistance.

7. Suggesting a Solution

Mediation is defined in numerous ways. A representative definition goes something like: "To act between parties in a non-binding, non-authoritarian manner to affect an agreement, compromise, or reconciliation." Nothing in this definition or in the grievance procedure itself demands that the committee play a passive role in its work. After hearing both parties to the grievance, the Committee may feel that it could help resolve it by having them hear how an impartial group of outsiders reacts to their respective cases, or by suggesting solutions or means of redress. The committee has every right to do so. In fact, in at least one grievance, both parties agreed to allow the Mediation Committee to arbitrate the dispute, and the solution mandated by the committee (with some agreed-to modifications) is now in effect.

8. Reports

There are three types of reports which the committee must make:

A. When it is all over, the committee must submit a brief
    report to the Senate Agenda Committee concerning the
    nature, processing, and outcome of the grievance, and
    containing any possible precedents established. Official
    statements pertaining to the resolution of the grievance,
    such as an arbitrator's finding (which is sent automati-
    cally to the Agenda Committee under Article F-5 of the
    current procedure) court decision, or final agreement
    should accompany the report. If there is disagreement
    within the committee concerning this or any other re-
    port, a minority report may be appended to it.

B. At any point in the procedure, the committee may sug-
    gest in writing to the Senate Agenda Committee (or its
    designee) changes in any of the practices, rules, or parts
    of the procedure itself. The Agenda Committee (or its
    designee) will give all such reports due consideration or
    will forward them to the appropriate agency (Step 4-
    05).

C. By June 1st of each academic year, the chairperson of
    each Mediation Committee whose grievance is not yet
    resolved must report to the Senate Agenda Committee
    on the current situation of the grievance, whether a
    "summer moratorium" (now in informal procedure,
    but included formally in Article 6-09 of the proposed
    revisions) is to come into effect by mutual agreement
    of the parties, and in general terms, whether and when
    all parties to the grievance (including the members of
    the Mediation Committee) will next be available to ef-
    fect a solution. At that time the Mediation Committee
    should resume its role and attempt to re-open commu-
    nication if the parties themselves have not already done
    so, or see that formal closure occurs.

Grievance Procedures:
Pace University

The text of the comprehensive faculty grievance procedure and transmittal letter from President Mortola to the faculty, dated November 29, 1982, is provided in full. This document references two other procedures dealing with salary and promotion. The provision for salary appeals shown below is excerpted from the Faculty Handbook. The procedure regarding promotion and tenure is issued annually by the Vice President for Academic Affairs; the text below, for the 1982 academic year, describes the appeals process.

Pace University
Faculty Grievance Procedure

Purpose

It is the purpose of this grievance procedure to secure prompt and equitable solutions to the grievances of faculty (including Adjunct Faculty) members.

Applicability of Procedure

This procedure shall apply to grievances relating the following:

Discrimination Claims: Allegations of unlawful discrimination on the basis of race, creed, color, national or ethnic origin, religion, age, sex (including sexual harassment), marital status or handicap in any educational or employment program, policy or practice of Pace University.

Contract Claims: Allegations by a faculty member or group of faculty members that a provision of the *Faculty Handbook* has been violated.

Non-Contract Claims: Allegations that any event or condition has adversely affected a faculty member regarding his/her welfare and/or terms and conditions of appointment not covered by the *Faculty Handbook.*

This procedure shall not apply to questions concerning level of compensation, rank, and/or title. Grievances relating to promotions in rank, tenure and salary, shall be handled in accordance with existing procedures for this purpose by either the CDFPT (Council of Deans and Faculty on Promotion and Tenure), or the Salary Review Board.

Definitions

Affirmative Action Officer (AAO): Administrator responsible for the coordination and implementation of University policy and procedure regarding discrimination claims.

University Grievance Reserve Pool (Pool): The group from which panelists will be drawn to hear grievances, shall be composed of administrators, faculty, staff and students to be selected by the University Senate in consultation with the AAO.

Discrimination Hearing Panel (Panel): Three member panel formed to conduct a hearing with respect to a formal written complaint alleging discrimination. Panel shall be selected from the Pool in the manner set forth below.

Procedures

Informal

(a)   Discuss the problem informally with the following persons:
   (i)   Department Chairperson
   (ii)   Dean of School
   (iii) Vice President for Academic Affairs
(b)   A faculty member may not proceed to formal review unless informal review with those cited above has been exhausted.

Formal

Contract Claims: If for any reason the grievance is not resolved informally to the satisfaction of the faculty member, he/she may obtain a hearing as follows:

(a) Within 30 days after a decision by the Vice President for Academic Affairs, or 45 days after submitting the question to the Vice President for Academic Affairs, whichever is later, the grievant shall notify the AAO that he/she desires a formal hearing.

(b) The AAO shall assist grievant in the preparation of a formal written complaint. In such complaint grievant shall designate whether the grievance contains any elements of discrimination. If discrimination is alleged, the matter shall be resolved in accordance with the discrimination claims procedure, *infra.*

(c) If no discrimination is alleged, as soon as practicable after preparation of the formal complaint, the AAO shall serve the complaint upon the respondent (if applicable) and upon the Grievance Committee (or other appropriate committee) of the Faculty Council of which the grievant is a constituent.

(d) The Grievance Committee, consistent with the Faculty Council By-Laws which govern its authority, may review the grievance and submit its findings to the President of the University (President) on an advisory basis.

(e) The final determination on the matter then rests with the President who will issue a decision as soon as practicable after receiving the report from the Faculty Council Committee.

Non-Contract Claims: It is recognized that disputes regarding matters not covered by the *Faculty Handbook* may arise. The settlement of such disputes is not a matter applicable to the grievance procedure cited above; however, certain channels of communication (i.e., Department Chairperson, Dean, Vice President for Academic Affairs) found in the grievance procedure are seen as proper channels through which non-contractual disputes may be processed and resolved. The Faculty and the University recognize that the use of expert advisory opinions may assist in a fair and expeditious settlement of non-contractual disputes. As such, the faculty member or the University may, if it deems necessary, introduce advisory opinions to support its position.

Contract or Non-Contract Claims Procedures to be Suspended if *Issue of Discrimination Arises on the Same Grievance*: If an issue of discrimination arises at any time during the course of the foregoing procedures, such procedures shall be suspended pending resolution of the discrimination issue pursuant to the discrimination claim procedure, *infra*.

Discrimination Claims: If for any reason the complaint is not resolved informally to the satisfaction of the faculty member, within a reasonable period of time, the faculty member should contact the AAO. The AAO shall assist the grievant in the preparation of a formal written complaint, or amend the written complaint drafted prior to the discovery of a discrimination issue.

As soon as practicable, after preparation of a formal complaint, the AAO shall:

(i)   Serve the complaint upon the respondent, if applicable.

(ii)   Convene a panel from the Pool.

Panel Selection:

(a) The grievant and the respondent shall each select one panelist from the Pool. The third panel member shall be selected by the aforesaid two panelists, and shall serve as Chairperson of the Panel.

(b) In the event that either party does not select a panel member, the AAO shall fill the vacancy or vacancies from the Pool.

(c) In the event the first two panelists selected cannot agree upon a third panelist, the AAO shall make such selection from the Pool.

(d) The AAO shall be an ex-officio non-voting member of the Panel.

Hearing Procedures: The hearing is not intended as a trial before a court of law and, therefore, adherence to the strict rules of evidence is not required. Questions relating to the competency, relevancy or materiality of evidence and the latitude in conducting questioning shall be based upon the Panel's determination as to what is just, fair and reasonable under the circumstances.

Procedural Guidelines:

(a) Each of the parties shall be afforded an opportunity to present an opening and closing statement.

(b) The grievant and his/her witnesses shall be heard first.

(c) The respondent shall be given an opportunity to testify and present evidence and witnesses, but shall not be compelled to testify against his/her will, nor shall an inference be drawn from the failure to testify.

(d) Each of the parties or their advisor shall have an opportunity to hear and question adverse witnesses.

(e) The decision of the Panel shall be based solely upon evidence presented at the hearing.

(f) A finding of the Panel shall be based on a fair preponderance of credible evidence.

(g) The burden of proof rests with the grievant.

(h) A tape recording of the hearing shall be made at the University's expense. Said recording shall be retained by the AAO for a period of one year. A party to the proceeding may obtain a written transcript or a copy of the tape recording at his/her expense.

(i) The failure of a party either to respond to the complaint or to participate in a hearing shall not preclude the Panel from proceeding and rendering its decision.

(j) Within thirty days after the conclusion of the hearing, the Panel shall prepare a written opinion as to whether the charges alleged in the complaint have been substantiated, stating the findings relied upon for such conclusion. A minority opinion and recommendation regarding action to be taken may be included. When such opinion is completed, the Panel shall serve copies thereof upon the parties and shall submit the opinion to the President. The Panel's opinion and recommendations are advisory in nature and are not binding upon the President.

Decisions and Notice of Decision: As soon as practicable after receipt of the Panel's opinion, the President shall render a written decision as to whether the charges have been substantiated. Such decision shall be communicated to the parties.

Miscellaneous General Provisions

Remedial Action: If the President finds that the grievant's charges have been substantiated, he shall confer with the grievant to determine appropriate corrective action. The University will implement corrective action upon receipt from the grievant of a signed statement releasing the University from all claims which the grievant might have arising out of the incidents or conditions upon which the grievance was based.

Time Limits: All time limits contained in the foregoing procedures may be extended by mutual written consent of the parties or by the AAO.

Confidentiality of Proceedings: The University shall take all reasonable steps to insure the confidentiality of all proceedings, hearings and the records produced therefrom. However, should any matter developed during the course of the proceedings become public knowledge, the University reserves the right to issue appropriate statements.

Use of This Grievance Procedure Not Available If Formal Complaint Is *Filed Outside The University On The Same Griev-*

ance: This procedure may not be used if a formal complaint has been filed with a governmental agency or a court action has been initiated based upon substantially similar facts, in which event any investigation or hearing then in progress shall be terminated.

Pace University
Salary Appeals Process

A faculty member may file a salary appeal within 30 days of issuance of the contract. All appeals should be handled according to established University procedure; the appropriate chairperson should first be consulted. Salary questions still unresolved should be taken up with the Dean and the Vice President for Academic Affairs. Should all such avenues be exhausted, appeal may be made through a Salary Review Board in those cases where a Review Board has been established (see below).

Salary Review Board. There are currently two Salary Review Boards, one serving the members of the New York Faculty Council, the other serving the members of the Pleasantville/ Briarcliff Faculty Council. These three-member Boards of faculty serve as an appeal body in connection with individual undergraduate faculty salary questions still unresolved after consultation with the appropriate chairperson, Dean and Vice President for Academic Affairs. To have the appropriate Salary Review Board convened, a faculty member should submit a request along with a sufficiently detailed statement of the basis for appeal to the Provost, who serves as ex officio member of both Boards. The Board then makes its recommendation directly to the President. The President makes the final decision and communicates with the appellant.

Members of the Salary Review Boards are nominated periodically by their respective Faculty Councils and appointed by the President. In New York, chairpersons of departments and directors of programs are ineligible for nomination to the Salary Review Board.

Pace University
Promotion and Tenure Appeals Process

Those faculty considered, but not supported, for promotion or tenure by the CDFPT (Council of Deans and Faculty on Promotion and Tenure) may direct appeals of that recommendation to the President of the University through the Office of the Vice President for Academic Affairs. In hearing the appeals, the President calls upon and takes into consideration the recommendation of a University-wide Appeals Committee. This Committee is currently composed of six members of the faculty (exclusive of the School of Law) who are not on the CDFPT and who are elected by their respective Faculty Councils; two from the Pleasantville/Briarcliff campus, two from the New York campus, and one from the White Plains campus as well as one from the Lubin Graduate School of Business. Six alternate members are similarly elected to be available in cases of inability to attend or challenge for cause. Alternates should attend all Appeals Committee meetings and receive all minutes and informational material. They may participate in the deliberative discussions when invited to do so, but have no vote in the Committee's decisions.

In addition, two members of the CDFPT, named by that group, will serve as non-voting liaison representatives to the Appeals Committee and, as with the CDFPT, the Vice President for Academic Affairs will serve as a resource person on matters of procedure. All communications between these individuals and members of the Appeals Committee are held in strictest confidence.

An individual faculty member has the right to appeal the CDFPT decision only as to himself or herself. A formal request for such appeal must be filed in writing to the President through the Office of the Vice President for Academic Affairs within thirty calendar days after the nominee has been sent written notification of the CDFPT decision. The appeal must set forth in sufficient detail the grounds upon which the appeal is based.

The President will arrange to have the first meeting of the Appeals Committee scheduled within fifteen calendar days after the latest date for filing an appeal, at which time the Committee will elect its chairperson. In this and, if necessary, subsequent meetings the Committee reviews each appeal and submits an oral report, followed by a written confirmation, on its recommendations to the President within forty-five calendar days after the latest date for filing an appeal. The Committee's recommendations are confidential and made available by the Committee only.

In judging the appeal, the Appeals Committee has access to the same Fact Sheet, evaluations, and dossier reviewed by the CDFPT, as well as the testimony offered by the CDFPT liaison representatives. Information which should have been available to the CDFPT but which was not made available in a timely and appropriate manner by the nominee may not be considered by the Appeals Committee. In judging the appeal, the Committee will determine one of two conditions: first, whether an appeal is warranted because procedural due process was not provided (e.g., information provided by the nominee in a timely and otherwise appropriate fashion was not presented to the CDFPT) in which case the President may remand the case to the CDFPT; or second, the Committee will determine whether the appellant is manifestly better qualified, on the basis of the relevant evidence provided and within the context of University policy on promotion, tenure and separation, than a candidate within an equivalent rank recommended by the CDFPT in the same year.

As with the CDFPT, the Appeals Committee is not bound by precedent; recommendations reached in a given year are mutually exclusive of those reached in prior years.

Within fifteen calendar days after receiving the Appeals Committee's written recommendation, the President will issue a decision in writing to the appellant with a copy to the members of the Appeals Committee and to the academic dean concerned.

Grievance Procedures:
Unity College

The following procedures were approved by the Unity College Board of Trustees in 1981.

Grievance Procedures

A. *The Grievance Committee* will consist of three members of the faculty, each serving three-year terms, with one normally expiring each year. Members will be elected at large by the faculty. No center chairperson or administrative officer, regardless of faculty rank, shall serve on the committee. The committee shall elect its own chairperson.

The Grievance Committee serves to investigate, to conciliate in an attempt to reach mutually agreeable settlements, to report its findings, to provide opportunity for a hearing of all interested parties in disputes, and to make recommendations concerning individual cases to the President or to other persons against whom grievances may be lodged. In its investigatory

247

role, impartiality is imperative; in its judgmental role, the committee is expected to be dispassionate. Members are expected to exercise prudence and caution, taking extreme care not to discuss cases in any but the appropriate committee meetings or to reveal either findings or recommendations of the committee except through the formal statements of the chairperson, who shall be sole spokesperson for the committee.

B. *Disqualification*
   1. When a petition for redress is submitted, either the petitioner or the person against whom the grievance is made is entitled to replacement of one or more members of the committee, or the committee member may disqualify him or herself, without prejudice.
   2. In the event of disqualification of one or more members, the Grievance Committee will select qualified replacements one at a time and at random until a committee of three, satisfactory to both parties, is established.
   3. For the duration of the case, the new committee performs all functions of the elected committee except that the duly elected chairperson continues to be responsible for all communications of the committee.

C. *Handling Grievances*
   Should any faculty member feel that he or she has cause for grievance in any matter—dismissal, non-reappointment, salary, assignment of duties, allotment of facilities, propriety of conduct, etc.—s/he may petition the elected faculty Grievance Committee for redress. The petition shall set forth in detail the nature of the grievance, and a copy shall be sent to the person against whom the grievance is directed at the same time the petition is submitted to the committee.
   1. Within ten working days of receipt of a petition, the chairperson will schedule a meeting of the Grievance Committee. The committee may call in the petitioner for clarification of his/her grievance. The committee will *decide* whether or not the case, as presented by the petitioner, warrants further action. The committee shall, as a result of this decision:

a. reject the petition with a written explanation to petitioner and to the person against whom the grievance is directed as to the reasons for rejection (petitioner may always submit a revision), or

b. decide that further evidence is needed or investigation is warranted, in which case the chairperson so notifies the concerned parties, with a request for pertinent statements and documents.

2. Following 1b above, the committee reconvenes within ten working days of the notification to weigh the evidence and statements at its disposal. As a result of this examination, the committee may:

a. attempt to mediate the differences, not by announcing judgment or making recommendations, but by bringing parties together voluntarily. The committee members shall not take the role of advocate in this process.

b. reject the petition, once more with written explanation to concerned parties.

c. decide that a hearing is justified.

3. Following 2c above, the chairperson of the committee so informs the petitioner and the President, who will arrange a formal hearing within thirty days of receipt of the notification, unless petitioner waives hearing. At this point, the petitioner may:

a. withdraw the petition without prejudice.

b. waive the hearing, asking that judgment and recommendations be reached on the basis of statements and documentary evidence submitted by both parties and available to both parties for examination and rebuttal. Having waived hearing, he/she is not entitled to a hearing after the committee's decision is announced.

4. A hearing is governed by the following rules:

a. The President of the College, consistent with his/her responsibility for the good order of the College, will decide whether the hearing is open or closed to the College community.

b.   The petitioner and his/her adversary have the right to be in attendance throughout, have the right to be represented by counsel, have the right to call witnesses and to cross-examine witnesses, have the right to remain silent. Witnesses have the right to be represented by counsel and have the right to remain silent.

c.   The Grievance Committee will announce to all parties its procedure, agenda, and rules of order at least one week before the hearing.

d.   A complete transcript of the proceedings will be kept at College expense. The petitioner and his/her adversary are entitled to purchase copies directly from the recorder.

5.   Following the hearing:

a.   Within 48 hours of the close of the hearing, the Grievance Committee will transmit, confidentially, its findings, arguments, and recommendations to the President.

b.   Within 48 hours of their receipt, the President may call a meeting of the Grievance Committee to discuss their findings, seek clarification, and suggest revisions.

c.   If a revision is suggested, the committee is obliged to respond, either with a revision or a rejection of the request, within 48 hours.

d.   Within 48 hours of receipt of the revision (or within 48 hours of the conference if no revision is requested), the President will transmit in writing, his/her decision to the Grievance Committee and to the petitioner. Only then will the recommendation and the President's decision be announced by the President, as spokesperson for the College.

6.   The Grievance Committee has, at this point, fully discharged its obligations and plays no further role. Because the case may yet be appealed, members shall not comment on the grievance proceedings.

7.   The petitioner may appeal the President's decision to

the Board of Trustees. To do so, s/he must make his or her request for appeal along with his/her reasons for doing so, in writing, to the President within 30 days of receiving the President's decision. The President will immediately transmit the request for appeal, along with the case records and transcript of the hearing as soon as it can be transcribed, to the Chairperson of the Board of Trustees.

The Board may follow whatever course of action it deems most appropriate. The Board's decision is final.

FURTHER READINGS

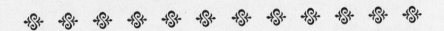

American Association of University Professors. "1972 Recommended Institutional Regulations on Academic Freedom and Tenure." In *AAUP Policy Documents and Reports*. Washington, D.C.: American Association of University Professors, 1973.

American Association of University Professors. "The Status of Part-Time Faculty." *Academe*, 1981, *67* (1), 29–39.

Benezet, L. T. "Do Presidents Make a Difference?" *Educational Record*, 1982, *63* (4).

Bok, D. "Balancing Responsibility and Innovation." *Change*, 1982. Excerpted from *Beyond the Ivory Tower: Social Responsibilities of the Modern University*. Cambridge, Mass.: Harvard University Press, 1982.

Brodsky, N., Kaufman, H. G., and Tooker, J. D. *University Industry Cooperation: A Preliminary Analysis of Existing Mechanisms and Their Relationship to the Innovation Process*. New York: New York University Center for Science and Technology Policy, 1979.

Bureau of National Affairs. *Sexual Harassment and Labor Relations*. Washington, D.C.: Bureau of National Affairs, 1981.

Chait, R. P., and Ford, A. T. *Beyond Traditional Tenure: A*

Guide to Sound Policies and Practices. San Francisco: Jossey-Bass, 1982.

Clark, D. L. "Discrimination Suits: A Unique Settlement." *Educational Record,* 1977.

Cohen, A. M., and Brawer, F. B. *The American Community College.* San Francisco: Jossey-Bass, 1982.

Crocker, P. L. "Annotated Bibliography on Sexual Harassment in Education." *Women's Rights Law Reporter,* 1982, 7 (2).

Cromie, W. *University-Industry Consortia in Microelectronics and Computers.* Oak Park, Ill.: Council for the Advancement of Science Writing.

Darknell, F., and Darknell, E. *State College Science and Engineering Faculty: Collaborative Links with Private Business and Industry.* Sacramento: California State University.

David, E. E., Jr. "Supporting Research with a Commercial Mission." *Change,* 1982.

Declercq, G. V. "Technology Transfer from Campus to Industry." *International Journal of Institutional Management in Higher Education,* 1979, *3.*

Farley, J. *Academic Women and Employment Discrimination.* Ithaca, N.Y.: New York State School of Industrial and Labor Relations, Cornell University, 1982.

Farley, J. (Ed.). *Sex Discrimination in Higher Education.* Ithaca, N.Y.: Cornell University, 1981.

Felicetti, D. A. "Retirement Options to Offer College Faculty." *Educational Record,* 1982.

Field, A. "Harassment on Campus: Sex in a Tenured Position?" *Ms. Magazine,* Sept. 1981.

Fishbein, E. A. "Sexual Harassment: Practical Guidance for Handling a New Issue on Campus." In *Higher Education: The Law and Emerging Issues and Trends.* Athens: Institute of Higher Education, University of Georgia, 1982.

Fowler, D. "What Barriers to Cooperation Have Been Encountered?—Industry and University Experience in University/Industry Relations." Paper presented at University of Wisconsin, Nov. 1982.

Fusfeld, H. I., Langlois, R. N., and Nelson, R. R. *The Changing Tide.* New York: New York University Center for Science and Technology Policy, 1981.

Gray, M. W., and Schafer, A. T. "Guidelines for Equality: A Proposal." *Academe,* 1981, *67* (6).

Johnson, E. C., and Tornatzky, L. G. "Academia and Industrial Innovation." In G. G.. Gold (Ed.), *New Directions for Experiential Learning: Business and Higher Education—Toward New Alliances,* no. 13. San Francisco: Jossey-Bass, 1981.

Kreinin, M. E. "Preserving Tenure Commitments in Hard Times, the Michigan State Experience." *Academe,* 1982.

Kruytbosch, C. E. *Annotated Bibliography on University-Industry Research Relationships.* Washington, D.C.: National Science Foundation.

Lee, B. A. "The Yeshiva Decision: An Ultimatum for Professionals?" *New York University Education Quarterly,* 1982, *5.*

Leslie, D. W., and others. *Part-Time Faculty in American Higher Education.* New York: Praeger, 1982.

Levenstein, A. "Confidentiality and Due Process." *Newsletter.* (National Center for the Study of Collective Bargaining in Higher Education and the Professions), 1981, *9* (4).

McCarthy, J. "Faculty Complaint Procedures: An Aspect of Preventive Management." *Lex Collegii,* 1982, *5* (3).

McCarthy, J. (Ed.). *New Directions for Higher Education: Resolving Conflict in Higher Education,* no. 32. San Francisco: Jossey-Bass, 1980.

McCarthy, J., and Ladimer, I. *Resolving Faculty Disputes.* New York: American Arbitration Association, 1981.

Marske, C. E., and Vago, S. "Law and Dispute Processing in the Academic Community." *Judicature,* 1980, *64* (4).

Massachusetts Institute of Technology, Office of Sponsored Programs. "Research Agreements with Industrial Sponsors: Review Draft." Cambridge, Mass.: Office of Sponsored Programs, Massachusetts Institute of Technology, 1981.

Mingle, J. R. and Associates. *Challenges of Retrenchment: Strategies for Consolidating Programs, Cutting Costs, and Reallocating Resources.* San Francisco: Jossey-Bass, 1981.

Mogee, M. E. *The Relationship of Federal Support of Basic Research in Universities to Industrial Innovation and Productivity.* Washington, D.C.: Congressional Research Service, Library of Congress, 1979.

National Center for the Study of Collective Bargaining in Higher

Education and the Professions. "Focus on the Part-Timer."
Newsletter, 1980.

Omenn, G. S. "University/Industry Research Linkages: Arrangements Between Faculty Members and Their Universities." Paper presented at the American Association for the Advancement of Science Symposium on the Impact of Commercial
Genetic Engineering on Universities and Non-Profit Institutions, Washington, D.C., Jan. 1982.

Peters, L. and Fusfeld, H. *Current U.S. University-Industry Research Connections.* New York: New York University Center
for Science and Technology Policy.

Prager, D. J., and Omenn, G. S. "Research, Innovation, and University-Industry Linkages." *Science,* 1980, *20F* (4429), 379–
384.

Project on the Status and Education of Women. "Sexual Harassment." *On Campus with Women,* 1980, *25.*

Robinson, D. F. "Reflections of a Trustee." *Academe, 68* (1).

Rosenzweig, R. M., and Trulington, B. *The Research Universities and Their Patrons.* Berkeley: University of California
Press, 1982.

"Sexual Harassment on Campus." *Journal of the National Association for Women Deans, Administrators, and Counsellors,*
1983, *46* (2).

Shapero, A. *University-Industry Interactions: Recurring Expectations, Unwarranted Assumptions, and Feasible Policies.*
Columbus: Ohio State University, 1979.

Steiner, D. "Technology Transfer at Harvard University." Discussion memorandum, Harvard University, Oct. 9, 1980.

Tatel, D. S., and Guthrie, R. C. 'The Legal Ins and Outs of University-Industry Collaboration." *Educational Record,* 1983.

Teisch, J. L. "Inventory of University-Industry Research Support Agreements in Biomedical Science and Technology."
Report prepared for the National Institutes of Health, Bethes-
da, MD, 1982.

Thackray, A. *University-Industry Connections and Chemical
Research: An Historical Perspective.* Philadelphia: University
of Pennsylvania.

Tornatzky, L. G., and others. *University-Industry Cooperative*

Research Centers: A Practice Manual. Washington, D.C.: National Science Foundation, 1982.

Tucker, A. and Mautz, R. B. "Academic Freedom, Tenure, and Incompetence." *Educational Record,* 1982, *63* (2).

Tuckman, H. P. "Part-Time Faculty: Some Suggestions of Policy." *Change,* 1981.

Weisberger, J. *Faculty Grievance Arbitration in Higher Education.* Monograph 5. Ithaca, N.Y.: Institute of Public Employment, Cornell University, 1976.

Zwingle, J. L. "Resolving Conflict in the Upper Echelons." In J. McCarthy (Ed.), *New Directions for Higher Education: Resolving Conflict in Higher Education,* no. 32. San Francisco: Jossey-Bass, 1980.

INDEX

259